Mathias Schnee

Fully Realistic Multi-Criteria Timetable Information Systems

Mathias Schnee

Fully Realistic Multi-Criteria Timetable Information Systems

Models, Algorithms, and Prototypes

Südwestdeutscher Verlag für Hochschulschriften

Impressum/Imprint (nur für Deutschland/ only for Germany)
Bibliografische Information der Deutschen Nationalbibliothek: Die Deutsche Nationalbibliothek verzeichnet diese Publikation in der Deutschen Nationalbibliografie; detaillierte bibliografische Daten sind im Internet über http://dnb.d-nb.de abrufbar.

Alle in diesem Buch genannten Marken und Produktnamen unterliegen warenzeichen-, marken- oder patentrechtlichem Schutz bzw. sind Warenzeichen oder eingetragene Warenzeichen der jeweiligen Inhaber. Die Wiedergabe von Marken, Produktnamen, Gebrauchsnamen, Handelsnamen, Warenbezeichnungen u.s.w. in diesem Werk berechtigt auch ohne besondere Kennzeichnung nicht zu der Annahme, dass solche Namen im Sinne der Warenzeichen- und Markenschutzgesetzgebung als frei zu betrachten wären und daher von jedermann benutzt werden dürften.

Verlag: Südwestdeutscher Verlag für Hochschulschriften GmbH & Co. KG
Dudweiler Landstr. 99, 66123 Saarbrücken, Deutschland
Telefon +49 681 37 20 271-1, Telefax +49 681 37 20 271-0
Email: info@svh-verlag.de
Zugl.: Darmstadt, TU, Diss., 2009

Herstellung in Deutschland:
Schaltungsdienst Lange o.H.G., Berlin
Books on Demand GmbH, Norderstedt
Reha GmbH, Saarbrücken
Amazon Distribution GmbH, Leipzig
ISBN: 978-3-8381-1780-5

Imprint (only for USA, GB)
Bibliographic information published by the Deutsche Nationalbibliothek: The Deutsche Nationalbibliothek lists this publication in the Deutsche Nationalbibliografie; detailed bibliographic data are available in the Internet at http://dnb.d-nb.de.

Any brand names and product names mentioned in this book are subject to trademark, brand or patent protection and are trademarks or registered trademarks of their respective holders. The use of brand names, product names, common names, trade names, product descriptions etc. even without a particular marking in this works is in no way to be construed to mean that such names may be regarded as unrestricted in respect of trademark and brand protection legislation and could thus be used by anyone.

Publisher: Südwestdeutscher Verlag für Hochschulschriften GmbH & Co. KG
Dudweiler Landstr. 99, 66123 Saarbrücken, Germany
Phone +49 681 37 20 271-1, Fax +49 681 37 20 271-0
Email: info@svh-verlag.de

Printed in the U.S.A.
Printed in the U.K. by (see last page)
ISBN: 978-3-8381-1780-5

Copyright © 2010 by the author and Südwestdeutscher Verlag für Hochschulschriften GmbH & Co. KG and licensors
All rights reserved. Saarbrücken 2010

Abstract

Millions of people use public transportation and consult electronic timetable information systems. A customer selects from the connections offered by the system according to personal preferences. The chosen connection is typically a compromise based on the importance of several criteria, including departure and arrival time, travel time, comfort and ticket cost. Consequently, multi-criteria optimization should be used to deliver "attractive" alternatives. We developed the concept of *advanced Pareto optimality* as an evolution of the classical Pareto optimality approach. It delivers more alternatives and removes unattractive solutions from the results to suit the notion of attractive connections for all potential customers.

Realistic modeling of the search for attractive connections leads to shortest-path algorithms. Fast search algorithms are needed to answer customer requests in only a few milliseconds since the schedules are modeled as large graphs (several hundred thousand edges and nodes). The graphs are either *time-expanded* or *time-dependent* to model the dimension of time.

In contrast to the majority of scientific work on the subject, our approach is *fully realistic* without simplifying assumptions. We extended the time-expanded graph model to an exact representation satisfying all constraints of a real schedule. Based on a generalization of Dijkstra's shortest-path algorithm, we developed our full-fledged multi-criteria timetable information system MOTIS (Multi Objective Traffic Information System). It delivers valid connections according to the principle of *advanced Pareto optimality*. A customer may actually buy a ticket for the connections determined by our system. Furthermore, we also explored the time-dependent model and built a prototype system working on that model as a proof of concept.

We also investigated several additional criteria that had not been considered before, for example special offers (reduced ticket cost under certain conditions, e.g. based on the availability of contingents) or the *reliability of interchanges*, a measure of how likely it is to catch all connecting trains of a trip. Moreover, we present approaches to the search for night trains with the additional objective of ensuring reasonable sleeping times without the need for train changes. Our algorithms respecting these criteria are fast and deliver attractive alternatives.

We explored and adapted existing speed-up techniques and developed new ones suitable for our scenario. In an extensive computational study we discuss the cost of regarding the criteria, the effect of various parameterizations of our algorithm, and the impact of the developed speed-up techniques. Applying these, we achieve runtimes of about one quarter of a second on average and solve most of the queries (95%) in less than a second.

Delays occur quite frequently in public transportation. They may invalidate connections as interchanges become infeasible. Current systems do not take that into account. At the utmost, they add changed departure or arrival times to connections calculated according to the static schedule. By incorporating information about delays into our model, we are able to deliver valid connections. We propose a multi-server architecture that allows several search servers to be updated by a central server distributing delay data. The simulation of a whole day with more than 6 million status messages takes less than two minutes. In our architecture, update phases may be scheduled to guarantee the availability of service at all times.

We have built user interfaces and visualization tools for our system. Additionally, we have created a new service: proactive route guidance. Within this service a planned trip is registered in CoCoAS (our Connection Controller and Alternatives System). While the passenger travels, the system continously checks the status of the connection. As soon as the system determines that the connection will break, it offers alternatives. By computing these alternatives as early as possible, an asset of our system, more and better options can be explored.

Contents

Abstract   i

Introduction   1

1 Setting   7
- 1.1 Terminology 7
- 1.2 Queries 8
  - 1.2.1 Specification of Queries 8
  - 1.2.2 Connections Matching a Query 9
- 1.3 Pre-Trip / On-Trip Searches 10
- 1.4 Fully Realistic Model 11

2 Multi-Criteria Optimization   13
- 2.1 Criteria 13
- 2.2 Pareto Optimality 13
- 2.3 Advanced Pareto Optimality 15
  - 2.3.1 Relaxed Pareto Dominance 15
  - 2.3.2 Tightened Dominance 18
  - 2.3.3 Advanced Pareto Dominance 19
- 2.4 Applying Advanced Pareto Dominance 23

3 Search Algorithms   25
- 3.1 Introduction 25
- 3.2 Dijkstra's Algorithm 26
- 3.3 Data Structures Speeding Up Dijkstra's Algorithm 28
  - 3.3.1 k-heap Implementation 28
  - 3.3.2 Binary Heap Implementation 31
  - 3.3.3 Fibonacci Heap Implementation 31
  - 3.3.4 Implementation Using Dial's Data Structure 31
  - 3.3.5 Priority Queues without decreaseKey-Operation 33

	3.3.6	Remarks on Data Structures and Shortest Path Search	34
3.4		The Multi-Criteria Version	35
	3.4.1	Problem Definition	35
	3.4.2	Number of Pareto Optimal Solutions (worst-case)	36
	3.4.3	Tractability and State of the Art	36
	3.4.4	A Generalization of Dijkstra's Algorithm	37
	3.4.5	Modifications	40

4 Graph Models   41
- 4.1 The Basic Time-Expanded Model 41
- 4.2 The Basic Time-Dependent Model 42
- 4.3 Non-Negligible Interchange Times 43
  - 4.3.1 Extending the Time-Expanded Graph 43
  - 4.3.2 Extending the Time-Dependent Graph 45
- 4.4 Discussion: Time-Expanded Vs. Time-Dependent Models 47

5 The MOTIS Algorithm   49
- 5.1 The Graph Model of MOTIS 49
  - 5.1.1 Realistic Interchange Rules 49
  - 5.1.2 Traffic Days 50
  - 5.1.3 Footpaths 50
  - 5.1.4 Edge Lengths for the Criteria 51
  - 5.1.5 Attributes NotIn/NotOut 53
- 5.2 Algorithm Refinements 53
  - 5.2.1 Realization of On-trip/Pre-trip Searches 53
  - 5.2.2 Meta Stations and Source-/Target-Equivalents 54
  - 5.2.3 Attribute Requirements and Class Restrictions 55
- 5.3 Implementation Details 55
  - 5.3.1 Edge Hierarchy 55
  - 5.3.2 Encoding Train Information 56
  - 5.3.3 Lazy Initialization and Reset 57
- 5.4 The Algorithm 57
- 5.5 MOTIS Search GUI 59
- 5.6 History of the MOTIS Algorithm 59

6 Additional Criteria and Special Search Forms   61
- 6.1 Seat Reservation 61
- 6.2 Search for Special Offers 62

		6.2.1	Introduction	63
		6.2.2	Modeling Regular Fares and Special Offers	63
		6.2.3	Details on the Search Algorithm	68
	6.3	Reliability of Transfers		69
		6.3.1	Reliability Measure	70
		6.3.2	Good Measure = Good Additional Criterion?	73
		6.3.3	Refinements	75
		6.3.4	Example Result Set	77
	6.4	Sleeping Time in Night Trains		78
		6.4.1	Introduction and Motivation	79
		6.4.2	Attractive Night Train Connections	81
		6.4.3	Approaches for Night Train Search	82

7 Delays   87

	7.1	Introduction and Motivation		88
	7.2	Up-To-Date Status Information		90
		7.2.1	Primary Delay Information	90
		7.2.2	Secondary Delays	91
	7.3	System Architecture		92
	7.4	Dependency Graph		94
		7.4.1	Graph Model	94
		7.4.2	Computation on the Dependency Graph	96
	7.5	Updating the Search Graph		98
	7.6	Traffic Days		99
		7.6.1	Memory Consumption Issues	100
		7.6.2	Moving from One Day to the Next	101
	7.7	Evaluation of the Prototype		102
		7.7.1	Overall Performance and Waiting Profiles	103
		7.7.2	Multi-Server Performance	106
	7.8	A New Service for Travelers		109
	7.9	Conclusions and Future Work		109

8 Speed-Up Techniques for Multi-Criteria Search   111

	8.1	Speeding up Dijkstra's Algorithm		111
		8.1.1	Early Termination	112
		8.1.2	Goal-Direction / Lower Bounding	113
		8.1.3	Priority Queues	114
		8.1.4	Reach Based	114

	8.1.5	Bidirectional Search	114
	8.1.6	Arc Flags and Geometric Containers	115
	8.1.7	Hierarchical Techniques	116
	8.1.8	Combinations	117
	8.1.9	Steps Towards Our Scenario	118
8.2	Multi-Criteria Approach	119
8.3	Goal-Directed Search	120
8.4	Domination by Labels at the Terminal	123
8.5	Lower bounds	124
	8.5.1	The Station Graph for Lower Bounds	124
	8.5.2	Interchange Graph	126
	8.5.3	Domination by Labels at the Terminal	127
	8.5.4	Usage in Goal-Directed Search	128
	8.5.5	Limiting the Search Horizon	128
8.6	Skipping Nodes in the Graph or Search	130
	8.6.1	Chaining Change-Arrival / Change-Departure Nodes	130
	8.6.2	Skipping Departure Nodes	130
	8.6.3	Bypassing Departure Nodes	131
8.7	Important Station Heuristics	132
	8.7.1	Skipping Nodes at Unimportant Stations	133
	8.7.2	Shortcuts in the Graph	134
8.8	The Priority Queue	135
	8.8.1	Smaller Relation for Priority Queues	135
	8.8.2	Different Priority Queue Types	136
	8.8.3	Reordering the PQ	137
	8.8.4	Avoid Inserting Minimum Labels	138
8.9	Edge-Blocking	138
	8.9.1	Mass Transportation Heuristic	138
	8.9.2	Route Blocking	139
	8.9.3	Shortcut Blocking	140
8.10	Bitonic Search	140
8.11	Speed-Up Techniques and Graph Updates	141
8.12	MOTIS Algorithm with Speed-Up Techniques	142
	8.12.1 Changes to the Graph	142
	8.12.2 Changes to the Algorithm	142
8.13	Further Thoughts on Speed-Up Techniques	144
	8.13.1 Ideas for Bidirectional Search	144
	8.13.2 Adapting Multi-Criteria SHARC	145

9 Computational Study — 147

- 9.1 Computational Study on Special Offers 148
  - 9.1.1 Computational Setup 148
  - 9.1.2 Searching for Multiple Tariffs 149
  - 9.1.3 Fast Search for Fixed Price Connections 151
- 9.2 Computational Study on Night Train Search 152
  - 9.2.1 Computational Setup 153
  - 9.2.2 Experiments 154
- 9.3 Computational Studies with Advanced Dominance 157
- 9.4 Computational Setup 157
  - 9.4.1 Testing Environment 157
  - 9.4.2 Measures and Test Procedures 158
- 9.5 Advanced Pareto Dominance 160
  - 9.5.1 Pareto to Relaxed Pareto to Advanced Pareto 160
  - 9.5.2 Tests with Dominance 162
- 9.6 Goal-Direction and Domination by Terminal 168
- 9.7 Lower Bounds 169
  - 9.7.1 Station Graphs 169
  - 9.7.2 Interchange Graph 170
  - 9.7.3 Summary Lower Bounds 172
- 9.8 Priority Queue 173
  - 9.8.1 Priority Queue Type and "Smaller"-Relation 173
  - 9.8.2 Weight for Interchanges in Goal-Direction 174
  - 9.8.3 Reordering the Priority Queue 175
  - 9.8.4 Decreasing the Number of Labels in the PQ 176
- 9.9 Reliability of Interchanges 177
  - 9.9.1 Number of Equivalence Classes 177
  - 9.9.2 Maximal Effective Reliability 178
- 9.10 Heuristics 179
  - 9.10.1 Bitonic Search 179
  - 9.10.2 Mass Transportation 179
  - 9.10.3 Routes Blocking 180
  - 9.10.4 Important Stations 182
  - 9.10.5 Shortcuts 184
  - 9.10.6 Combination of the Four Heuristics: Important Station, Shortcuts, Mass Transportation, and Routes 186
- 9.11 Detailed Figures for the Reference Version 187

         9.11.1 Configuration 187
         9.11.2 Detailed Number Of Significant Operations 188
         9.11.3 Number of Optima 189
    9.12 Significant Operations 190
    9.13 Analysis of Heavy-Weight Searches 190
    9.14 Example Connections 192
    9.15 Conclusion 193

10 A Time-Dependent Timetable Information System   **195**
    10.1 Realistic Time-Dependent Graph Model 196
         10.1.1 Basic Time-Dependent Model 197
         10.1.2 Transfers 197
         10.1.3 Fully Realistic Model 198
    10.2 Multi-Criteria Dijkstra and Speed-Up Techniques 199
         10.2.1 Algorithm 199
         10.2.2 Speed-Up Techniques 200
    10.3 Computational Study 201
         10.3.1 Train Network and Test Cases 201
         10.3.2 Computational Environment 201
         10.3.3 Experiments 201
    10.4 Conclusions and Future Work 206

11 Developed Software Tools   **207**
    11.1 GUI Architecture 207
         11.1.1 MOTIS Backbone 207
         11.1.2 GUIs 207
    11.2 Search GUI 208
    11.3 Connection Controller and Alternatives System 210
    11.4 Others 214
    11.5 System Architecture: The Big Picture 215

12 Conclusion and Outlook   **219**

Appendix A: Transitivity   **225**
    A.1 The Time Difference Formula 225
    A.2 The Hourly Wage Tightening 230

Appendix B: Speed-Up Techniques   **231**
    B.1 Lower Bounds 231
    B.2 Important Station and Shortcuts Heuristics 233
    B.3 Search Space 233

List of Algorithms	**235**
List of Tables	**239**
List of Figures	**242**
Bibliography	**253**

Introduction

Millions of people use public transportation every day. The federal German railroad company, *Deutsche Bahn AG*, transported 1.4 billion passengers and those traveled more than 70 billion person kilometers[i] per year in 2007 and 2008 [Deu09]. Timetable information systems are available either in the internet, in the form of ticket machines at stations, or at a counter, where railway staff employ them to determine the desired connections for customers. The company providing timetable information for Deutsche Bahn AG, HaCon,[ii] claims that their servers calculate over 20 million connections per day [Haf09]. Realistic modeling of the search for attractive connections leads to shortest-path algorithms. Fast search algorithms are needed to answer customer requests in only a few milliseconds since the schedules are modeled as large graphs (several hundred thousand edges and nodes). The graphs are either *time-expanded* or *time-dependent* to model the dimension of time.

A customer decides which connection to select, according to personal preferences. It is a *multi-criteria* choice based on: time, ticket cost, and number of interchanges. Information systems present those values together with the itinerary. Then the user may pick a connection suiting his desired travel time, comfort, and budget.

Surprisingly, previous scientific work has put little effort in true multi-criteria optimization. Some systems simply minimize each of the criteria alone and deliver fastest, most convenient (least number of interchanges) and cheapest connections. The price of a connection has been neglected for a long time and only recently came into focus. These connections only fit assumed *purist* customer profiles, concentrating on a single criterion. However, customers usually do not have *purist* preferences. Rather, the typical customer regards all of these criteria important, with different individual preferences. Unfortunately, interesting compromises are not produced with this approach. For example, sometimes a slightly slower connection than the fastest high-speed train is much less expensive - and preferable over a slow alternative that uses only regional trains but is not much cheaper.

Furthermore, the classical multi-criteria approach may be extended to produce a higher number of alternatives which are even more attractive. Think of two connections that differ in travel time by just two minutes but depart half an hour apart from each other, within the classical approach only the faster one is found. Additionally, we may want to suppress

---

[i]passengers times average travel length, long-distance and regional rail traffic without urban traffic
[ii]Their system HAFAS is present in 16 countries, among them Germany, UK, France, and Switzerland.

obviously unattractive alternatives, e.g. one alternative that travels 1 hour longer but saves only 2 Euros.

We present an algorithm based on Dijkstra's algorithm that computes shortest paths on a suitably constructed time-expanded graph. It respects the multi-criteria nature of the problem and the aforementioned extensions to the classical multi-criteria approach. Our algorithm is an exact multi-criteria algorithm optimizing the two criteria: travel time and number of interchanges. Many railways employ complicated tariff rules that make finding the cheapest connection really challenging. The algorithm has been extended to efficiently search for various types of tariffs (regular fares and special offers). We illustrate and emphasize the flexibility of the multi-criteria approach by adding new criteria. For example, the *reliability of transfers* (i.e. how likely it is to catch all connecting trains of a trip), and the search for night trains.

Still, in contrast to most other scientific work on the subject, our algorithm solves the *fully realistic* timetable information problem. We do not make any simplifying assumptions and satisfy all constraints of real schedules. The algorithm produces valid connections for which a customer may actually buy a ticket.

In public transportation delays occur quite frequently. Research on timetable information approaches that correctly treat delay information is still in its infancy. Current practice is to determine connections according to the original schedule and add delay information to the departure and arrival times, afterwards. In the process, invalid connections may be reported as interchanges can break due to the delayed arrival of a train in the chain. We have built a system that takes this information into account. It updates the representation of the schedule according to the delays and delivers only valid connections. Furthermore, our system is able to do more than just that, it also facilitates a new service: proactive route guidance for planned itineraries, i.e. our system can confirm whether the trip is still possible as planned. It continuously checks the status, while the passenger travels, and may offer alternatives as soon as the connection becomes highly likely to break. By computing these alternatives as early as possible, and earlier than without our system, more and better options can be explored.

We have a long-term cooperation with Deutsche Bahn AG in the field of timetable information. They provided us with real-world schedules, rules of operation, meta data, and real delay messages.

Our Contribution and Overview In this work we present our full-fledged, fully realistic timetable information system MOTIS (Multi Objective Traffic Information System). We will discuss the core algorithm, the *time-expanded* graph model, and the chosen multi-criteria approach. Besides, we explore additional criteria and the alternative *time-dependent* graph model.

We also study the proper treatment of information about delays and outline the service of proactive route guidance (status checks for connections and calculation of alternatives).

We propose a multi-server architecture to allow search servers to be updated on request by a central server distributing delay information. This allows each search server to be available 99.9% of the time and spend only the remaining tiny amount of time on updates and maintenance. Amongst several search servers the update phases can easily be scheduled to allow for permanent availability of the service.

The fully realistic model, the aim of multi-criteria optimization, and the consideration of dynamical changes to the schedule due to delays are challenging. Straightforward implementations require several minutes to answer queries for connections. We explored and adapted existing and developed new speed-up techniques for our scenario to achieve average runtimes of about one fourth of a second. We are able to solve 95% of the queries in less than one second. Furthermore, we implemented user interfaces to the search engine and the system to supervise connections and calculate alternatives.

The thesis is organized as follows: We start by stating basic terminology and details that have to be considered to make timetable information fully realistic. Moreover, we define queries and properties of connections matching these queries in Chapter 1: *Setting*.

The general multi-criteria approach is introduced in Chapter 2: *Multi-Criteria Optimization*. First, we explain the classical Pareto version. Then we enhance the approach to *relaxed Pareto* by adding relaxation functions (to find the slightly slower but much later connection from above, too). Finally, we present our extension to the concept of *advanced Pareto* (removing unattractive solutions and improving the set of results by defining trade offs, e.g. save x Euro by traveling at most y minutes longer).

Next, in Chapter 3: *Search Algorithms*, we introduce Dijkstra's algorithm for single-criterion shortest path search. We discuss various data structures for the algorithm, generalize the algorithm and eventually present a multi-criteria version.

In Chapter 4: *Graph Models*, we describe the *time-expanded* and *time-dependent* graph models suitable for the representation of schedules. Both of these models allow the application of a shortest-path algorithm to find optimal train connections. The time-expanded model represents each departure and arrival event of a train as a node. Edges with fixed lengths represent traveling in trains, changing and waiting at stations. In the basic time-dependent model there is only one node per station. The edges again encode traveling, changing and waiting, but now one edge represents many possibilities to travel from one station to another. The edge lengths are determined according to when they are used and thus change over time.

The algorithmic core is explained in detail in Chapter 5: *The MOTIS Algorithm*. We refine the algorithm from Chapter 3 to support the search for *advanced Pareto optimal* connections and modify the time-expanded model from Chapter 4 to obtain a fully realistic yet efficiently searchable graph. In Section 5.6 we give a brief overview of the history and evolution of the MOTIS system.

Chapter 6: *Additional Criteria and Special Search Forms*, is devoted to additional criteria.

First, we show an illustrative example: seat reservation. Afterwards, in Section 6.2.2, we present the search for different fare types. We discuss various regular fares and discounts, including contingent based special offers like traveling for a reduced or fixed price as long as a corresponding contingent is available in all used trains. The new concept of the *reliability of transfers*, which is especially interesting in case of delays, is introduced in Section 6.3, thereafter. We define a measurement for the reliability of transfers and show how to extend the search to cover this criterion as well. At the end of the chapter, in Section 6.4, we discuss the search for night trains, with the additional objective of ensuring reasonable sleeping times without need for train changes. We present two approaches to the search for night trains. One method enumerates all suitable night trains, which is possible due to the small number of night trains to be considered for a query. The other one models sleeping time as an additional criterion in our multi-criteria approach.

The consideration and integration of delay information is treated in Chapter 7: *Delays*. Delay information is given as a permanent stream of status messages (over 6 million messages per day, real data from our cooperation partner Deutsche Bahn). We show how to propagate delays due to waiting connecting trains and how to manage the delay information. A whole day can be simulated in less than two minutes. This makes the task obviously manageable. Additionally, we address the issues of fast graph updates and required adjustments to the graph model. A multi-server architecture and the benefit of updating in batches is introduced there, as well.

Chapter 8: *Speed-Up Techniques for Multi-Criteria Search* deals with speed-up techniques. The main challenges are the realism of our model, the multi-criteria nature of the problem (that requires a set of "optimal" connections), the schedule requiring a time-expanded (or time-dependent) graph, the fact that real-world requests specify departure or arrival intervals in times rather than single points, and the graph updates according to delay information. After a concise overview on techniques for shortest path search in general, we show how to adapt some of the techniques to our complex scenario and develop some new techniques.

An extensive computational study follows in Chapter 9: *Computational Study*. We evaluate the search forms for special offers and night trains and the concept of *relaxed Pareto dominance*. From Section 9.3 onwards, we work with *advanced Pareto optimality*, and thoroughly examine the speed-up techniques and influences of various aspects of the algorithm (e.g. combinations of the different criteria, varying parameterizations, exact and heuristic speed-up techniques, etc.).

Although we chose the *time-expanded* model for our algorithm, we also investigate the *time-dependent* model. Our prototype based on that graph model is discussed in Chapter 10: *A Time-Dependent Timetable Information System*.

Finally, in Chapter 11: *Developed Software Tools* we introduce our GUIs and visualization tools. The two major topics are the MOTIS search GUI and CoCoAS (Connection Controller and Alternatives System), our proactive route guidance system which handles status updates of journeys and computation of alternatives in the presence of delays.

We close with a conclusion and an outlook in Chapter 12: *Conclusion and Outlook*.

Acknowledgments

First of all, I would like to thank my supervisors, Karsten Weihe and Matthias Müller-Hannemann. I appreciate their collaboration, guidance and impulses regarding my research in general and this thesis in particular.

I am grateful towards our cooperation partner Deutsche Bahn and especially Wolfgang Sprick and Christoph Blendinger for fruitful discussions, insights into the business, and the supply of data: schedules, coordinates, status messages, and meta data.

I also enjoyed productive conversations with many researchers from other universities, most notably Annabell Berger (MLU Halle-Wittenberg), Daniel Delling, Dominik Schultes, and Frank Schulz (all three formerly at TH Karlsruhe).

Many students have been involved in the development of MOTIS in one or the other way, including theses, practical courses, research projects and seminars. The following students wrote a thesis contributing to the whole framework (in alphabetical order): Miriam Graue [Gra04], Peter Jung [Jun06], Torsten Gunkel [Gun07, GMS07, GMS09], Kai Mehringskötter [Meh07], Yann Disser [Dis07, DMS08], Lennart Frede [FMS08, Fre08], Mohammad Keyhani [Key09], Daniel Mäurer [Mäu09], Konstantin Tennhard, and Christian Weber. The last two are currently writing their Bachelor's theses in our group.

Special thanks go to our long-time student assistants: Mohammad Keyhani (assistance in implementation and algorithm design) and Konstantin Tennhard (GUIs, communication, and maintenance) and my new colleague and PhD student Daniel Mäurer. They provided invaluable assistance during the writing of the thesis.

I want to thank my girlfriend, Christiane, and my parents, Heidemarie and Vinzenz, for their love, support and encouragement. Furthermore, I would like to thank Benjamin Knopp and Jana Kaiser for proofreading and improving my English skills. Last but not least, thank you to all members of the Algorithms Group at TU Darmstadt for their support and assistance.

Parts of this thesis have been published in refereed proceedings and journals [MSW02, MS06, GMS07, MS07, DMS08, FMS08, MS09, GMS09].

Chapter 1

Setting

In this chapter, we want to introduce and clarify basic terminology. We specify queries and the necessary requirements for connections to match a query. Furthermore, we will discuss different search forms, either classical *pre-trip* search from a planning stage, or *on-trip* search, when already at the station or traveling. Finally, we will illustrate the constraints to consider in fully realistic timetable information.

> A train station is a station where a train stops.
> - Then, tell me, what is a workstation?

1.1 Terminology

Trains. The term *train* will be used for all means of transportation, including trains (of course) but also trams, busses, subways and even ferries. Two different trains do not necessarily need to be physically different. A train, e.g. "ICE 158" might reach its final destination, get renamed and head back as "ICE 190", which will be considered a different train.

Stations. Each place a train can stop at in order to allow for boarding and disembarkment of passengers is a *station*. This includes railway-stations (major railway stations like Frankfurt or Paris, small ones like in my hometown with just a single track and a ticket machine), bus stops, subway stations, landing stages for ferries and so on.

Train classes. Each train is associated a specific *train class* in the global data. This includes high-speed trains such as the German ICE and French TGV; ICs and ECs; local trains, "S-Bahn" and subways; busses and trams.

Attributes. Trains have *attributes* describing additional services they provide. Such attributes are, for example: bike transport possible, sleeping car, board restaurant, compartment for disabled, place for wheelchairs.

Traffic days. Most trains do not operate on a daily basis. There is a lot of change during the year. Some trains only operate on workdays, others only on Sundays. National and local holidays, as well as school holidays, affect the days of operation.

Footpaths. Sometimes a passenger has to walk short distances, like from the long distance platform to the one for local transport, or from the railway station to the bus station in front of it. There are a number of these so-called *footpaths* in the German timetable. A passenger may use any footpath at any point in time. This makes a footpath very different from all other means of transportation, which may only be used at specific points in time, namely when the corresponding train departs from the station.

Connections. A *connection* consists of an ordered list of trains and possibly also of footpaths, the list of stations the trains passes and the list of stations where train changes occur. If footpaths are involved, source and target station, length, and description of the footpath are included, too.

Realistic interchange times We count every time a train change occurs as an interchange. The German time table data provides a lower bound for the time between the arrival of a train and the departure of its connections. This bound does not depend only on the train classes and the size of the station. In fact, there is a list of different rules that may be applicable to determine whether a train change is feasible or not. The following list enumerates the rules for interchanges, arranging them from the most general to the most specific one.

- *Interchange rules at stations.* Every station has an interchange time as a default for all interchanges at this station.
- *Transfers between transfer classes.* Each train is associated with a *transfer class*. The time needed for the train change depends on the transfer classes of the coming train at arrival and the leaving train at departure.
- *Line to line transfers.* Similar to the *transfer classes*, each train may be associated with a *line* it serves and specific rules for line changes.
- *Service to service transfers.* The most specific interchange rule gives interchange times between individual trains.

1.2 Queries

1.2.1 Specification of Queries

A *query* to a timetable information system usually includes the following: The (start or) *source station* of the connection, the *target station* and an *interval* in time in which either

1.2 Queries

the departure or the arrival of the connection must be, depending on the *search direction*, the user's choice whether to provide the interval[i] for departure ("forward search") or arrival ("backward search"). Additional query options are:

Vias and duration of stay. A query may contain one (or more) so called *vias*, stations the connection is required to visit and where at least the specified amount of time can be spent, e.g. from Cologne to Munich via Frankfurt with a stay of at least two hours for shopping in Frankfurt.

Train class restrictions. The *query* may be restricted to a subset of all *train classes*. By excluding high speed trains one might be able to find cheaper connections.

Attribute requirements. A user can specify attributes a connection has to satisfy or is not allowed to have. We allow Boolean operators for specifying *attribute requirements* like:

(a restaurant OR a bistro) AND bike transportation.

Passenger related attributes. Additional attributes are relevant for the fare calculation. The query contains the desired *comfort class* (i.e. first or second class). In order to determine possibilities for discounts, the query also includes the number of passengers, and for each passenger the type of discount card which is available (if any). For families with children the age of each child must be specified.

1.2.2 Connections Matching a Query

A connection needs to be feasible and must satisfy all requirements of the query specification to match the query. Some additional feasibility requirements are:

Meta Stations and Source-/Target-Equivalents. For a passenger the starting station might not be important, as long as these stations are relatively close together. Virtual *meta stations* group such stations together (like the railway station and bus stops that can be found right next to each other at the central station of any city). *Source/target-equivalents* group stations together in a similar fashion, but not as a new virtual station: Every *source/target-equivalent* consists of a station and its possible replacements.
Meta-stations or source/target-equivalents may appear as the source and target station as well as any *via* in a query.

Special attributes: NotIn / NotOut. There are some train and station related attributes that do have a special meaning for the stops of a train. Although a train stops at a station, boarding or disembarking the train or both may not be allowed. Especially for night and high-speed trains there are some stations near the origin of the train where one is only allowed to enter the train and some stations near the end where one is only allowed to leave it. In a night

---

[i]Note that the specification of an interval is crucial for typical pre-trip queries although previous work often assumes single point intervals.

train passengers should not be disturbed by too much "traffic" inside the train. In both cases the trains should not be used only for a short transfer. Passengers are encouraged rather to use local transportation.

1.3 Pre-Trip / On-Trip Searches

Most timetable information systems consider a pre-trip scenario: The user is at home and requests a connection from station s_1 to s_2 departing or arriving around some time τ or inside an interval $[\tau_1, \tau_2]$. In such a scenario, it is important that the search delivers all attractive connections with respect to several criteria which suit the query. Even if you use information systems at a station or click "Right-now" in an online system you will usually be offered several alternatives.

In an *on-trip* scenario one is much closer to an earliest arrival problem. We differentiate two cases of the on-trip search:

1. A customer is at a certain station and wants to travel right now. Either he comes without a travel plan (for example, he was unable to plan the end of some meeting) or he may have just missed a connecting train.

2. The customer sits already in a train and wants to search for alternatives, for example, because he has been informed that a connecting train will be missed.

In both cases travelers want to reach their destination as fast and convenient as possible. In case of delays many railway companies even remove restrictions on train-bound tickets, so it might be possible to completely forget about ticket costs, since the ticket is already paid and the passenger may use any means of transportation available. If there is a restriction like "no high speed train" (like the German ICE or French TGV) which is not revoked, an on-trip search with train category restrictions should be supported.

On-trip search at a station. While in a pre-trip search travel time is measured as the difference between the arrival at the destination and the departure with the first used train, on-trip search measures the travel time from "now" on and takes it as one of the optimization goals. However, in the presence of delays it may become more important to search for reliable connections (cf. Section 6.3).

On-trip search in a train. In case the user currently travels in a train, the on-trip search is different from the scenario at a station. Instead of leaving the train and standing at a station with the connecting train long gone (or canceled), we can often do better if we know of this problem in advance. Interesting additional alternatives may either be to leave the train before arriving at the station where the connection breaks, or to stay longer in the train to change trains at a subsequent station.

1.4 Fully Realistic Model

Our model of the timetable is fully realistic. We did not make any simplifying assumptions. You can actually buy a ticket for connections computed by our MOTIS system. All interchange rules are realized and only connections with valid change times are computed. Trains operate according to their real traffic days. We consider footpaths between stations as well as meta stations and source/-target-equivalents and respect the specific attributes prohibiting boarding or disembarking at certain times and stations.

Chapter 2

Multi-Criteria Optimization

In this chapter we will introduce our multi-criteria approach for the search for attractive train connections.

2.1 Criteria

We want to base our discussion in this chapter on the following criteria:

- *Travel time* (time) is the classical optimization criterion in timetable information systems.

- The *number of interchanges* (ic) is a measure for the convenience and reliability of a connection.

- Another important criterion for rating a connection is *ticket cost* (cost).

- As we will introduce further criteria in Chapter 6, we will use an *additional criterion* (add) in our discussions, where needed. Think of a measure for the reliability of interchanges or sleeping time in night trains, for example.

The remainder of this chapter is devoted to the questions of how to compare connections using multiple criteria and how to obtain all attractive connections. In the subsequent chapters we will see what algorithm to use and how to design a timetable representation to find "attractive" connections according to multiple criteria.

2.2 Pareto Optimality

Measuring the Quality of Connections

Most timetable information systems only regard one criterion, namely *travel time* (as observed in [MSWZ07]). As mentioned before we want to focus on the three criteria, travel time, ticket

Name	Departure time	Travel time (minutes)	Number of interchanges	Price	Pareto optimal
c_1	7 : 30	110	1	75€	
c_2	8 : 00	100	1	75€	✓
c_3	8 : 00	160	0	60€	✓
c_4	8 : 00	200	2	35€	✓
c_5	8 : 00	260	2	34€	✓
c_6	8 : 15	120	1	50€	✓

Table 2.1: Example connections for Pareto dominance and extensions.

costs, and number of interchanges. Simply minimizing any of these three independently (or all three separately) is obviously not the method of choice. In the *weighted multi–criteria* case an evaluation function f may look like:

$$f = \varphi \cdot \text{time} + \xi \cdot \text{ic} + \vartheta \cdot \text{cost}.$$

Different choices for the set of parameters $P = \{\varphi, \xi, \vartheta\}$ express the difference in importance of the three criteria (called a *preference profile*). Users may never see some interesting alternatives (for them) if either they or a system/operator sets the wrong parameters.

To overcome this problem, the concept of *Pareto optimality* treats all criteria simultaneously. For two given k-dimensional vectors $x = (x_1, \ldots, x_k)$ and $y = (y_1, \ldots, y_k)$, we define x dominates y (denoted by $x <_p y$) if

$$x_i \leq y_i \qquad \text{for all } 1 \leq i \leq k \text{ and}$$
$$x_i < y_i \quad \text{for at least one } i \in \{1, \ldots, k\}.$$

The *smaller relation* $x <_p y$ is an irreflexive, transitive relation. Together with the canonical multidimensional equality we have a partial order $x \leq_p y$ (a reflexive, antisymmetric, and transitive relation). Our approaches will depend on the transitivity, antisymmetry and irreflexivity of the smaller relation. Note that vectors can be incomparable, that is, neither $x <_p y$ nor $y <_p x$ holds even though $x \neq y$. Vector x is *Pareto optimal* in set X if there is no $y \in X$ that dominates x. Here, we assume for simplicity that all cost criteria shall be minimized. In our scenario we compare 3-dimensional vectors encoding travel time, ticket cost, and the number of interchanges of our connections. Each of the x_i is called a *Pareto criterion*. This approach is easily extendable to cover further criteria.

Consider the connections of Table 2.1: Connections c_2 to c_6 are Pareto optimal. Neither the single-criterion nor weighted-criteria approaches (for some parameters) find c_6, which is probably the most promising connection for the majority of people. Unfortunately, the classical Pareto approach has its limits as well: Suppose connection c_6 does not exist in the list. Although connection c_1 is dominated by c_2 it still arrives earlier at its destination. A passenger using a timetable information system at the departure station might prefer c_1 as it leaves more time to get to his final destination from the target station instead of waiting 30 minutes at the departure station. In spite of being Pareto optimal, connection c_5 is of no practical use at all. Alternative c_4 is much faster and only minimally more expensive.

Antisymmetry, irreflexivity, and transitivity Suppose our smaller relation $<'$ were neither antisymmetric nor irreflexive and we wanted to compare two connections A and B. If both $A <' B$ and $B <' A$ hold, it would depend on the order of the evaluation, as to whether we keep A or B. This is clearly undesirable.

Due to the desired use in dominance testing, during algorithm execution, we also require our smaller relation to be transitive.

2.3 Advanced Pareto Optimality

2.3.1 Relaxed Pareto Dominance

To tackle the drawbacks of the simple Pareto dominance approach we *relax* the dominance rule in the *relaxed Pareto dominance* case (as published in [MS07]). This means that more pairs of connections become mutually incomparable. In addition to the four cost criteria, travel time, ticket cost, number of train changes, and our additional criterion, further aspects are taken into account to define the smaller relation between connections.

Formally, we now consider n-dimensional (integral or real-valued) vectors

$$x = (x_1, \ldots, x_k, x_{k+1}, \ldots, x_n) \in S,$$

where the first k components are cost criteria and the remaining $n - k$ components encode additional data (like departure and arrival time, highest used train class). Furthermore, for each cost criterion we have a non-negative *relaxation function* $f_i : S \times S \mapsto \mathbf{R}_0^+ \cup \{+\infty\}$. For any two $x, y \in S$ we now define that x dominates y *(in the relaxed sense)* if

$$\begin{aligned} x_i + f_i(x, y) &\leq y_i & \text{for all } 1 \leq i \leq k \text{ and} \\ x_i + f_i(x, y) &< y_i & \text{for at least one } i \in \{1, \ldots, k\}. \end{aligned}$$

We will denote relaxed Pareto dominance by $x <_r y$.

In order to be able to apply relaxed Pareto dominance in the computation of attractive connections, it is essential that dominance is a transitive relation. This restricts the set of reasonable relaxation functions.

Next we give examples of how to specify suitable relaxation functions f_i.

- The larger the time difference between the departure and arrival times of two connections, the less these connections should influence each other.

  Suppose we want to compare connections A and B which have departure times d_A, d_B, arrival times a_A, a_B and travel times $time_A, time_B$ (all data given in minutes), respectively. Then connection A dominates B with respect to the criterion travel time if A overtakes B or

  $$time_A + \alpha(A,B) \cdot \min\{|d_A - d_B|, |a_A - a_B|\} < time_B, \tag{2.1}$$

  where, e.g., we may choose $\alpha(A,B) := \frac{1}{2} time_A / time_B$.

  With this relaxation, connection c_1 is no longer dominated by c_2.

- Different kinds of connections shall not dominate each other (e.g., connections using night trains or no night trains, or an event train (e.g. a special train to a sports event). Using night trains a customer does not want to arrive as fast (and/or cheap) as possible. He would rather arrive relaxed and even save a night's stay at a hotel. Neither of these alternatives should be dominated by connections using other kinds of transportation. This can be modeled by defining a relaxation function to be $+\infty$ if the encoding of the train class attributes forbids a mutual domination.

Incomparable connections do not dominate each other, thus attractive alternatives are not suppressed. It is easy to check that all the proposed relaxation functions preserve the desired transitivity of our Pareto dominance relation. In Section 6.2 it will turn out that this concept can also be used to handle special offers in pricing systems.

Antisymmetry and irreflexivity For two connections A and B we have

$$c_A + f(A,B) \leq c_B \;\Rightarrow\; c_A \leq c_B,$$

due to the fact that $f(A,B) \geq 0$, and, obviously,

$$c_A \leq c_B \wedge c_A \geq c_B \;\Leftrightarrow\; c_A = c_B.$$

Pareto smaller $<_p$ only holds if, at least in one of the dimensions, the inequality is fulfilled by a strict smaller. Thus, antisymmetry and irreflexivity follow immediately for all relaxations.

2.3 Advanced Pareto Optimality

Transitivity Suppose we have $A <_r B$ and $B <_r C$ for three connections A, B, and C. Looking at a criterion c and the associated relaxation function $f(\cdot, \cdot)$ we have

$$c_A + f(A, B) \leq c_B \text{ and } c_B + f(B, C) \leq c_C.$$

If we replace c_B in the second inequality with the left hand side of the first inequality, we get

$$c_A + f(A, B) + f(B, C) \leq c_C.$$

Thus, the classical triangle-inequality

$$f(A, B) + f(B, C) \geq f(A, C)$$

is sufficient for the transitivity of our relation.

Examples for suitable relaxation functions

The classical triangle-inequality obviously holds for the following types of relaxation functions:

- constant non-negative additive term $\delta \geq 0$:

$$c_A + \delta < c_B$$

- addition of non-negative fraction (constant multiplicative term $\delta \geq 0$):

$$c_A + \delta \cdot c_A = c_A \cdot (1 + \delta) < c_B$$

- non-negative weighted additive term using another criterion, weight $\delta \geq 0$:

$$c_A + \max\{x_B - x_A, 0\} \cdot \delta < c_B$$

- addition of non-negative fraction (multiplicative term using another criterion), weight $\delta \geq 0$:

$$c_A + \max\{x_B - x_A, 0\} \cdot \delta \cdot c_A < c_B$$

Arbitrary combinations of these types of functions do not violate the desired properties of our relation. This can be shown by a simple inductive argument.

See Appendix A.1 for a proof of transitivity for our relaxation of travel time as modeled in Inequality 2.1.

2.3.2 Tightened Dominance

In order to remove undesired optima from the set of solutions we want to tighten the dominance. One approach could be to subtract non-negative real valued functions instead of adding them like in relaxed dominance. We give two examples:

- The travel time spent for getting less expensive connections has to yield a fair *hourly wage*, say of δ_{cost} Euros per hour. (In the examples of Table 2.1 an hourly wage of less than one Euro is not enough to make connection c_5 worth considering.) This can be modeled as follows. Suppose we want to compare connections A and B with associated costs $cost_A, cost_B$ in Euros and travel times $time_A, time_B$ in minutes, respectively. Then connection A dominates B with respect to the cost criterion only if

$$cost_A - \frac{\max\{time_A - time_B, 0\}}{60} \cdot \delta_{cost} < cost_B. \tag{2.2}$$

- One might even argue that a faster connection with too many additional interchanges is not desired. This can be achieved by tightening the travel time criterion with

$$time_A - \max\{ic_B - ic_A, 0\} \cdot \delta_{ic} < time_B \text{ or}$$

$$time_A - \max\{ic_B - ic_A, 0\} \cdot \frac{\delta'_{ic}}{100} \cdot time_A < time_B$$

for the number of interchanges ic_A, ic_B, respectively, and constants $\delta_{ic}, \delta'_{ic} > 0$. Now each additional interchange must be compensated for by at least δ_{ic} minutes less travel time or by at least a δ'_{ic} percent shorter travel time.

We will denote tightened Pareto dominance by $x <_t y$.

Tightening and transitivity Unfortunately, tightening does not harmonize well with transitivity. Looking at a straightforward idea for a tightening function, namely subtracting a constant, we already get a counter-example:

$$A <_t B \Leftrightarrow cost_A - \delta < cost_B.$$

For three connections A, B, and C with costs $cost_A = 9$, $cost_B = 6$, and $cost_C = 2$ with $\delta = 5$ we have:

$$cost_A - \delta = 9 - 5 < 6 = cost_B \Rightarrow A <_t B \text{ and}$$
$$cost_B - \delta = 6 - 5 < 2 = cost_C \Rightarrow B <_t C, \text{ but}$$
$$cost_A - \delta = 9 - 5 \not< 2 = cost_C \Rightarrow A \not<_t C$$

2.3 Advanced Pareto Optimality

The function is not even antisymmetric, for the same connections A and B we have

$$cost_A - \delta = 9 - 5 < 6 = cost_B \Rightarrow A <_t B \text{ and}$$
$$cost_B - \delta = 6 - 5 < 9 = cost_A \Rightarrow B <_t A, \text{ but}$$
$$A \neq B.$$

Hourly wages: properties of the smaller relation

In the hourly wage example, transitivity does not hold if ticket cost is the only criterion (see Appendix A.2). Besides, neither asymmetry nor irreflexivity hold.

However, let us consider a combination of two criteria, the hourly wage tightening for ticket cost and non-tightened dominance on travel time. From $A <_t B$ and $B <_t C$ we have $time_A \leq time_B$ and $time_B \leq time_C$. Furthermore, the following two inequalities

$$cost_A - \max\{time_B - time_A, 0\} \cdot \frac{\delta_{cost}}{60} \leq cost_B \tag{2.3}$$

and

$$cost_B - \max\{time_C - time_B, 0\} \cdot \frac{\delta_{cost}}{60} \leq cost_C \tag{2.4}$$

hold and the differences in the $\max\{\cdot\}$ terms are always non negative. We insert 2.3 (left) for c_B into 2.4 and receive:

$$\begin{aligned}
&cost_A - (time_B - time_A) \cdot \tfrac{\delta_{cost}}{60} - (time_C - time_B) \cdot \tfrac{\delta_{cost}}{60} \\
=\ &cost_A - (time_C - time_A) \cdot \tfrac{\delta_{cost}}{60} \\
\leq\ &cost_C.
\end{aligned}$$

Here, $A <_t B$ and $B <_t C$ guarantee that at least one of the less-or-equal relations (either regarding time, cost, or both) between A and B, as well as between B and C, is a strict less. Consequently the same holds between A and C, thus $A <_t C$. No other evaluations of the $\max\{\cdot\}$ term will ever occur due to the travel time criterion.

2.3.3 Advanced Pareto Dominance

In this section we will discuss how to combine the concepts of relaxation and tightening, which will result in what we call *advanced Pareto dominance*. We will first look at an example. Suppose we want to minimize the following criteria: travel time, number of interchanges, ticket cost, and an additional criterion (*add*) measured in some unit U. The last criterion acts as a wildcard for the further criteria (a measure for the reliability of interchanges and the sleeping time in night trains among others) that we will introduce in Chapter 6.

Using Pareto optimality, all connections in Table 2.2 except connection F are optimal. Now we define our desired goal as

- the travel time should be a relaxed Pareto criterion,
- the number of interchanges should be a Pareto criterion,
- we want an hourly wage of at least 5€ in ticket cost, and
- we want an hourly wage of at least $10U$ in the additional criterion.

We relax the travel time using our time difference formula

$$rel_{time}(AB) = \alpha(A,B) \cdot \min\{|d_A - d_B|, |a_A - a_B|, \omega(A,B)\} \qquad (2.5)$$

with the third argument to $\min(\cdot)$

$$\omega(A,B) = \begin{cases} 0 & \text{if } A \text{ overtakes } B \\ 100,000 & \text{otherwise} \end{cases}$$

to void the relaxation if A overtakes B and $\alpha(A,B) = \frac{1}{2} time_A/time_B$ as introduced on Page 16. To use tightening on ticket cost and our additional criterion we define

$$\Lambda_{AB}(c) := \max\{c_B - c_A, 0\}$$

for criterion c. Let the relation symbol $\preccurlyeq$ describe the concept of "less or equal in all dimensions and less in at least one of the dimensions."

Ruleset (I) Our first set of rules (I) consists of these inequalities:

$$\begin{aligned} time_A + rel_{time}(AB) &\preccurlyeq time_B \\ ic_A &\preccurlyeq ic_B \\ cost_A - \Lambda_{AB}(time) \cdot \delta_{cost} &\preccurlyeq cost_B \\ add_A - \Lambda_{AB}(time) \cdot \delta_{add} &\preccurlyeq add_B \end{aligned}$$

with the parameters $\delta_{cost} = 5€/h$ and $\delta_{add} = 10E/h$. With this set of rules we relax the time criterion, have interchanges as a Pareto criterion and tighten the additional and cost criteria requiring hourly wages.

Now all but connections D and E are optimal. The time difference formula ensures that connection F is not dominated by connection A. Connections B and C achieve the desired decrease in either ticket cost or our additional criterion for the additional hour travel time. Connection D is dominated by connection A as it fails to reach the desired hourly wages.

2.3 Advanced Pareto Optimality

Name	Departure time	Criteria				Dominance Rules			
		time	ic	add	cost	Pareto	I	II	III
A	8:00	120	1	$50U$	90 €	✓	✓	✓	✓
B	8:00	180	1	$50U$	84 €	✓	✓		✓
C	8:00	180	1	$39U$	90 €	✓	✓		✓
D	8:00	180	1	$42U$	86 €	✓		✓	✓
E	8:00	240	1	$49U$	89 €	✓			
F	8:45	125	1	$50U$	90 €		✓	✓	✓

Table 2.2: Example connections for advanced Pareto dominance and different sets of rules. Hourly Wages of 5€ for ticket cost or $10U$ in our additional criterion are assumed.

Ruleset (II) However, connection D obtains an hourly wage of 4€ and $8U$ simultaneously and therefore could be considered attractive as well. We might even want connection D to dominate connections B and C (and not be dominated itself). To this end we may use $\Delta_{AB}(c) := c_B - c_A$ instead of adding or subtracting $\Lambda_{AB}(c) := \max\{c_B - c_A, 0\}$. In doing so, we are able to reward and penalize for a single criterion at the same time. As we replace the maximum term by a simple difference, we automatically gain transitivity, asymmetry, and irreflexivity (see Page 23). This leads to our second, alternative set of rules (II):

$$time_A + rel_{time}(AB) \preccurlyeq time_B$$

$$ic_A \preccurlyeq ic_B$$

$$cost_A - \Delta_{AB}(t) \cdot \delta_{cost} - \Delta_{AB}(add) \cdot \overline{\delta}_{add} \cdot \delta_{cost} \preccurlyeq cost_B \quad (2.6)$$

$$add_A - \Delta_{AB}(t) \cdot \delta_{add} - \Delta_{AB}(cost) \cdot \overline{\delta}_{cost} \cdot \delta_{add} \preccurlyeq add_B \quad (2.7)$$

$$time_A - \Delta_{AB}(add) \cdot \overline{\delta}_{add} - \Delta_{AB}(cost) \cdot \overline{\delta}_{cost} \preccurlyeq time_B \quad (2.8)$$

where $\overline{\delta}_i = \frac{1}{\delta_i}$.

In the formulae the terms $\Delta_{AB}(c) \cdot \overline{\delta}_c$ are used to determine the tradeoff in time from the difference in criterion c. By multiplying it with $\delta_{c'}$, we obtain the tradeoff in criterion c', e.g. a difference of $15U$ is equivalent to 7.50€, because we have

$$\Delta_{AB}(add) \cdot \overline{\delta}_{add} \cdot \delta_{cost} = 15E \cdot \frac{1h}{10E} \cdot \frac{5€}{1h} = \frac{3h}{2} \cdot \frac{5€}{1h} = 7.5€.$$

The Inequalities 2.6, 2.7, and 2.8 convert time, ticket cost and the additional criterion into only one of them. Either of them is suitable to make our connections A and D optimal and allow connection D to dominate connections B and C, but only one of them is needed. So, although we have four criteria, only three equations are necessary.

Ruleset (III) If we do not want to lose connections B and C, we only need to keep separate inequalities for the ticket cost and the additional criterion. Note that we will again use $\Delta_{AB}(c)$

instead of $\Lambda_{AB}(c)$. Our rule set (III) is:

$$\begin{aligned} time_A + rel_{time}(AB) &\preccurlyeq time_B \\ ic_A &\preccurlyeq ic_B \\ cost_A - \Delta_{AB}(time) \cdot \delta_{cost} &\preccurlyeq cost_B \\ add_A - \Delta_{AB}(time) \cdot \delta_{add} &\preccurlyeq add_B \\ time_A - \Delta_{AB}(add) \cdot \overline{\delta}_{add} - \Delta_{AB}(cost) \cdot \overline{\delta}_{cost} &\preccurlyeq time_B \end{aligned} \quad (2.9)$$

This is essentially the rule set (I) plus Equation 2.8. Thus we keep the tightening for ticket cost and the additional criterion (protecting connections B and C) as well as the weighted sum that protects connections reaching a "combined" hourly wage, like connection D.

We could also incorporate our trade-off for the number of interchanges from Section 2.3.2. For example by adding

$$-\Delta_{AB}(ic) \cdot \frac{\delta'_{ic}}{100} \cdot time_A$$

on the left hand side of Formula 2.9.

Reformulation by sorting If we sort the terms on the left and right hand side in Formula 2.9 appropriately, we obtain

$$time_A - add_A \cdot \overline{\delta}_{add} - cost_A \cdot \overline{\delta}_{cost} \preccurlyeq time_B - add_B \cdot \overline{\delta}_{add} - cost_B \cdot \overline{\delta}_{cost}.$$

That is, we only compare two weighted sums as our fifth criterion. Similarly, we may sort the whole rule set (III) to look as follows:

$$\begin{aligned} time_A + rel_{time}(AB) &\preccurlyeq time_B \\ ic_A &\preccurlyeq ic_B \\ time_A \cdot \delta_{cost} + cost_A &\preccurlyeq time_B \cdot \delta_{cost} + cost_B \\ time_A \cdot \delta_{add} + add_A &\preccurlyeq time_B \cdot \delta_{add} + add_B \\ time_A - add_A \cdot \overline{\delta}_{add} - cost_A \cdot \overline{\delta}_{cost} &\preccurlyeq time_B - add_B \cdot \overline{\delta}_{add} - cost_B \cdot \overline{\delta}_{cost} \end{aligned} \quad (2.10)$$

In fact, this leads to our final formulation for advanced Pareto Dominance.

Formulation for Advanced Pareto Dominance
Given k criteria and r inequalities, we can formulate each of our inequalities (i) for $i \in \{1, \ldots, r\}$ as

$$(i) \quad \sum_{j=1}^{k} \alpha_{c_j}^i c_{j_A} + rel_i(A, B) \preccurlyeq \sum_{j=1}^{k} \alpha_{c_j}^i c_{j_B} \quad (2.11)$$

2.4 Applying Advanced Pareto Dominance

i	a^i_{time}	a^i_{ic}	a^i_{add}	a^i_{cost}	$rel_i(AB)$
1	1	0	0	0	$rel_{time}(AB)$
2	0	1	0	0	0
3	δ_{cost}	0	0	1	0
4	δ_{add}	0	1	0	0
5	1	0	$\overline{\delta}_{add}$	$\overline{\delta}_{cost}$	0

Table 2.3: The coefficients a^i_c and relaxation terms $rel_i(A, B)$ in Formula 2.11 for rule set (III).

with c_{jA} and c_{jB} denoting the value of criterion c_j for connections A and B. Function $rel_i(A, B)$ is our relaxation for criterion c_i, e.g. a constant or the time difference rule (Formula 2.5).

The coefficients for the rule set (III) are shown in Table 2.3. For example, we have $\alpha^4_{time} = \delta_{add}$, $\alpha^4_{add} = 1$, $rel_4(A, B) = 0$, for the fourth formula, and all $\alpha^4_{c_j} = 0$ for all other criteria c_j.

Transitivity, Antisymmetry, and Irreflexivity
We compare only weighted sums of the criteria in an extension of the fundamental Pareto formulation, which is of course transitive, antisymmetric, and irreflexive. Applying relaxation using functions of the type discussed in Section 2.3.1 does not violate the desired properties of our smaller relations.

Expressiveness of Our Formulation Our formulation for advanced Pareto dominance can model all introduced variants of multi-criteria dominance. Classical Pareto dominance and relaxed Pareto dominance are obtained, with $k = 4$, $r = 4$ and $a^i_{c_j} = 1$ for $i = j$, and $a^i_{c_j} = 0$, otherwise. With relaxation functions $rel_i(AB)$ we get relaxed Pareto dominance. Without relaxation functions we have Pareto dominance. We will use these formulations in the computational study in Section 9.5. There, they are also given in a less condensed form including coefficient tables like Table 2.3.

Using only one equation ($r = 1$) and weights $a^1_{c_j} \neq 0$ for each of the criteria c_j, we have a simple weighted sum. If all but one of the $a^1_{c_j}$ are zero with $r = 1$, we model dominance on a single criterion.

2.4 Applying Advanced Pareto Dominance

The relaxed approach requires additional computational effort during the search, otherwise we miss desired connections. The tightening, on the other hand, does not need to be considered before a search has been completed. It suffices to only use it in the final filtering step before presenting the connections to the customer. However, if this filter is applied anyway, it may be used during the search to improve runtime.

One can opt for any of these modus operandi:

1. Relaxed Pareto dominance during the search, final filtering using advanced Pareto dominance, or

2. advanced Pareto dominance using a *widely accepted parameter set* during search with additional final filtering, or

3. advanced Pareto dominance using a *customer specific parameter set* so that only interesting alternatives for this customer are found.

We believe that the first modus is never needed, for two reasons: a) Relaxed Pareto dominance finds far too many connections, and these have to be filtered before presenting them to a customer. So there is no reason to waive some sort of early filtering. And b) a widely accepted parameter set exists, e.g. at least 1 Euro per additional hour travel time. Additionally, virtually nobody would want to spend more than double the travel time for saving one interchange.

It might also qualify as natural, that a faster connection should save at least 5 minutes travel time per additional interchange. On the other hand, some might argue the point of not producing the fastest connection.

In Section 9.5, we will discuss the changes in the solutions and computational effort when moving from Pareto to relaxed Pareto and to advanced Pareto. There, we will also study the impact of the second and third modus changing wage profiles in Section 9.5.2.5.

Our overall goal is to determine the complete set of connections not dominated by *advanced Pareto dominance*. However, some other aspects are still not covered. Such as: the reliability of interchanges of a connection, i.e. how likely is it to realize all interchanges (cf. Section 6.3), the aim of using a sleeping cart for a reasonable time during the night (cf. Section 6.4), the maximization of a stay at "nicer" locations, scenic views etc.

Chapter 3

Search Algorithms

In this chapter, we will introduce shortest-path search on graphs with non-negative edge lengths using Dijkstra's algorithm. We will discuss different priority queue implementations and generalize Dijkstra's algorithm to cover multi-criteria optimization.

3.1 Introduction

A *directed graph* or *digraph* is a pair $G = (V, E)$. V is the set of *nodes* and $E \subseteq V \times V$ the set of *edges*. We will frequently be referring to the cardinality of V and E and will denote $|V|$ by n and $|E|$ by m. An edge (v, w) is directed from v to w. A node v is *adjacent* to node w if either $(v, w) \in E$ or $(w, v) \in E$ or both.

A *path* P in G is an ordered collection of nodes and edges:

$$P = (v_0, e_1, v_1, \ldots, v_{m-1}, e_m, v_m)$$

with $v_i \in V$ and $(v_i, v_{i+1}) \in E$ for $0 \leq i < m$. An $(s\text{-}t)$-path is a path from s to t, i.e. $s = v_0$ and $t = v_m$.

For any length function $\ell : E \to \mathbf{R}$ and any path $P = (v_0, e_1, v_1, \ldots, e_m, v_m)$ the *length* $\ell(P)$ of P is defined by: $\ell(P) := \sum_{i=1}^{m} \ell(e_i)$. The definition for the *general shortest path problem* reads as follows:

THE GENERAL SHORTEST PATH PROBLEM
Instance: A digraph $G = (V, E)$,
 lengths $\ell : E \to \mathbf{R}$,
 and two vertices $s, t \in V$.
Task : Find an $(s\text{-}t)$-path of minimum length.

The problem is hard to solve in case of arbitrary edge lengths. Namely, if all lengths are -1 then the $(s\text{-}t)$-paths of length $1 - |V|$ are precisely the Hamiltonian $(s\text{-}t)$-paths. Deciding whether such a path exists is NP-complete. However, the problem becomes much easier, if it is restricted to non-negative lengths, referred to as the *shortest path problem* throughout this text.

In this thesis, we will only consider non-negative lengths, as all natural cost functions for our application (travel time, number of interchanges, fares) have this property. We will see in Chapter 6 how additional criteria can be modeled and handled to fit into this scenario as well.

3.2 Dijkstra's Algorithm

The *distance* from s to t (with respect to ℓ), denoted by $dist(t)$, is equal to the minimum length of any $(s\text{-}t)$-path. If no $(s\text{-}t)$-path exists, $dist(t)$ is set to $+\infty$.

Dijkstra's algorithm [Dij59] maintains a distance label $d(v_i)$ for each node v_i, which is an upper bound on the shortest path length to node v_i. The algorithm divides the nodes into two groups at any intermediate step: For any *permanently labeled* node the distance label is exactly the shortest distance from the source to that node. The distance label of any *temporarily labeled* node is an upper bound on the shortest path distance to that node.

The basic idea is to start at s and to permanently label nodes in the order of their distance to s. Initially, only s is permanently labeled, $d(s)$ is set to zero. For any node v, a finite label is the length of an $(s\text{-}v)$-path whose nodes are all permanently labeled except v. The algorithm takes the temporarily labeled node v with minimum label (breaking ties arbitrarily), labels it permanently and scans all arcs leaving v to update the distance labels of adjacent nodes.

Algorithm 1 is a textbook version of Dijkstra's algorithm (from [KV00]), the nodes $v \in R$ are permanently labeled, those in $V \setminus R$ are temporarily labeled. Distance $d(v)$ is the length of a shortest s-v-path, which consist of a shortest $(s\text{-}p(v))$-path together with the edge $(p(v), v)$. If v is not reachable from s, then $d(v) = +\infty$ and $p(v)$ is undefined.

Note that the node t is not part of the input. Dijkstra's algorithm in fact calculates shortest paths from s to all other nodes in G (or the information that a node is not reachable from s in G).

Definition 3.1. *A directed tree is a digraph $T = (U, A)$ in which exactly one node r, the root, has no entering edge and there is a unique $(r\text{-}v)$-path for all $v \in U \setminus \{r\}$. The depth of a node $v \in U$ is the length of the unique $(r\text{-}v)$-path.*

Definition 3.2. *A directed tree $T = (U, A)$, with root node s, is called a shortest paths tree for a graph $G = (V, E)$ and a length function $\ell : E \to \mathbf{R}_+$, if $U \subseteq V$ is the set of vertices reachable from s and $A \subseteq E$ such that for each $t \in V'$ the $(s\text{-}t)$-path in T is a shortest $(s\text{-}t)$-path in G.*

Lemma 3.3. *Dijkstra's algorithm correctly determines a shortest paths tree with root s for a graph $G = (V, E)$ and a length function $\ell : E \to \mathbf{R}_+$.*

3.2 Dijkstra's Algorithm

Proof. Trivially, $d(v) \geq dist(v)$ for all v, throughout all iterations. We prove that throughout the iterations, $d(v) = dist(v)$ for each $v \in R$ (all permanently labeled nodes). After the initialization this is trivial (as $R = \{s\}$).
Consider any iteration. It suffices to show that $d(v) = dist(v)$ for the chosen $v \in V \setminus R$. Suppose $d(v) > dist(v)$. Let $(s = v_0, e_1, v_1, \ldots, e_k, v_k = v)$ be a shortest $(s$-$v)$-path. Let i be the smallest index with $v_i \in V \setminus R$. Then $d(v_i) = dist(v_i)$. Indeed, if $i = 0$ then $d(v_i) = d(s) = 0 = dist(s) = dist(v_i)$. If $i > 0$, then (as $v_{i-1} \in R$): $d(v_i) \leq d(v_{i-1}) + \ell((v_{i-1}, v_i)) = dist(v_{i-1}) + \ell((v_{i-1}, v_i)) = dist(v_i)$. This implies $d(v_i) \leq dist(v_i) \leq dist(v) < d(v)$, contradicting the choice of v. □

Theorem 3.4. *Dijkstra's algorithm solves the shortest path problem in $\mathcal{O}(n^2)$.*

Proof. The correctness follows from the previous Lemma. The computational time is allocated to the following two basic operations:

1. *Node selections* (in line ♭)
   This operation is executed $\mathcal{O}(n)$ times, each execution requires the scanning of each temporarily labeled node. The total time spent on node selection is $\sum_{i=1}^{n} i \in \mathcal{O}(n^2)$.

2. *Distance updates* (in line ♯)
   The algorithm performs this operation at most $|\{(v, w) : (v, w) \in E\}|$ times for all v, thus the total time is $\sum_{v \in V} |\{(v, w) : (v, w) \in E\}| = |E| \in \mathcal{O}(m)$ for updating all distance labels.

Input : A digraph $G = (V, E)$,
edge weights $c : E \to \mathbf{R}_+$,
and a vertex $s \in V$.
Output: Shortest paths from s to all $v \in V$ and their lengths.
More precisely distances $d(v)$ and predecessors $p(v)$ for all $v \in V$.
begin
$\quad d(v) := \begin{cases} 0 & : v = s \\ \infty & : \text{otherwise} \end{cases}$
$\quad$ **for all** $v \in V$ **do** $p(v) := \bot$;
$\quad R := \emptyset$;
$\quad$ **while** $R \neq V$ **do**
♭ $\quad\quad$ Find a vertex $v \in V \setminus R$ such that $d(v) = \min_{w \in V \setminus R} d(w)$;
$\quad\quad R := R \cup \{v\}$;
$\quad\quad$ **for** $w \in V \setminus R, (v, w) \in E$ **do**
$\quad\quad\quad$ **if** $d(w) > d(v) + \ell((v, w))$ **then**
♯ $\quad\quad\quad\quad d(w) := d(v) + \ell((v, w))$ and $p(w) := v$;
end

Algorithm 1: Textbook version of Dijkstra's algorithm.

This runtime is clearly best possible for dense graphs, i.e. graphs where $|E| \in \Theta(n^2)$.

3.3 Data Structures Speeding Up Dijkstra's Algorithm

The bottleneck operation in Dijkstra's algorithm is node selection. If $|E|$ is asymptotically smaller than n^2 the runtime of Dijkstra's algorithm can be reduced by storing the nodes according to their distance labels, instead of scanning all temporarily labeled nodes at each iteration to find the one with minimum distance label. In this section, four data structures will be discussed that all speed up Dijkstra's algorithm by decreasing the computational time required for node selection. All of them can be treated as different implementations of the abstract data type *priority queue*. A priority queue PQ stores a collection of objects, each with an associated real number called its *key*. It provides the following operations:

- *createPriorityQueue()*. Create an empty priority queue.

- *extractMin()*. Find, return and remove an object of minimum key from the priority queue.

- *decreaseKey(o, val)*. Reduce the key of object o from its current value to val which must be smaller than the key it is replacing.

- *insert(o, val)*. Insert a new object o with key val.

In an implementation of Dijkstra's algorithm using a priority queue, the priority queue is the collection of nodes with finite temporary distance labels with their distance values as key. An implementation is given in Algorithm 2.

There are now two different versions of the *distance update* operation if the test in ♮ succeeds: If the distance label of any node is to be updated the first time, it is set from ∞ to a finite value, the node with the distance label as its key is to be inserted into the PQ (in line ♭). If a node is already stored in the PQ the distance update requires a $decreaseKey(\cdot, \cdot)$ operation (in line ♯).

Clearly the operations $extractMin()$ and $insert(\cdot, \cdot)$ are executed at most n times, the operation $decreaseKey(\cdot, \cdot)$ at most m times. We now analyze the runtimes and discuss the data structures for different implementations of the priority queue.

3.3.1 k-heap Implementation

A k-heap is a data structure that stores the elements in a *tree* $T = (U, A)$. Each node has at most k children. Nodes are added to the tree in increasing depth, and for the same depth value from left to right. Formally this *contiguity* property reads as follows:

3.3 Data Structures Speeding Up Dijkstra's Algorithm

$$d(v) := \begin{cases} 0 & : v = s \\ \infty & : \text{otherwise} \end{cases}$$
for all $v \in V$ **do** $p(v) := \perp$;
$R := \emptyset$;
$PQ := createPriorityQueue()$;
$PQ.insert(s, d(s))$;
while $PQ \neq \emptyset$ **do**
    $v = PQ.extractMin()$; $R := R \cup \{v\}$;
    for $w \in V \setminus R$, $(v, w) \in E$ **do**
        if $d(w) > d(v) + \ell((v, w))$ **then**
            if $d(w) = \infty$ **then**
                $d(w) := d(v) + \ell((v, w))$ and $p(w) := v$;
                $PQ.insert(w, d(w))$;
            else
                $d(w) := d(v) + \ell((v, w))$ and $p(w) := v$;
                $PQ.decreaseKey(w, d(w))$;

Algorithm 2: Dijkstra's algorithm using a priority queue.

Property 3.5 (Contiguity).

1. At most k^i nodes have depth i.

2. At most $(k^{i+1} - 1)/(i - 1)$ nodes have depth between 0 and k.

3. The depth of a k-heap containing n nodes is at most $\lfloor \log_k n \rfloor$.

The ordering of the elements satisfies the following invariant:

Property 3.6 (Heap Order). $d(v) \leq d(w)$ for all $(v, w) \in A$.

As a consequence the root node has the smallest $d(\cdot)$-value of all elements.

During heap-operations Property 3.6 may be violated but after completion of any operation both properties hold again. We need two procedures to restore the heap order property after any operation on the heap.

The *siftup()* procedure restores the heap order property after $d(v)$ has decreased for a $v \in U$ and $d(w) > d(v)$ for a $(w, v) \in A$. It repeatedly swaps v and its parent node until either v is the root or $d(v) < d(x)$ for all $(v, x) \in A$. The depth of node v decreases $\mathcal{O}(\log_k n)$ times, since its initial depth is in $\mathcal{O}(\log_k n)$ by item 3 of Property 3.5. Therefore the runtime of *siftup()* is in $\mathcal{O}(\log_k n)$.

The *siftdown()* procedure lets a node "sink" in the heap if for some reason $d(v) > d(w)$ for $(v, w) \in A$. It repeatedly swaps v and the smallest of its children until either v is a leaf or $d(v) \leq d(x)$ for all $(v, x) \in A$. The depth of node v increases $\mathcal{O}(\log_k n)$ times, since the max depth of the tree is in $\mathcal{O}(\log_k n)$ again by item 3 of Property 3.5. Finding the minimal child of v requires $\mathcal{O}(k)$ time, thus the runtime of *siftdown()* is in $\mathcal{O}(k \log_k n)$. Inductive arguments show that both procedures correctly restore the heap order property.

An array can be used to store a k-heap in an ordered fashion: Nodes of same depth are ordered from left to right and all nodes are ordered by increasing depth. The parent of node v at position i is stored at $\lceil (i-1)/k \rceil$, the children at positions $ik - k + 2$ to $ik + 1$. Utilizing an additional array that stores the position of each node and a variable *last* specifying the number of elements stored in the heap all operations can be implemented efficiently.

All *priority queue* operations are implemented as described here:

- *extractMin()* The node of minimum distance to be returned is the root r of the heap. The last node x is placed at the root, the number of elements is decreased by one and *siftdown()* is called for x if necessary. Clearly, this operation takes $\mathcal{O}(k \log_k n)$ time.

- *decreaseKey(o, val)*. After the key of node o is decreased to val, *siftup()* restores the heap order property if violated. This takes $\mathcal{O}(\log_k n)$ time.

- *insert(o, val)*. First variable *last* is incremented by one, then node o with key val is placed at position *last*, and finally operation *siftup()* restores the heap order property if violated. This also takes $\mathcal{O}(\log_k n)$ time.

The performance of k-heaps can be summarized as follows:

Theorem 3.7. *The k-heap data structure requires $\mathcal{O}(\log_k n)$ runtime to perform each of the operations $insert(\cdot)$ and $decreaseKey(\cdot,\cdot)$ and $\mathcal{O}(k \log_k n)$ runtime to perform $extraxtMin()$.*

If a k-heap implementation for the priority queue is used in Algorithm 2 the runtime is in $\mathcal{O}(m \log_k n + nk \log_k n)$. The $extractMin$ operation for node selection is executed $\mathcal{O}(n)$ times. $\mathcal{O}(m)$ times either a new node is inserted or a label is decreased, these operations take $\mathcal{O}(\log_k n)$ time each. An optimal choice of k is $k = max\{2, \lceil \frac{m}{n} \rceil\}$ obtained by equating the two terms $m \log_k n$ and $nk \log_k n$. The resulting runtime is $\mathcal{O}(m \log_k n)$.

Theorem 3.8. *The shortest path problem can be solved in $\mathcal{O}(m \log_k n)$ using a k-heap.*

The runtime is even linear for non sparse graphs (i.e. $m \in \Omega(n^{1+\epsilon})$ for some $\epsilon > 0$), as

$$\mathcal{O}(m \log_k n) = \mathcal{O}(\frac{m \log n}{\log k}) \stackrel{(*)}{=} \mathcal{O}(\frac{m \log n}{\log n^\epsilon}) = \mathcal{O}(\frac{m}{\epsilon}) = \mathcal{O}(m).$$

For the equality marked with $(*)$ remember our choice of $\mathcal{O}(k) = \mathcal{O}(\frac{m}{n}) = \mathcal{O}(\frac{n^{1+\epsilon}}{n}) = \mathcal{O}(n^\epsilon)$. The last equality is true since ϵ is a constant. For very sparse networks (i.e. $m \in \mathcal{O}(n)$) the runtime is $\mathcal{O}(n \log n)$.

3.3.2 Binary Heap Implementation

A binary heap is the simplest form of a k-heap for $k = 2$. As a Corollary from Theorem 3.7 for the special case $k = 2$ we have:

Theorem 3.9. *The* binary heap *data structure requires $\mathcal{O}(\log n)$ runtime to perform each of the operations $insert(\cdot)$, $extraxtMin()$ and $decreaseKey(\cdot, \cdot)$.*

Therefore, the runtime of Algorithm 2 is $\mathcal{O}(m \log n)$ if a *binary heap* implementation of the *priority queue* is used. For very dense graphs (i.e. $m \in \Theta(n^2)$) this is slower than the original implementation of Dijkstra's algorithm in $\mathcal{O}(n^2)$, but faster when $m \in \mathcal{O}(\frac{n^2}{\log n})$.

Theorem 3.10. *The shortest path problem can be solved in $\mathcal{O}(m \log n)$ using a binary heap.*

3.3.3 Fibonacci Heap Implementation

The *Fibonacci heap* is a data structure that performs the heap operations more efficiently than k-heaps. The data structure was named after the well-known *Fibonacci numbers* that are used to prove its runtime bounds. Basically, a Fibonacci heap is a dynamically changing collection of directed trees that all satisfy the heap order property (Property 3.6). Basic operations are linking two trees together or cutting a tree into two. To discuss Fibonacci heaps in full detail is beyond the scope of this work, a nice introduction to Fibonacci heaps can be found in [AMO93]. The runtimes for the various *priority queue* operations are summarized in:

Theorem 3.11. *The Fibonacci heap data structure requires $\mathcal{O}(1)$ amortized time to perform each of the operations $insert(\cdot, \cdot)$ and $decreaseKey(\cdot, \cdot)$ and $\mathcal{O}(\log n)$ time to perform the operation $extractMin()$.*

If a Fibonacci heap implementation for the priority queue is used in Algorithm 2, the runtime reduces to $\mathcal{O}(n \log n + m)$.

Theorem 3.12. *The shortest path problem can be solved in $\mathcal{O}(n \log n + m)$ using a Fibonacci heap.*

This bound is better than that of binary heaps, k-heaps and Dial's data structure (discussed in the next section).

Unfortunately, the better worst-case bound does not make Fibonacci heaps the data structure of first choice. The overhead of the dynamically changing structure hidden in the $\mathcal{O}(\cdot)$ notation is enough to let other heap implementations do far better in empirical studies.

3.3.4 Implementation Using Dial's Data Structure

Dial's algorithm from [Dia69] uses the following fact to store the objects in a sorted fashion:

Property 3.13. *The distance labels of permanently labeled nodes are nondecreasing throughout the execution of the algorithm.*

This fact follows from noting that the algorithm permanently labels a node v with smallest temporary label $d(v)$ and, while scanning the nodes adjacent to v, does not decrease the distance label of any temporarily labeled node below $d(v)$, as all edges have non-negative length.

Let $C = \max_{e \in E} \ell(e)$. Than nC is an upper bound on the distance label of any finitely labeled node. Nodes with infinite distance label need not to be stored until they receive a finite distance label for the first time. Dial's algorithm stores nodes in $nC + 1$ sets, called *buckets*. Bucket k contains all nodes v with temporary distance label $d(v) = k$.

We scan buckets $0, 1, 2 \ldots$ until we identify the first nonempty bucket, say i. Each node v in bucket i has a minimum distance label. For each of these nodes v all adjacent nodes are scanned and their distance labels are updated, v is permanently labeled and removed from bucket i.

If the label of node w is updated from d_1 to d_2, node w is deleted from bucket d_1 and inserted into bucket d_2. Property 3.13 ensures that $d_2 \geq k$ for all updated node labels, thus scanning resumes with buckets $k, k+1, \ldots$ in the following iteration to find the next nonempty bucket.

Storing the content of each bucket as a doubly linked list and keeping pointers from each node v to its distance label in bucket $d(v)$ the following operations require $\mathcal{O}(1)$ time each:

1. checking whether a bucket is empty or not,
2. removing an element from a bucket,
3. inserting an element into a bucket.

The algorithm performs each distance update in $\mathcal{O}(1)$ time and thus requires a total of $\mathcal{O}(m)$ time for all distance updates. The scanning of $nC + 1$ buckets is the bottleneck of this implementation. The runtime of Dial's algorithm is in $\mathcal{O}(m + nC)$.

Due to the large number of $nC + 1$ buckets the memory requirements can be prohibitively large. The following fact allows a significant reduction in the number of required buckets:

Property 3.14. *If v is permanently labeled at the beginning of an iteration, then at the end of the iteration all finitely labeled nodes $w \in V \setminus R$ have labels $d(w) \leq d(v) + C$.*

The fact follows from (a) $d(x) \leq d(v)$ for all $x \in R$ (from Property 3.13) and (b) for each finitely labeled node $w \in V \setminus R$, $d(w) = d(x) + \ell((x,w))$ for some node $x \in R$ (by the property of distance updates). Consequently, $d(w) = d(x) + \ell((x,w)) \leq d(v) + C$. The values of all finite temporary labels are in $[d(v), d(v) + C]$. Thus, all nodes with finite temporary distance labels can be stored in $C + 1$ buckets.

3.3 Data Structures Speeding Up Dijkstra's Algorithm

So in a modified version, the buckets are numbered $0, 1, 2, \ldots, C$. Every temporary labeled node w with distance label $d(w)$ is stored in bucket $d(w) \mod (C+1)$. Therefore during the execution of the algorithm bucket k contains nodes with temporary distance labels $k, k+(C+1), k+2(C+1)$, and so on in that order. However, due to Proposition 3.14 this bucket will hold only nodes with the same distance label at any point in time. If bucket k contains a node with minimum distance label, buckets $k+1, k+2, \ldots, C, 0, 1, \ldots, k-1$ store nodes in increasing values of the distance labels.

The buckets are examined sequentially in a wrap-around fashion to identify the first nonempty bucket, i.e. after bucket C has been tested, bucket 0 is next. Let k be the bucket where the minimum was found. In the subsequent iteration Dial's algorithm reexamines the buckets starting at bucket k.

Compared to the original implementation with runtime $\mathcal{O}(n^2)$ and linear space requirement, the amount of storage required for large C may still be too large. Furthermore, because the algorithm might take as many as $n-1$ wrap-arounds, the computational time in $\mathcal{O}(m+nC)$ is large or not even polynomial, e.g. if $C = n^5$ the algorithm runs in $\mathcal{O}(n^5)$ or requires even exponential runtime in the worst case, if $C \in \mathcal{O}(2^n)$.

However, the bound of $\mathcal{O}(m+nC)$ is almost never touched. In most domains the size of C is modest and the number of passes through all of the buckets is much less than $n-1$. In consequence, the runtime of Dial's algorithm is much better than that indicated by its worst-case complexity.

Implementing the priority queue interface using Dial's data structure

Dial's data structure can be used as the priority queue PQ in Algorithm 2, as well, since all functions of the *priority queue* interface can be implemented using Dial's data structure:

- *createPriorityQueue()*. Create $C+1$ empty buckets.
- *extractMin()*. Find next empty bucket, return an element from it and remove this element from the bucket.
- *decreaseKey(o, val)*. Remove element of node o from bucket $(d(o) \mod (C+1))$ and insert it into bucket $(val \mod (C+1))$.
- *insert(o, val)*. Insert a new object o into bucket $val \mod (C+1)$.

Theorem 3.15. *The shortest path problem can be solved in $\mathcal{O}(m+nC)$ using Dial's data structure.*

3.3.5 Priority Queues without decreaseKey-Operation

A *priority queue* with fewer operations (namely without a $decreaseKey(\cdot, \cdot)$ operation) allows an even more compact and easier to implement version of Algorithm 2 and is described in Algorithm 3:

```
     ⎧ 0  :  v = s
d(v) := ⎨
     ⎩ ∞  :  otherwise
for all v ∈ V do p(v) := ⊥;
R := ∅;
PQ := createPriorityQueue();
PQ.insert(s, d(s));
while PQ ≠ ∅ do
    v := PQ.extractMin();
 ♭  if v ∈ R then continue;
    R := R ∪ {v};
    for w ∈ V \ R, (v, w) ∈ E do
        if d(w) > d(v) + ℓ((v, w)) then
 ♯          d(w) := d(v) + ℓ((v, w)) and p(w) := v;
            PQ.insert(w, d(w));
```

Algorithm 3: Dijkstra's algorithm using a priority queue without decreaseKey.

If the value of $d(w)$ is decreased (in line ♯), a new entry $(w, d(w))$ is inserted into the priority queue. Note that $d(\cdot)$ never increases. So multiple labels for w may be stored in PQ. Labels of nodes that have already been permanently labeled may simply be ignored (in line ♭). The algorithmic complexity using one of the introduced priority queue types is the same as if the entry $(w, d(w))$ is decreased and the position of the label in the priority queue is adjusted accordingly: There are at most m $insert(\cdot, \cdot)$ operations as no more than m edges are to be inspected and so the number of executions $extractMin()$ is restricted to m as well.

But in contrast to the other version, ignoring all $v \in R$ does not require pointers from v to $(v, d(v))$ in the PQ and is easier to implement, as there are only $insert(\cdot, \cdot)$ and $extractMin()$ operations on the PQ.

3.3.6 Remarks on Data Structures and Shortest Path Search

This introduction to shortest path algorithms relies on [AMO93] and [Sch03]. The first algorithm discussed in this chapter was suggested by Dijkstra [Dij59]. The use of heaps was introduced by Williams [Wil64]. The use of k-heaps is due to Johnson [Joh77]. Fibonacci heaps were introduced by Fredman and Tarjan in [FT84]. Dial's data structure was suggested by Dial [Dia69].

Although Dial's implementation has a poor worst-case runtime bound it has led to algorithms with better worst case behavior. An improved version that runs better in practice can be found in [DGKK79]. Researchers have extensively tested shortest path algorithms empirically. Computational results [HD88, DH90] suggest that Dial's implementation is the fastest algorithm for many classes of graphs.

Variants and combinations of data structures achieve even better theoretical runtime bounds, e.g. with the priority queue due to Van Emde Boas et al. [EKZ76] in $\mathcal{O}(m \cdot \log \log C)$ and with a combination of Radix and Fibonacci Heaps in $\mathcal{O}(m + n\sqrt{C})$ [AMOT90].

3.4 The Multi-Criteria Version

3.4.1 Problem Definition

Multi-criteria shortest-path problems with non-negative edge lengths occur in many applications. To mention just a few, problems of this kind arise in communication networks (cost vs. reliability), in individual route planning for trucks and cars (fuel costs vs. time), in route guidance [JMS00], and in curve approximation [MZ00, MZ01]

Formally, we have a digraph $G = (V, E)$ and for a fixed positive integer k a k-dimensional length-function $\ell : E \to \mathbf{R}^k$ that assigns a k-dimensional length vector $\ell(e) = (\ell_1(e), \ldots, \ell_k(e))$ to each edge $e \in E$. For any path $P = (v_0, e_1, v_1, \ldots, e_m, v_m)$ the *length* $\ell(P)$ of P is defined by:

$$\ell(P) := \sum_{i=1}^{m} \ell(e_i) = \left(\sum_{i=1}^{m} \ell_1(e_i), \sum_{i=1}^{m} \ell_2(e_i), \ldots, \sum_{i=1}^{m} \ell_k(e_i) \right)$$

The path P has k lengths $\ell_j(P) = \sum_{i=1}^{m} \ell_j(e_i)$, $j = 1, \ldots, k$.

Recall our Definition in Section 2.2 of Pareto dominance and Pareto optimality.

Like in the normal shortest path problem ($k = 1$) it makes sense to consider the node-to-node case, i.e. computing all Pareto optimal paths P_{opt} of all paths $P_{s,t}$ from $s \in V$ to $t \in V$.

Variants

Interesting variants of optimization in the multi-criteria Pareto case are:

1. finding the so-called *Pareto curve* which is the set of all Pareto optimal solution vectors (i.e. lengths of the Pareto optimal paths);

2. finding all Pareto optimal paths;

3. finding just one Pareto optimal path;

4. finding some lexicographically interesting Pareto optimal path(s) (e.g. find among all paths that minimize one criterion the paths that minimize a second criterion).

We are mainly interested in finding the set of all Pareto optimal paths. In fact, we will extend the algorithm in Chapter 5 to even find all *advanced Pareto optimal* solutions as discussed in Section 2.3.3.

The definition for the *multi-criteria shortest path problem* with non-negative edge lengths reads as follows:

> THE MULTI-CRITERIA SHORTEST PATH PROBLEM
> Instance: A digraph $G = (V, E)$,
>   a positive integer k,
>   lengths $\ell : E \to (\mathbf{R}_+)^k$,
>   and two vertices $s, t \in V$.
> Task   : Find all Pareto shortest $(s\text{-}t)$-paths.

3.4.2 Number of Pareto Optimal Solutions (worst-case)

Lemma 3.16. *The number of Pareto optima can be exponentially large even in the two criteria case.*

Proof. We construct a class of instances, each of which is basically an acyclic chain, with two alternative paths between node v_{2i} and v_{2i+2}, see Figure 3.1. Formally, let $G = (V, E)$ be a digraph with $n+1$ nodes, numbered from 0 to n. The edge set consists of the edges (v_{2i}, v_{2i+1}) and (v_{2i+1}, v_{2i+2}) with lengths $(2^{i+1}, 2^i)$ and the edges (v_{2i}, v_{2i+2}) with lengths $(2^{i+1}, 2^{i+2})$.

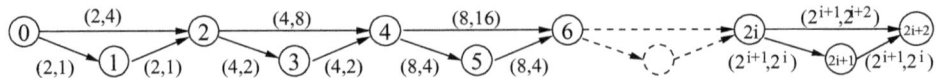

Figure 3.1: Example for exponentially many Pareto optimal paths.

Now it is easy to prove by induction, that there are as many as 2^i different Pareto optimal paths at node $2i$ (in fact, every directed path is Pareto optimal). The objective values of the Pareto optimal labels at node $2i$ are of the form $(2^i + 2^j, 2^{i+1} - 2^j)$ for $j = 0, 1, \ldots, 2^i - 1$ and $i \geq 1$. (Example from [MW01]). □

3.4.3 Tractability and State of the Art

We sketch the previous work on multi-criteria shortest path problems only briefly. For a more complete overview, we refer to the section on shortest paths in the recent annotated bibliography on multi-objective combinatorial optimization [EG00].

The standard approaches to the case that *all* Pareto optima have to be computed are generalizations of the standard algorithms for the single-criterion case. Instead of one scalar distance label, each node $v \in V$ is assigned a number of k-dimensional vectors, which are the lengths of all Pareto optimal paths from s to v (clearly, for $k = 1$ the Pareto optima are exactly the distance labels). For the bi-criteria case, generalizations of the standard label setting (Dijkstra's algorithm) [Han79, Mar84] and label correcting [SA00] methods have been developed. In the monograph of Theune [The95] algorithms for the multi-criteria case are described in detail in the general setting of cost structures over semi-rings. A *two-phase method* has been proposed by Mote et al. [MMO91]. They use a simplex-type algorithm to find a subset of all Pareto optimal paths in the first place, and a label-correcting method to find all remaining Pareto optimal paths in the second phase.

The crucial parameter for the runtime and the space consumption is the total number of Pareto optima over all visited nodes. The insight that this number is exponential in $|V|$ in the worst case has motivated the design of approximation algorithms. Hansen [Han79] and Warburton [War87] both present a fully polynomial-time approximation scheme (FPTAS) for finding a set of paths which are approximately Pareto optima for the bi-criteria shortest-path problem. The *(resource)-constrained* or *weight-restricted shortest-path problem* [MZ00] is a simplifying (yet still $\mathcal{NP}$-hard) variation of the bi-criteria case. Here only one Pareto optimal path is to be computed, namely the one that optimizes the first criterion subject to the condition that the second criterion does not exceed a given threshold value. More than two criteria have mostly been studied in the field of network communications, Tsaggouris and Zaroliagis presented an FPTAS for multi-objective optimization problems with application in traffic optimization [TZ06]. A theoretical study on the size of the Pareto set in practical applications appeared in [MW01, MW06].

There are several experimental studies. Mote et al. [MMO91] investigate problem instances on random graphs and grid graphs with a positive correlation between the two length values of each edge. More precisely, the first length value is randomly generated from a uniform distribution within a certain range, whereas the second length value is a convex combination of the first length value and a randomly generated value from the same distribution. Their experiments indicate that the number of Pareto optimal paths decreases with increasing correlation and that the overall number of such paths is quite small. Brumbaugh-Smith and Shier [BSS89] studied implementations of label-correcting algorithms on graphs where pairs of edge lengths are randomly generated from a bivariate normal distribution. For such instances, their empirical observation was that the asymptotic runtime of the label-correcting method has a very good fit for $\mathcal{O}(m\sqrt{p})$, where p denotes the average number of labels per node.

3.4.4 A Generalization of Dijkstra's Algorithm

In the case that *all* Pareto optimal paths have to be computed, a generalization of Dijkstra's algorithm for the single-criterion case is applicable (see Algorithm 5 on page 39).

It is not at all clear how to organize the priority queue as there are most likely labels of paths P and P' with neither $\ell(P) <_k \ell(P')$ nor $\ell(P') <_k \ell(P)$ in the priority queue at some time during the execution of the algorithm. So no straightforward generalization of any priority queue discussed for the single-criterion case by simply replacing the smaller relation by Pareto dominance is applicable. Let us assume the priority queue is implemented in a fashion that allows the following operations:

- insert a label $(P, \ell(P))$,
- remove a label $(P, \ell(P))$,
- *extractMin()* return some label $(P, \ell(P))$ with $(P', \ell(P')) \not<_k (P, \ell(P))$ for all other labels $(P', \ell(P')) \in PQ$.

Many unnecessary steps may be saved in the following algorithm depending on certain properties of the order in which *extractMin()* returns the labels. Note that the correctness does not depend on the order in which the labels are extracted from the priority queue. Any order suffices to calculate all Pareto optimal paths, only the number of updates and *extractMin()* operations changes. The advantages and disadvantages of implementing such a priority queue in one or another fashion may differ from application to application so we will not describe any implementation at this point. However, the influence of different priority queues in our application of calculating train connections will be discussed in Section 8.8.2 and the ordering criterion on our priority queue will be discussed when dealing with speeding up multi-criteria search in general (see Section 8.3).

Each node $v \in V$ is assigned a number of *labels* stored in a list *nodelist(v)*. Each label stores the path P and the k-dimensional length $\ell(P)$ for its corresponding $(s$-$v)$-path. Throughout the execution of the algorithm *nodelist(v)* satisfies the following invariant at the beginning and end of each iteration.

Property 3.17. *The paths of labels in* `nodelist(v)` *are Pareto optimal in the set of all $(s$-$v)$-paths computed so far.*

To prove that the property holds we need the following two simple facts:

Fact 3.18. *Pareto dominance is transitive.*

---

updateNodeList$(v, (P, \ell(P)))$:
begin
    for *all labels* $(P', \ell(P')) \in$ `nodelist(v)` **do**
        if $\ell(P') <_k \ell(P)$ **then** exit;
        if $\ell(P) <_k \ell(P')$ **then**
            remove $(P', \ell(P')$ from `nodelist(v)` and PQ;
    insert new label $(P, \ell(P))$ into `nodelist(v)` and PQ;
end

Algorithm 4: Procedure `updateNodeList(...)` for Algorithm 5.

3.4 The Multi-Criteria Version

```
d(v) := { (0,...,0)  : v = s
         { ∞         : otherwise
for all v ∈ V do nodelist(v) = ∅;
PQ := createPriorityQueue();
PQ.insert({s},(0,...,0));
begin
    while PQ ≠ ∅ do
        ((P,ℓ(P))) = PQ.extractMin();
        v := last node of P;
        for all edges (v,w) ∈ E do
            P' := P ∪ {(v,w),w};
            updateNodeList(w,(P',ℓ(P')));
end
```

Algorithm 5: Generalization of Dijkstra's algorithm for the multi-criteria case.

Fact 3.19. *If P is a Pareto optimal path, then any sub-path P' of P must also be Pareto optimal.*

As all nodelists are initially empty, Property 3.17 trivially holds. If a new path P with length $\ell(P)$ reaches v, the *updateNodeList(v,·)* -procedure (see Algorithm 4) restores Property 3.17 if it has been violated during the current iteration.

If any label in nodelist(v) dominates $\ell(P)$ (in line ♭), P is not only not Pareto optimal, but all paths $\hat{P}$ that start with P are not Pareto optimal either and need not be inspected, due to Fact 3.19.

If the label $(P,\ell(P))$ is inserted into nodelist(v) (in line ♮) there is no label $(\hat{P},\ell(\hat{P}))$ in nodelist(v) with $\ell(\hat{P}) <_k \ell(P)$, thus label $(P,\ell(P))$ is Pareto optimal in the set of all (s-v)-paths computed so far.

If for any label $(\hat{P},\ell(\hat{P}))$ in nodelist(v) $\ell(P) <_k \ell(\hat{P})$ holds, label $(\hat{P},\ell(\hat{P}))$ is not Pareto optimal. Again due to Fact 3.19 no path P^i with sub-path $\hat{P}$ has to be considered at all, therefore the label is not only removed from nodelist(V) but also from the priority queue PQ.

If a label $(P^*,\ell(P^*))$ is removed while updating nodelist(v) (in line ♯), the new label $(P,\ell(P))$ is later inserted into nodelist(v) (in line ♮). Assume for a contradiction $\ell(P) <_k \ell(P^*)$ and $\exists P' \in$ nodelist(v) such that $\ell(P') <_k \ell(P)$. Due to the transitivity of Pareto dominance (Fact 3.18) $\ell(P') <_k \ell(P) <_k \ell(P^*)$. This implies $\ell(P') <_k \ell(P^*)$ violating Property 3.17 as $P', P^* \in$ nodelist(v) at the beginning of the iteration. Contradiction.

As soon as the priority queue is empty, all Pareto optimal paths to node v are stored in the labels in nodelist(v) for all $v \in V$ and nodelist(t) contains all Pareto optimal (s-t)-paths.

Theorem 3.20. *The multi-criteria shortest path problem can be solved by a generalization of Dijkstra's algorithm.*

3.4.5 Modifications

3.4.5.1 Generalizing the s-t-Case

Consider the scenario where the input does not consist of two nodes s and t but of start nodes $s_1, s_2, \ldots, s_u$ and target nodes $t_1, t_2, \ldots, t_v$ with either $u > 1$ or $v > 1$ or both $u, v > 1$.

Our algorithm can easily be modified to handle more than one source at a time: A new start node s is added to V. Let $E' := E \cup \{(s, s_i)\}$ and set $\ell((s, s_i))$ to zero for all new edges (s, s_i). Any shortest path from s to t in $G' = (V \cup \{s\}, E')$ is a shortest path from an s_i to t.

By connecting all target nodes t_j to a new target t with edge cost zero in the same fashion, more than one target can be handled, too. Thus, all shortest s-t-paths are a shortest path from a start node s_i to some target node t_j.

The new nodes and edges need not be introduced into the graph (as this would require many changes for each search). The search can more efficiently be initialized by setting

$$d(v) := \begin{cases} 0 & : \ v = s_i \text{ for some } i \\ \infty & : \ \text{otherwise} \end{cases}$$

and inserting all labels $(s_i, d(s_i))$ into the priority queue.

Labels representing optimal paths are gathered at all t_j once the priority queue is empty.

3.4.5.2 Limited Priority Queue

A limited priority queue data structure that only supports insertion of labels and extraction of a minimum label is sufficient as for the standard Dijkstra algorithm (cf. Section 3.3.5). Since there are now multiple labels for one node a set storing the nodes that are permanently labeled is replaced by flags in the labels themselves. These flags are initialized to *valid*. Every time a label is removed from a nodelists its flag is set to *invalid* instead of removing the label from the priority queue. After every *extractMin()*-operation the flag of the new label is checked. The label is ignored if its flag is set to *invalid*. This one bit information saves a pointer from the label in the nodelist to its position in the priority queue as there is no need to access the latter from anywhere in the algorithm except in the *extractMin()*-operation.

Chapter 4

Graph Models

There are basically two approaches for modeling public transportation timetable data: the *time-expanded* [PS98, SWW00, MW01, Sch04, Gra04, Sch05, MS07, PSWZ04b, PSWZ08], and the *time-dependent* approach [CH66, OR90, OR91, KW93, Nac95, BJ04, PSWZ04b, PSWZ08]. The common characteristic of both is that a query can be answered by applying a shortest path algorithm (as introduced in the previous chapter) on a suitably constructed digraph.

4.1 The Basic Time-Expanded Model

In a basic version of the time-expanded graph (as described e.g. by Schulz, Wagner and Weihe in [SWW00]) each arrival or departure of a train is called an *event* and is represented by a node of a directed graph $G = (V, E)$. Each event has its timestamp. There are two types of edges: *train edges* and *waiting edges*. We call a connection between two stations A and B *elementary* if the train departs from station A and arrives at station B without stopping in between. For every elementary connection c in the timetable, node v corresponding to its departure event at station S_d is connected by a directed edge (v, w) to node w corresponding to its arrival event at station S_a. This type of edge is called a *train edge*. Put differently: The set of all elementary connections in the timetable is equivalent to the set of train edges $E_Z \subset E$, whose endpoints induce the set of nodes V.

To facilitate the description of the second set E_W of edges, we order the nodes of V. For each Station S, all nodes belonging to S are arranged according to their time values. In case that there are several nodes sharing the same time stamp, the arrival events are placed before the departure events.

Let $v_1, v_2, \ldots, v_k$ be the nodes of a station S. Two successive nodes v_i, v_{i+1} are linked by a *waiting edge* representing waiting within a station. Let t_u, t_v be the time stamps of two nodes u, v, respectively. Then the length of edge $(u, v) \in E$ is $t_v - t_u$.

In the time-expanded graph there is a directed path for every connection and under our simplifying assumptions the reverse is true as well (see Figure 4.1 for an example).

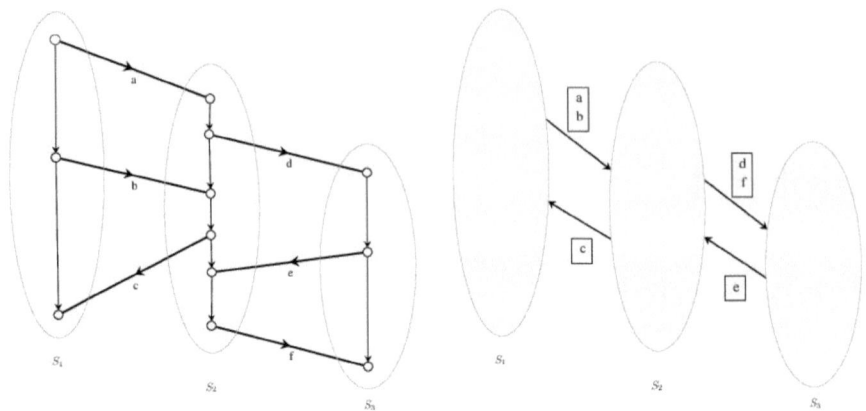

Figure 4.1: The time-expanded (left) and time-dependent (right) model for the same small timetable with three stations S_1, S_2 and S_3. There are two elementary connections, a and b, from S_1 to S_2, one from S_2 to S_1 (connection c), two between S_2 and S_3 (connections d and f), and one direct connection (e) from S_3 to S_2.

The construction of a time-expanded graph usually leads to very large but sparse graphs, i.e. $m \in \mathcal{O}(n)$.

This model appears to be the a natural representation of scheduled traffic.

4.2 The Basic Time-Dependent Model

Alternatively, a timetable may be represented by a so-called time-dependent digraph. This description follows Brodal and Jacob [BJ04]. In this graph $G = (V, E)$ there is only one node per station. The set of nodes V consists of all stations of the associated train network. Two nodes v and w are connected by an edge (v, w) if, at some time, there is an elementary connection from station v to station w.

The length (or cost) of an edge (v, w) depends on the point in time when it is used. More specifically, every edge $e = (v, w)$ has an associated *link-traversal function* $f_e : \mathcal{T} \to \mathcal{T}$, where $\mathcal{T}$ represents the time domain. The cost $\ell((v, w))$ of (v, w) can be calculated by $f_{(v,w)}(t) - t$, where t is the departure time from v and $f_{(v,w)}(t)$ is the earliest possible arrival time at w.

If the function $f : \mathcal{T} \to \mathcal{T}$ satisfies $f(t) \geq t$ for all $t \in \mathcal{T}$, f is said to have *non-negative delay*. Function f is called *monotonic*, if $t \leq t'$ implies $f(t) \leq f(t')$.

Definition 4.1 (Timed path). *A timed path in G is a sequence $v_1, v_2, \ldots, v_k$ of nodes in G and a sequence $t_1, t_2, \ldots, t_k$ of times, $t_i \in \mathcal{T}$, such that $(v_i, v_{i+1}) \in E$ and $f_{(v_i, v_{i+1})}(t_i) = t_{i+1}$ for all $1 \leq i < k - 1$.*

The vertex v_1 is called the departure location or source of the path, t_1 the departure time, v_k the destination, and t_k the arrival time. The corresponding timed path is denoted as a timed (v_1, v_k, t_1)-path.

It can be proven that a modified version of Dijkstra's algorithm can be used to find fastest train connections in a time-dependent graph given the link-traversal functions are monotonic and have non-negative delay.

Brodal et al. showed in [BJ04] that for every timed (v_A, w_B, t)-path in G there is an equivalent train connection, and that for every connection c from A to B there is a path which arrives not later at B than connection c does.

4.3 Non-Negligible Interchange Times

Towards a more realistic scenario we need to take the time necessary for changing trains into account as well. Therefore, we will now extend both models to cover non-negligible interchange times.

4.3.1 Extending the Time-Expanded Graph

In a first step, we extend the basic time-expanded model to cover constant interchange times, which we will modify further at the end of this section to be applicable to variable interchange times as well.

4.3.1.1 Constant Interchange Times

Pyrga et al. [PSWZ04a] propose the concept of change nodes in the time-expanded graph. In this approach a copy of all departure and arrival nodes is kept for each station. These are called *change nodes*. The waiting edges are only introduced between change nodes, linking them by increasing time values at each station. For every original arrival node there are two additional outgoing edges: one, called *entering edge*, connecting a change node to the departure node of the same train and the other, called *leaving edge*, connecting an arrival node to the change node whose time stamp is no less than the time stamp of the arrival event plus the minimum interchange time for this station.

In order to describe the model formally, let S, S' be stations, z be a train, d_S^z the departure node at station S belonging to train z, and a_S^z the arrival node at station S for train z. Then $G = (V, E)$, with $V = D \cup A \cup C$ and $E = Z \cup W \cup L \cup E \cup Y$, where

- D is the set of departure nodes,

- A is the set of arrival nodes,

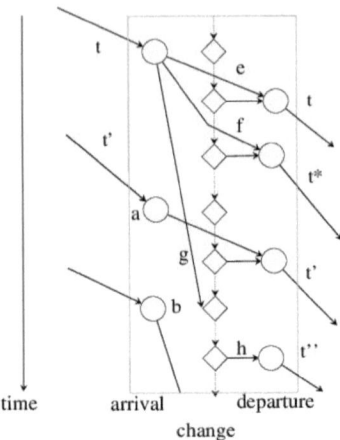

Figure 4.2: Example for the time-expanded model with change nodes for constant interchange times and the extension with a special-interchange edge (f) for non-constant interchange times. Edge f allows the change from t to t^* although the change to the later departing t' is not allowed.

- C is the set of change nodes with $|C| = |D \cup A|$,

- $Z = \bigcup_{SS'} Z_{SS'}$ is the set of train edges, where for each pair of stations S, S': $Z_{SS'} = \{(d_S^z, a_{S'}^z) : d_S^z \in D, a_{S'}^z \in A, z \text{ is a train}\}$,

- $W = \bigcup_S W_S$ is the set of waiting edges connecting a change node to the next change node at the same station, where $W_S = \{(c_S, c'_S) : c_S, c'_S \in C\}$,

- $L = \{(a_S^z, c_S) : a_S^z \in A, c_S \in C\}$ is the set of edges for leaving a train,

- $E = \{(c_S, d_S^z) : c_S \in C, d_S^z \in D\}$ is the set of edges for entering a train, and

- $Y = \{(a_S^z, d_S^z) : a_S^z \in A, d_S^z \in D\}$ is the set of edges for staying in a train, connecting the arrival of a train at a station to the departure of the same train at that station. An example can be seen in Figure 4.2.

4.3.1.2 Variable Interchange Times

As mentioned in Section 1.1, there are several different interchange times in the German timetable data. In the case that these interchange times depend on the train class, we see two possibilities to further extend the model.

4.3 Non-Negligible Interchange Times

(a) *The platform model.* At each station we introduce virtual platforms p_i, $i \in P_S$. The change nodes are organized not only in one cycle per station but there is a cycle for each of the virtual platforms p_i. The arrival event a of a train at virtual platform p_i at time τ is connected to the event v_j at platform p_j with timestamp $\tau + \tau_{ij}$ where τ_{ij} is the time needed for a transfer from a train at platform p_i to a train at platform p_j.

(b) *Adding special-interchange edges.* Instead of introducing virtual platforms, we can add what we call *special-interchange edges*. We define τ_χ to be the maximum over all interchange times at station S for a train arriving at node a with time τ. Arrival node a is connected to the change node c with time stamp $\tau' \geq \tau + \tau_\chi$ by a regular leaving edge. For all departure events d_i with a time stamp $\tau_i < \tau + \tau_\chi$ which can be reached according to the interchange regulations, an additional special-interchange edge (a, d_i) is introduced.

An example for the second model is provided in Figure 4.2.

If there are many events reachable from a before $\tau + \tau_\chi$ but not many platforms the platform-based model is better in terms of memory consumption. But note that the second model can easily be extended to handle a range of different kinds of interchanges independent of platforms and train classes.

4.3.2 Extending the Time-Dependent Graph

Pyrga, Schulz, Wagner and Zaroliagis proposed two approaches for modeling the Earliest Arrival Problem with non-zero interchange time using a time-dependent graph [PSWZ04a]. One is based on *platform information*, the other incorporates *train routes*. Both variants are applicable for constant as well as variable interchange times. We will only show the extensions to model constant interchange times using train routes.

Constant interchange times using train routes

Nodes $v_1, v_2, \ldots, v_k$, $k > 0$ form a *train route* if there is a train starting its journey at v_1, and visiting $v_2, \ldots, v_k$ consecutively. If there is more than one train following the same schedule (with respect to the order in which they visit the above nodes) all these trains belong to the same train route R. Note that it can be $v_i = v_j$ for $i \neq j$, for example when the train performs a loop.

For $u \in \mathcal{S}$, let Σ_u denote the set of different train routes that stop at u. Let R_u be the set containing exactly one node at u for each of the train routes R in Σ_u. We define $\rho(u) = |R_u|$ and $\mathcal{R} = \bigcup_{u \in \mathcal{S}} R_u$. Then the new node set of the time-dependent graph $G = (V, E)$ is $V = \mathcal{S} \cup \mathcal{R}$. For $u \in \mathcal{S}$ let p_i^u, $0 \leq i < \rho(u)$, denote the node representing the i-th train route $R \in \Sigma_u$.

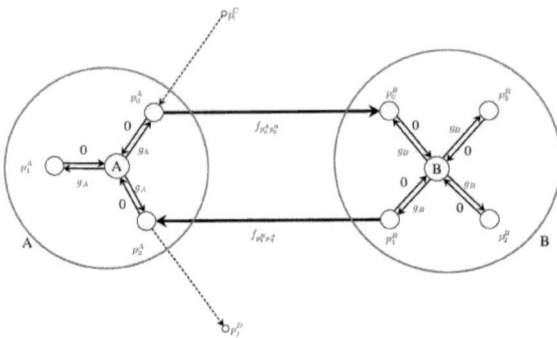

Figure 4.3: An example for modeling a time-dependent graph with non-negligible constant interchange times using train routes.

Again, the edge set $E = A \cup D \cup \hat{D} \cup R$ consists of four different types of edges, namely the following:

- $A = \bigcup_{u \in S} A_u$, where $A_u = \bigcup_{0 \leq i < \rho(u)} \{(p_i^u, u)\}$,

- $D = \bigcup_{u \in S} D_u$, where $D_u = \bigcup_{0 \leq i < \rho(u)} \{(u, p_i^u)\}$,

- $\hat{D} = \bigcup_{u \in S} \hat{D}_u$, where $\hat{D}_u = \emptyset$ if all trains that stop at u have identical interchange time, and $\hat{D}_u = \bigcup_{0 \leq i,j < \rho(u), i \neq j} \{(p_i^u, p_j^u)\}$ otherwise, and

- $T = \bigcup_{u,v \in S} T_{uv}$, where $T_{uv} = \emptyset$ if there is no train route visiting u and v successively and

$$T_{uv} = \bigcup_{\substack{0 \leq i < \rho(u) \\ 0 \leq j < \rho(v)}} \{(p_i^u, p_j^v) : p_i^u, p_j^v \text{ being the corresponding route-nodes}\},$$

otherwise.

Edges $e \in T$ are called *train edges* and edges $e \in A \cup D \cup \hat{D}$ are called *transfer edges*. The modeling with train routes is based on the following assumption.

Assumption 4.2. *For any two nodes p_i^u, p_j^v connected by a train edge $(p_i^u, p_j^v) \in T$ and departure times τ_d, τ_d' from p_i^u, for the respective arrival times τ_a, τ_a' at p_j^v it holds that*

$$\tau_d \leq \tau_d' \Rightarrow \tau_a \leq \tau_a'.$$

In other words, there is no train t_1 serving the same connection as t_2 which departs later than t_2, overtakes t_2, and arrives earlier than t_2 at the next station. In case the assumption is violated the train route concerned is split into two (or more) different train routes, for example by separating the trains into different speed classes.

Using a graph constructed in this way a fastest connection can be calculated by a time-dependent variant of Dijkstra's algorithm.

Further Extending the Time-Dependent-Model For more steps towards a realistic scenario we refer to the description of our prototype of a time-dependent timetable information system in Chapter 10.

4.4 Discussion: Time-Expanded Vs. Time-Dependent Models

For single–criterion shortest path search, the time-dependent model seems to be more attractive due to its smaller sized graph that drastically speeds up the search. This advantage does not hold for more realistic scenarios. In their experiments for computing all Pareto optima for two criteria Pyrga et al. [PSWZ04b] did not show a big advantage for time-dependent models. Not only did the size of the graph significantly grow due to the modeling – as we have seen – of constant interchange times (which are still far from reality), the computational time required for solving the problem on the time-expanded graph was only 58% higher than for the time-dependent graph. Their constructions in [PSWZ04a] show how difficult the extension to model more realistic scenarios is. The general interchange rules and the special attributes disallowing boarding and disembarkment even violate assumptions made for the most realistic model of interchanges known for time-dependent graphs. The time-dependent approach seems not to be as easily extendable to attribute requirements and train class restrictions as the time-expanded approach as already observed in [MSW02]. It is well suited for solving the earliest arrival problem given a time of departure. Considering time intervals instead of a single point in time for the departures, searching from each departure in the interval separately is not an option. Alternatively, many more labels have to be made mutually incomparable than due to multi-critiera search alone.

As a consequence of these reasons and especially the flexibility and extendibility of the time-expanded model we used it for our algorithm MOTIS. However, we also investigated the possibilities of an algorithm on a time-dependent graph in Chapter 10.

Chapter 5

The MOTIS Algorithm

The MOTIS-algorithm basically is a multi-criteria version of Dijkstra's algorithm as introduced in Chapter 3 on a graph based on a time-expanded graph model from the previous chapter. In this chapter, we will present the algorithm itself and some issues affecting graph model and algorithm likewise.

5.1 The Graph Model of MOTIS

5.1.1 Realistic Interchange Rules

All interchange rules introduced in Section 1.1 can be modeled using only the station dependent interchange time and service to service transfers by adding service to service transfers for all interchanges defined by transfers between transfer classes or lines.

If boarding is permitted we have an *entering edge* from the change node copy to the original departure node. If leaving a train is possible, we have one *leaving edge* connecting the arrival node to the appropriate change node. Namely the node at the time from which on all other events are reachable, i.e. the time difference of this node to the arrival is the maximum over the interchange times required by all change rules concerning this train at this station. For all trains reachable before this point in time we have *special-interchange edges* from the arrival to the departure nodes of the corresponding trains.

Example See Fig. 5.1 for an exemplary excerpt. It is easy to see that we have indeed covered all interchange rules. Arriving with train t we can either stay-in-train t (use stay-in-train edge e) or change to t^* which is possible due to some interchange rule e.g. service to service transfer (special-interchange edge f). However, we can not take t' (for example, if the minimum interchange time at the station does not allow this). Therefore, we needed the special interchange edge to reach t^* and not to reach t' from t although entering t' is allowed from the change level. Every event from time b on is again reachable (using leaving edge g to the change node at time b), e.g., we can take train t'' (via entering edge h).

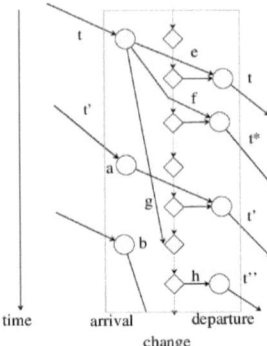

Figure 5.1: Example for the time-expanded model with change nodes and special-interchange edges.

5.1.2 Traffic Days

Recall that not all trains operate on a daily basis, e.g. some only on workdays, others only on Sundays. To correctly model the traffic days of trains and still achieve a bearable memory footprint, the days of operation are coded into the train edges only. All time values of nodes are taken modulo a single day (more precisely 1440 minutes, as the granularity of the schedule is one minute). During construction of the graph, an additional waiting edge from the last change node before to the first change node after midnight. Let t_u, t_v be the time stamps of two nodes u, v, respectively. Then the length of edge $(u, v) \in E$ is $t_v - t_u$ (mod 1440).

We maintain the exact time t throughout the execution of the algorithm (i.e. not only modulo a single day). Every time an edge is considered the exact departure time is known. The time of day is determined by $t \mod 1440$ and the traffic day is $\lfloor t/1440 \rfloor$. A look-up in the traffic days of the involved train shows whether the edge is available at that day or can be ignored.

5.1.3 Footpaths

Inserting all the footpaths into the graph straightforwardly would result in a tremendous increase in the number of edges, as we would have to insert all footpaths of a station directly "behind" each arrival event. To avoid this problem the idea is to store the footpaths at the station and calculate the correct arrival node at the target station S of the footpath with a search in the node list of station S. Thus, the footpaths are inserted without time dependency. They are always available and have constant length.

We calculate the reflexive, transitive hull of the "footpath-relation" using a textbook ver-

5.1 The Graph Model of MOTIS

sion of Floyd-Warshall algorithm (Algorithm 6). To this end we set the walking time from station S_X to station S_X to zero and remove these loops afterwards. Using this modified "footpath-relation" we never need to consider more than one footpath in a row without traveling edges in between and still find all feasible connections containing any number of footpaths.

Input : Digraph $G = (V = \{1,...,n\}, E)$ with nonnegative edge weights $0 < \ell_{ij} < \infty$ for all $(i,j) \in E$.
Output: A matrix $D = (d_{ij})_{1 \leq i,j \leq n}$ where d_{ij} is the length of a shortest path from i to j if it exists and $d_{ij} = \infty$ otherwise.

for $i,j \in V$ **do** $d_{ij} := \begin{cases} 0 & : i = j \\ \ell_{ij} & : (i,j) \in E \\ -\infty & : \text{otherwise} \end{cases}$;

for $j := 1$ **to** n **do**
  for $i := 1$ **to** n **do if** $i \neq j$ **then**
    for $k := 1$ **to** n **do if** $k \neq j$ **then**
      $d_{ik} = \max\{d_{ik}, d_{ij} + d_{jk}\}$;
return D;

Algorithm 6: Floyd-Warshall algorithm.

Masking in Iterators Footpaths virtually connect arrival nodes to change-departure nodes. The footpaths of a station are stored once per station. They are only considered when iterating over the leaving edges of an arrival node.

Start Labels after Footpaths Footpaths affect the creation of start labels, as well. Consider the departure interval specified to be $[\tau_{first}, \tau_{last}]$ and the footpaths $f_1, \ldots, f_k$, $k > 0$ from the departure station $\mathcal{A}$ to the stations $S_1, \ldots S_k$ in time $\tau_1, \ldots, \tau_k$. We collect all departure events $d_j^{S_i}$ at station S_i with departure time in $[\tau_{first} + \tau_i, \tau_{last} + \tau_i]$. Start labels for the events $d_j^{S_i}$ need to be initialized with the duration τ_i of footpath f_i and the footpath as first travel edge, whereas all other start labels do not have a first travel edge.

5.1.4 Edge Lengths for the Criteria

We associate component-wise non-negative cost vectors to the edges. Here we describe only the choice for forward search, the necessary modifications for backward search should be obvious.

travel time For the cost criterion travel time, the cost for edge $e = (v,w)$ is the difference between the timestamps of the nodes w and v.

number of interchanges For the cost criterion number of train changes, all entering edges and all special-interchange edges get a cost value of 1, and all other edges a value of 0.

ticket cost Ticket costs are more difficult to handle:

Pricing systems of railway companies are very complex. Unfortunately, ticket costs are typically not proportional to the distance traveled. In distance-based fares the cost of the distance traveled in one train depends not only on the number of kilometers but also on its train class and other train classes used in the connection. Additionally, there are relation-based fares for which origin-destination pairs and regional corridors determine the cost. Currently there are different supplementary fares for the different higher speed train classes. For more details see our discussion of regular fares in Section 6.2.2. Furthermore, the system undergoes rapid change. In building timetable information systems it should not be the task to rebuild pricing components.

To be resistant to the changes in the pricing system (to some degree) we have a black-box pricing component (BPC) that can be used to calculate the ticket cost for some connection. Unfortunately, one call to this black-box routine is very costly: The path information stored in labels has to be converted into structures for the BPC. Much additional information like attributes on the train edges has to be set to get a correct price. Therefore, it is not at all possible to calculate the correct price for every label and achieve a bearable runtime.

As a consequence we use price estimates in the labels that are updated during the search. The distance between the two stations of a train edge is taken as the straight line distance obtained from the coordinates of the stations. For every train edge the price estimate is increased by the distance times a factor depending on the train class used. The supplementary fare is paid once and only for the highest train class involved.

This simplified model provides helpful estimates for the search. After a search is completed, all connections are correctly priced by the BPC and advanced Pareto dominance can be applied to true fares.

Here another benefit of the Pareto relaxation (compare Section 2.3.1) comes into play, enabling us to model some exceptions: For example, there might be a special offer (like "Schönes-Wochenende-Ticket" in Germany) for traveling on weekends for a fixed price independent of the distance but valid only on non-high speed trains. The relaxation allows us to make connections using no high speed trains and connections with high speed trains on weekends incomparable. We come back to the edge lengths regarding ticket cost in Section 6.2 when talking about special offers.

In Chapter 6 we will introduce some additional criteria and how the edge lengths for these are defined and calculated.

5.1.5 Attributes NotIn/NotOut

Handling the special attributes forbidding boarding or disembarkment of a train at one of its stops during the execution of the algorithm calls for many exceptional rules:

1. We may not enter a train, if boarding is not allowed.

2. We may not leave a train, if disembarkment is not allowed.

3. If we reach our destination but may not leave the used train, we have to continue our journey until we reach the destination again (and are allowed to leave the train).

4. No start label is to be created for a departure event at station A where boarding is not allowed.

The first two problems can be solved on the graph level: If boarding a train is not allowed, the corresponding departure event has no entering edge. Analogously, if disembarkment is not allowed, the corresponding arrival event has no leaving edge.

The last two issues are treated in the algorithm itself: Whenever a label at (one of the) terminal station(s) is created, we only consider the terminal as "reached" (and thus the connection as complete) if leaving the train is allowed. During the creation of start labels only departure nodes with entering edges are considered as start labels.

Let us again take a look at Figure 5.1 on Page 50 for an example. Train t' stops at the station only for boarding (no leaving edge for the arrival at time a). If it is not possible to enter train t^* there will be neither the entering edge to the departure of t^* nor the special-interchange edge f.

5.2 Algorithm Refinements

5.2.1 Realization of On-trip/Pre-trip Searches

5.2.1.1 Start Interval for Pre-Trip Searches

Pre-trip search amounts to a multi-source shortest path problem from all departure events in the departure interval. We create start labels at all departure nodes in the given interval at the source station and if applicable all its meta replacements. At any station reachable via a foot edge of length τ minutes from any of these stations we also create start labels in the departure interval shifted by τ minutes. These have the foot edge as first edge and τ minutes travel time so far. Respecting the attributes prohibiting entering a train, start labels are not created for a train when boarding is forbidden at that station.

5.2.1.2 On-Trip Searches

In contrast, both on-trip searches can be realized as single-source shortest path problems in our timetable information system using different starting events. We either

- create only a single start label at the change level of the source station and measure travel time including the waiting time before taking any train (on-trip station), or

- create only a single start label at the arrival event of the train edge the traveler uses when receiving the information about a connecting train that will be missed[i] (on-trip train).

Note that in the on-trip train case, using the arrival node of the train instead of any of the departure nodes, the modeling of interchanges in the time expanded graph guarantees that only valid train changes at the first stop after receiving the information are used. It would not be feasible to solve the on-trip train case with a single departure at that station, because we need to ensure that the departure of the train with which one arrives, all departures below the station dependent change time (through special interchange rules) and all later departures are considered and all but the first case are counted as an additional interchange.

5.2.2 Meta Stations and Source-/Target-Equivalents

Recall the concept of new virtual *meta stations* and of stations grouped in *source/target-equivalents* from Section 1.2.1. Both may be represented as a pair $(S, (R_1, R_2, ..., R_n))$. The sole difference is that for *meta stations* S is a new station and $S \neq R_i$ for all i while for *Source/target-equivalents* $S = R_i$ for some $i \in \{1, ..., n\}$.

During the execution of the algorithm it is irrelevant whether $(S, (R_1, R_2, ..., R_n))$ describes one or the other possibility. Every time S is source, target or via in a query, it is "replaced" by all the R_i. Thus we change the creation of start labels and the test whether the terminal is reached:

- start labels are created at all R_i in the interval for departure/arrival, depending on the search direction. Only footpaths reaching stations $T \neq R_i$ for all i are allowed as first footpaths in a connection.

- The terminal in any iteration ending at S is reached, if any of the R_i is reached. (cf. Generalizing the s-t-Case in Section 3.4.5.1).

---

[i]or the train edge in use when the traveler is ready to change, cf. Section 11.3

5.2.3 Attribute Requirements and Class Restrictions

Possible attribute requirements and train class restrictions with respect to a given query can be handled quite easily. We simply mark train edges as *invisible* for the search if they do not meet all requirements of the given query. With respect to this visibility of edges, there is a one-to-one correspondence between feasible connections and paths in the graph.

Checking Attribute Combinations Specifying wanted and excluded *attributes* is not just giving a list of attributes. Wanted attributes may appear in groups as there are e.g. many *attributes* for "bike transportation possible" specifying, for example, a place to store up to eight bikes in a coach where passengers are allowed or a whole coach only for bikes ("Fahrradtransportzug").

The attribute requirements are given in n groups of required attributes and m excluded attributes b_k. Each group of required attributes consists of $n_i \geq 1$ attributes $a_i j$. The requirement:

$$\left(\bigwedge_{i=1}^{n} \left(\bigvee_{j=1}^{n_i} a_{ij} \right) \right) \wedge \left(\bigwedge_{k=1}^{m} \neg b_k \right)$$

is satisfied by an attribute combination if of each group of required attributes at least one attribute a_{ij} is in the combination and none of the excluded attributes b_k.

Instead of checking the attribute requirements every time a train edge is used during the search, we check each of the attribute combinations in a preprocessing step of a search and mark them as either admissible or not. Thus, we only have to check less than 1000 combinations once per search.

5.3 Implementation Details

5.3.1 Edge Hierarchy

We use seven different types of edges, which we designed using two levels of inheritance. The complete edge type hierarchy is depicted in Figure 5.2. All edges are derived from an abstract base class MetaEdge. On the second level of abstraction we differentiate between the classes FootEdge and Edge.

Foot edges connect stations and not nodes and are treated differently from standard edges. They have no time dependency, store their length, and are allowed only when iterating over the leaving edges of arrival nodes, see also Section 5.1.3).

Class Edge is an abstract class for all edge types connecting two nodes in the timeexpanded graph. An instance of class Edge can be of one of the following types representing traveling, waiting or changing:

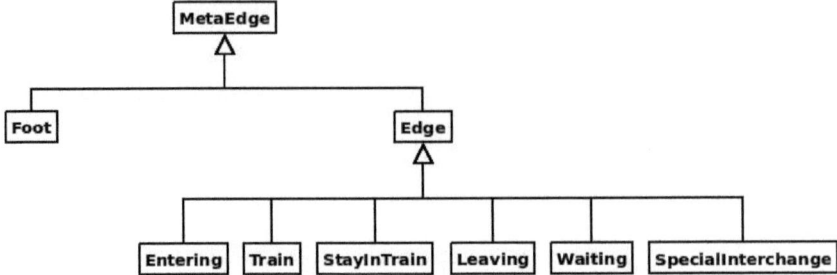

Figure 5.2: The edge class hierarchy in MOTIS

- Train edges connect a departure node at a station to the corresponding arrival node at the next station of the train.

- Stay-in-train edges connect an arrival node to a departure node belonging to the same train at the same station.

- Leaving edges connect an arrival node to the first feasible (according to interchange rules) change-departure node at the same station.

- Entering edges connect a change-departure node to a departure node at the same station at the same point in time.

- Special-interchange edges connect an arrival node to a departure node at the same station realizing all interchanges possible below the station dependent interchange time.

- Waiting edges connect two nodes on the waiting level of one station.

The length of any of these edge types is the time difference between the time stamps of the tail and head nodes.

5.3.2 Encoding Train Information

On many subsequent train edges the relevant information about the train like its name and number, category, class, and attributes does not change. Therefore, we use a struct `ConnectionInfo` to bundle this information and only store pointers to these objects in the train edges themselves. Thus, we just need roughly 1.5 times the number of trains many of these structs instead of storing the data on each train edge separately.

This and some other ideas to save memory have been introduced in [MSW02].

5.3.3 Lazy Initialization and Reset

The graph representing a time table usually consists of several million nodes, not all of which are touched during a search. Instead of iterating over all nodes and reseting its label list and a "visited"-flag, we keep an iteration counter for each station and each node. Any node or station touched with an iteration counter different from the current iteration is touched for the first time during this search. In the clean-up phase only the flags and lists of nodes at stations with iteration counter matching the current iteration need to be considered. This saves iterating over a large portion of the graph and especially speeds up the clean-up phase after quick searches that only visit few nodes.

5.4 The Algorithm

Our algorithm is an "advanced Pareto version" of Dijkstra's algorithm using multi-dimensional labels. In Algorithm 7 we present a pseudo-code formulation for the core of our algorithm. Each label is associated with a node v in the search graph. A label contains key values of a connection from a start node up to v. These key values include the travel time, the number of interchanges, a ticket cost estimation and some additional information. For every node in the graph we maintain a list of labels that are not dominated by any other label at this node. Every time a node is extracted from the priority queue, its outgoing edges are scanned and (if they are not infeasible due to traffic days, attributes and train class restrictions etc.) labels for their head nodes are created. Such a new label is compared to all labels in the list at the head node. It is only inserted into that list and the priority queue if it is not dominated by any other label in the list. On the other hand, labels dominated by the new label are removed. Our dominance relation is advanced Pareto dominance as introduced in Chapter 2, the specific parameters will be introduced in Section 9.5.1 after the introduction of some additional criteria and special search forms in Chapter 6.

In the following short overview we mention some of the details and points to consider in the individual steps or method calls:

createStartLabels() in pre-trip search labels for all nodes in the start interval, maybe at
    metas and stations reachable via footpaths as well, respecting attribute NotIn,
    in on-trip search either at one arrival node or one change-departure node.

outgoing edge `e=(v,w)` all leaving edges, for arrival nodes additionally the foot edges stored
    for this station

isInfeasible(`e`) edge e is infeasible due to traffic days, attribute requirements, or train class
    restrictions

isDominated (`newLabel`) test against other labels at the same node

```
Input: a timetable graph and a query
Output: a set of advanced Pareto optimal labels at the terminal
foreach node v do
 │ labelListAt(v) := ∅;
PriorityQueue pq := ∅;
createStartLabels();

while ! pq.isEmpty() do
 │ Label label := pq.extractLabel();
 │ foreach outgoing edge e=(v,w) of v=label.getNode() do
 │  │ if isInfeasible(e) then continue; // ignore this edge
 │  │ Label newLabel := createLabel(label, e);
 │  │ if isDominated(newLabel) then continue;
 │  │ // newLabel is not dominated
 │  │ if isTerminalReached(newLabel) then
 │  │  │ terminalList.insert(newLabel);
 │  │ else
 │  │  │ labelListAt(w).insert(newLabel);
 │  │  │ labelListAt(w).removeLabelsDominatedBy(newLabel);
 │  │  │ pq.insert(newLabel);
filterList(terminalList);
```

Algorithm 7: Pseudocode for the MOTIS algorithm.

isTerminalReached(·) if leaving allowed (attribute NotOut) at a node belonging to the terminal station (or any of the meta replacements)

filterList(`terminalList`**)** after a final evaluation of the complete connections represented by the labels in `terminalList` remove dominated labels

Correctness

The construction of the graph and the associated edge costs guarantee that a valid connection exists for each path in the graph and that the key characteristics (travel time, number of interchanges) are computed correctly.

See Möhring [Möh99] or Theune [The95] for correctness proofs for a multi-criteria Dijkstra. Since the employed *advanced Pareto dominance* relation is transitive and antisymmetric, it may replace classical Pareto dominance.

Ticket cost is only estimated, therefore we cannot guarantee optimal results regarding prices. However, the results are much better than that of the commercial systems currently in use. Because they rely on heuristics only, our advanced Pareto approach outperforms these systems even with estimates.

5.5 MOTIS Search GUI

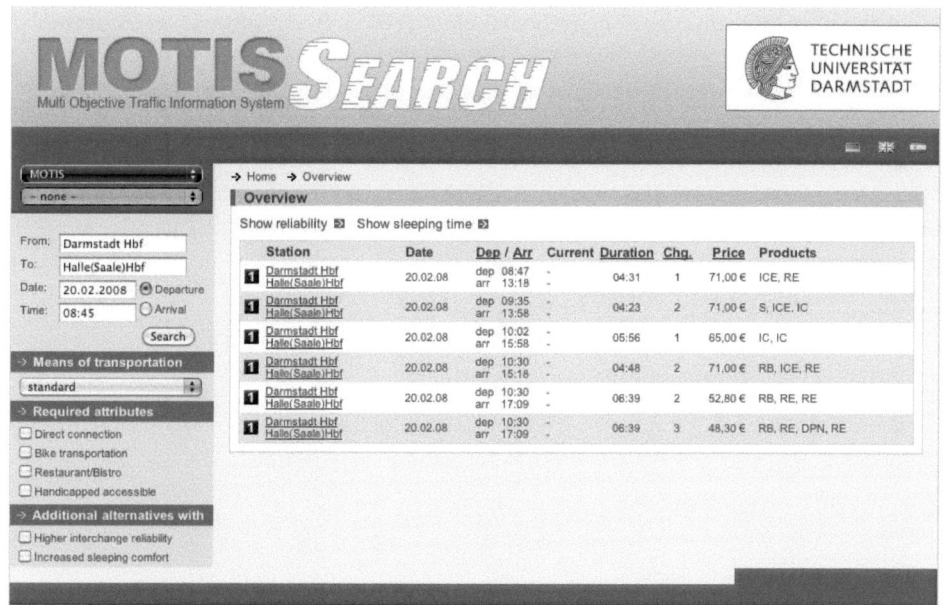

Figure 5.3: Search results for a search from Darmstadt to Halle (Saale).

5.5 MOTIS Search GUI

Our graphical user interface for querying the system and displaying the computed connections will be introduced in Section 11.2. Figure 5.3 shows a screen-shot for the query from Darmstadt to Halle. We can see the fastest connection (the second) with 2 interchanges for 71€. There are alternative with less interchanges (first, third), one of them is only slightly slower (first), the other significantly slower but less expensive (third). The fifth and sixth connection do not use high-speed trains and are much cheaper, albeit much slower.

5.6 History of the MOTIS Algorithm

As a predecessor to the MOTIS Algorithm we developed our early fully realistic timetable information system PARETO [MSW02, Sch04]. It used the simpler time-expanded graph model introduced in Section 4.1 and Pareto dominance (cf. Section 2.2). Due to the treatment of train changes on the algorithmic level rather than on the graph level, we could not guarantee optimality of our results, but already outperformed commercial systems. We redesigned the algorithm, changed to the current graph model and introduced the idea of relaxed Pareto dominance [Gra04, MS07] (cf. Section 2.3.1). We then studied the application of relaxed Pareto dominance to the search for special offers [MS06] (cf. Section 6.2.2) and developed two approaches for night train search [Gun07, GMS07, GMS09] (cf. Section 6.4). Afterwards, we investigated the time-dependent model [DMS08, Dis07] (cf. Chapter 10) and started our research on incorporating and dealing with delay information [FMS08, Fre08, Key09, MS09] (cf. Chapter 7). The latter motivated our investigation of the reliability of interchanges as an additional criterion [Meh07] (cf. Section 6.3). The ideas of advanced Pareto dominance have been around for some time and were finalized for this thesis (cf. Section 2.3.3). Throughout the whole development, we worked on the design of speed-up techniques [Jun06, Mäu09] (cf. Chapter 8) and built visualization tools and GUIs (cf. Chapter 11).

Chapter 6

Additional Criteria and Special Search Forms

In this chapter, we will present ways of modeling and treating other concepts and search goals to fit into our multi-criteria approach.

We start with a simple yet descriptive example, the possibility to reserve a seat. Afterwards, we will introduce a way of modeling and actively improving the likelihood of catching all connecting trains by our concept of "reliability of transfers." In Section 6.2 we will talk about efficiently searching for special price offers, like a $x\%$ discount ticket or a fixed price ticket subject to some restrictions. The chapter will end with two different approaches to searching for night trains, one using a different kind of algorithm, the other an additional optimization criterion.

6.1 Seat Reservation

An illustrative example of how we can use the tools of multi-criteria optimization is the search for connections with the possibility of seat reservations. We assume that it is too costly to constantly query the reservation server therefore we use a "traffic light encoding" for the reservation status of each train section:

red All seats are already reserved.

yellow Only a few seats are left for reservation.

green There are still many seats left that can be reserved.

These status information flags for all train sections can be updated in regular intervals. Thus, no queries to a reservation server are required during individual searches. The flags may be used for serving a number of connection requests between updates. As usually only high-speed trains allow seat reservations, the total amount of reservation data is relatively small.

If we now search with an additional criterion "seat reservation desired", we define the status of a connection as follows:

red At least one section is red.

yellow At least on section is yellow and no section is red.

green There are neither yellow nor red sections.

The possibility to reserve a seat is considered good for green connections, maybe possible for yellow connections and impossible for red connections. Upon selecting a connection for booking, a request to the reservation sever is made for yellow and green connections. We code red, yellow, and green as 2, 1, and 0, respectively, and minimize the additional criterion seat reservation.

When comparing two connections a green connection may dominate any other connection, yellow connections may only dominate yellow and red connections and red connections may not dominate any other than red connections. Thus, we expect to find alternative connections with a more promising reservation status with the typical trade off being a potential loss in the quality of the other criteria. If even the best connections have status green, no additional alternative needs to be returned.

The benefit of treating reservability as an additional criterion instead of a constraint is the chance to deliver these alternatives after one search. If we used a constraint and found no reservable connection, we would need an additional search (without the constraint). Furthermore, a customer might originally want a seat reservation but decide against it, in case a large detour is required.[i] On the other hand, a reservable connection may be not much worse in the other criteria. Thus, a customer not very interested in seat reservation might opt to take the reservable one nonetheless.

6.2 Search for Special Offers

Finding cheap train connections for long-distance traffic is algorithmically a hard task due to very complex tariff regulations. Several new tariff options have been developed in recent years. In such an environment, it becomes more and more important that search engines for travel connections are able to find special offers efficiently.

The purpose of this section is to show by means of a case study how several of the most common tariff rules (including special offers) can be embedded into our multi-objective search tool MOTIS. These results have been published in [MS06].

---

[i]This information would require the results of the constrained search.

6.2.1 Introduction

Pricing systems of railway companies are very complex and actual fares depend on many parameters. In recent years, railway companies faced higher competition caused by the strong increase of low-cost airlines. As a reaction to this development, marketing departments of railway companies answer with the introduction of different types of special offer tariffs. For origin-destination pairs with a low-cost competitor the relation-based prices are occasionally decreased.

For this and several other reasons, the fare of a connection cannot be modeled in an exact way as an additive function on the edges of a graph which can simultaneously be used for a fastest connection search.

Apart from our initial work (published in [MS07]) we are not aware of any previous work which takes fares as an optimization criterion into account. There is even no literature to heuristic approaches concerning minimizing ticket cost.

Our Contribution. Usually, marketing experts design a new tariff with respect to expected sales but without considering how such an offer can be found in an efficient way. It seems that Germany has one of the most complicated tariff systems of the world, providing us with the most challenging task to find cheap connections systematically.

In this section, we analyze the different tariff options with respect to searchability. We show that a systematic, simultaneous search for different tariffs can be integrated into a suitable graph model and a generalized version of Dijkstra's algorithm. In particular, we focus on tariff options which are based on the availability of contingents, yielding either a fixed price or a certain discount.

Overview. The rest of the section is organized as follows. In Subsection 6.2.2, we present a systematic overview on fare regulations. For each tariff class we analyze the algorithmic consequences for efficient searchability of connections which fall into this class. Thereafter, we present more details on the modifications to the search algorithm of MOTIS and introduce specialized search modes as subroutines in Subsection 6.2.3.

6.2.2 Modeling Regular Fares and Special Offers

The purpose of this subsection is to provide an overview on the many different classes of tariffs commonly used by train companies.

As the number of different tariffs is very large, they differ considerably from country to country, and they are subject to frequent changes, this overview is far from being comprehensive. However, we try to group the most commonly used tariffs into certain classes. For each tariff class, we analyze how a search for connections which fall under this class can be modeled and incorporated into our general framework of MOTIS.

In some rare cases it might be profitable to partition the desired connection into smaller connections. To each partial connection a different tariff option may apply, yielding an overall saving if several tickets are bought. However, this is very impractical and potentially confusing for the customer. In this section, we therefore restrict our discussion to a single tariff for each connection.[ii]

6.2.2.1 Regular Fares

Regular fares apply at any time to everyone without any restrictions. To calculate regular fares, two main principles are in use: distance-based and relation-based fares.

Distance-based fares. For this type, regular fares are modeled by piecewise affine-linear functions which depend on the number of kilometers of the connection and the used train classes. These functions are encoded in tables and the calculation of fares is done with a table look-up. For example, regular fares in France (SNCF) follow this scheme.[iii]

Relation-based fares. For long-distance travel in a highly connected network like that of Germany the regular fare is more often based on relations, i.e. origin-destination pairs associated with a regional corridor. The corridor of a relation describes what is considered as a common route. A relation can only be applied to a connection if the connection passes stations from a relation-specific set which specifies the corridor.

If a connection leaves the corridor of a relation, the fare has to be determined by partitioning the entire connection into smaller connections. The details of this procedure are beyond the scope of this work.

Marketing considerations influence the price for each relation. In general, the fare of a relation is derived from the travel distance, but it may be changed in either direction.

Properties of regular fares. In most cases, we can assume that regular fares are monotonously increasing and sub-additive. That is, for a connection c from station s to station t via station v, the price $p_c(s,t)$ satisfies

$$p_c(s,t) \leq p_c(s,v) + p_c(v,t).$$

Distance-based fares are degressive functions in the travel kilometers. Hence, they are always strictly sub-additive.

[ii]Note that a combination of tariffs is necessary in multi-vendor systems.
[iii]see http://www.voyages-sncf.com/guide/voyageurs/pdf/calcul_prix_tarif_normal.pdf (retrieved September, 8th, 2009).

6.2 Search for Special Offers

In dominance tests, good lower bounds are of crucial importance for the efficiency of the search (discussed in detail in Section 8.5). Hence, we need a lower bound on the price of a connection. With distance-based fares, we get a lower bound on the distance of a connection from the distance traveled from s to v plus a lower bound on the distance from v to t.

In sharp contrast, valid lower bounds are hard to obtain for relation-based fares as these may even violate our sub-additivity assumption. But even if we assume sub-additivity, it is not clear how to get a reasonably tight lower bound on the price of a connection from s to t given the prices from s to v and from v to t.

Frequent user cards. For holders of frequent user cards (like "BahnCard") a general $x\%$ discount applies to the regular fare. As this kind of discount yields the same reduction rate for all connections, our price estimation merely needs a flag indicating whether such a card is available or not. The flag is necessary for a comparison with other tariff options.

Sometimes the discount is only available for tickets above some minimum ticket cost. This condition can easily be evaluated to determine the actual ticket cost before comparing prices.

Approximation of regular fares. We use a simple and efficiently computable model to approximate regular fares. Basically, we simulate a distance-based fare and associate a travel distance with each edge. The distance between the two stations of a train edge is taken as the straight line distance obtained from the coordinates of the stations. During the search, we add for each train edge the travel distance times a constant factor (in Euros/km) depending on the train class used.

6.2.2.2 Surcharges

An additive surcharge applies to certain trains (night trains, ICE sprinter) or train classes (IC,EC). It has to be paid once, if such a train is used. If a connection uses several trains to which a surcharge applies, then usually only the highest surcharge has to be paid once.

During the search, the amount of the surcharge is added to the price estimation when a partial connection first enters a train with a surcharge. In order to guarantee that a surcharge is paid only once, the labels characterizing a partial connection store in flags which surcharges have already been applied.

6.2.2.3 Contingent Based Discount Fares

Contingent-based offers are intended to increase (and balance out) the average passenger load on high-speed trains. For each train in a connection for such an offer, a contingent of available seats must not be exceeded by previous bookings. For high-speed trains the contingent may be something like 10% of all seats. For local trains, there is typically no contingent restriction, i.e. the contingent is regarded as being unlimited. As a consequence, such offers are only valid for connections which contain at least one contingent-restricted train.

Many train companies offer discounted fares on long-distance travel under certain restrictions. These restrictions typically include that

- the ticket has to be bought a certain time in advance
  (for example, at least three days in advance),
- passengers restrict themselves to a particular day and a certain connection which has a contingent available,
- passengers make a return journey to and from the same station.

Discount rates may also be subject to weekend restrictions. For example, Deutsche Bahn AG offers "Savings Fare 50" ("Sparpreis 50") only if the following restrictions apply: For trips starting from Monday to Friday, the return trip cannot be any sooner than the following Sunday. If you travel on Saturday or Sunday you may return that same day.

To incorporate such types of offers into the search, we add and maintain a *contingent flag* in our labels. It is a Boolean flag which is set to true if and only if all previous high-speed train edges of this connection have a contingent available.

6.2.2.4 Fixed Price Offers

Contingent-Based Restrictions. Certain special tariffs offer fixed price tickets within a limited time period (of several weeks or even months, like "Summer Special") subject to the availability of contingents.

A further restriction is that the itinerary of a connection from station A to B must use a "common route". This rule is to prevent possible misuse by making round-trips or stop-overs during the travel for which one usually would have to buy several tickets or at least to pay for the deviation.

The easiest way to model common routes is to impose the restriction that the length of an itinerary of a connection shall not be more than a certain percentage, say 20%, longer than the shortest route from A to B. Alternatively, the travel time shall not be more than a certain percentage longer than the fastest route from A to B.

The modification of our model for this kind of tariff is similar to the previous case. We also maintain a contingent flag in each label indicating whether a contingent has been available on all previous edges. As contingents for discounts and for fixed prices may be different, we use different kind of contingent flags. At each intermediate station, we also check whether the partial connection up to this station can still be extended in such a way that it stays on a "common route". To this end, we use lower bounds for the remaining path from this intermediate station to the final destination.

6.2 Search for Special Offers

Time Interval Restrictions. Tickets allowing unlimited travel may be available for a fixed price provided the time of the trip falls into a certain time interval.

For example, Deutsche Bahn AG offers a "Happy-Weekend-Ticket" which can be used on all trains except high-speed trains on Saturdays or Sundays between 12 a.m. until 3 a.m. of the following day for a fixed price. Another example would be a fixed price ticket valid from 7 p.m. until the end of the same business day ("Guten-Abend-Ticket").

Such offers can be handled in the following way. For a given query, we first check whether the given start interval falls into the interval of a special offer. If not, the corresponding tariff is definitely not applicable. In case the offer has no train class restrictions, we can use the standard multi-objective search. For each alternative found by this search, we finally have to check whether the complete connection falls into the time interval. If this is the case, the price for this connections is the minimum of the regular fare and the fixed price.

If train class restrictions apply, we could use two independent searches, one with train class restriction and one without. However, it is more efficient to treat train class restrictions as a further criterion in the multi-criteria search and to run just a single simultaneous search for both cases.

Rail Passes. Many train companies also offer different kinds of so-called *rail passes* which allow unlimited travel. Prices depend on country and number of days. Rail passes may be restricted to special user groups (students, disabled, unemployed), restrictions may be based on the age (children, seniors), or restrictions on the place of permanent residence apply.

Further restrictions may be imposed on the set of allowed train classes. For example, a regional rail pass like "Hessenticket" offered by Deutsche Bahn AG is only valid for local trains.

Passengers with rail passes can use the standard multi-objective search on the basis of regular fares which delivers, in particular, all attractive connections with respect to travel time and convenience. The price information can simply be ignored. The search has only to make sure that the whole connection lies within the region where the rail pass is valid.

6.2.2.5 Discounts for Groups

Groups of 2 or more passengers either get an $x\%$ discount on the regular tariff which can be applied to all trains, or they get an even larger discounts of $y > x\%$ based on the availability of certain contingents.

During the search, both options can be handled in the same way as for single passengers.

6.2.2.6 Further Possibilities for Discounts

Discounts for single passengers or groups may also be restricted to certain Boolean conditions which depend only on properties of the travelers but not on the particular trip they are going to make. For example, if the group is a family with children below a certain age, then special discounts apply. Another example would be discounts for employees of certain companies (corporate clients).

6.2.3 Details on the Search Algorithm

6.2.3.1 Simultaneous Search

The aforementioned modeling of the various tariffs allows the search for combinations of tariffs simultaneously. This is preferable over having individual searches for each of the tariff rules that apply in a scenario and can be done without sacrificing search speed (as we will show in the computational study in Section 9.1).

However, as the number of tariff rules increases, more and more labels become mutually incomparable. For example, consider two labels representing partial connections that can gain a fixed price or discounted fare, respectively. Either connection might not be extendable to a connection from source to target with contingents available on all edges. So neither of them can dominate the other depending on an estimate of the special price. Furthermore, they cannot even be compared regarding the estimation for the regular price, as the final price may differ substantially if a special tariff is applicable.

The dominance test between a connection that has already reached the terminal station and a partial connection has to compare the lowest possible price reachable by extending the partial connection to the actual price of the complete connection. So it is even more important to have a fast and cheap connection at the terminal fairly early in the search process.

6.2.3.2 Fast Search for the Fastest Fixed Price Connection

For several reasons we implemented a specialized version of our algorithm to search for fixed price connections. Our motivation was

1. to have a stand alone tool to find one fixed price connection, and
2. to strengthen our dominance with terminal labels (a speed-up technique introduced in Section 8.4), or
3. to have a certificate that no fixed price connection is available at all. In the latter case, we can turn off our fixed price search.

Our specialized algorithm for fixed price search ("fixed price Dijkstra") is a single-criterion goal-directed search algorithm (see Section 8.3 for details on goal-direction). It determines a fastest connection among all connections using only available contingent edges and edges without contingent restrictions.

6.2.3.3 Determining Lower Bounds in the Preprocessing Phase

The initialization phase now consists of up to two searches: First we use the standard single-criterion goal-directed search algorithm to determine a fastest connection from source to target. It keeps track of the contingent information, and

- either finds a connection with a fixed price (it includes a high-speed train and contingents are available on all contingent edges),
- or finds a connection without high-speed trains (therefore no fixed price is possible for it). As it is the fastest connection, we may use it for dominance testing later on. It is also quite often cheaper than the fixed price (see Subsection 9.1.3).
- Otherwise, it triggers the specialized algorithm for fixed price search.

If triggered, the "fixed price Dijkstra" algorithm

- either finds a connection with a fixed price (it includes a high-speed train, contingents are available on all contingent edges, and it is within the allowed margin (here 20% more travel time) compared to the fastest connection),
- or finds a connection without high-speed trains (therefore no fixed price is possible for it). If a fixed price connection exists, it must be slower than this connection.
- Otherwise, it finds a connection with contingents available on all contingent edges but that does not stay within the allowed margin. In this case no fixed price connection exists (as all other connections with contingents available are even slower).

In the latter case the following multi-criteria search is performed with the option to search for fixed price connections turned off. Note, that in case two the algorithm fails to compute a connection with a fixed price although one may exist. However, it delivers an alternative connection for dominance testing that is faster than any fixed price connection, if there are any, and in most cases cheaper than the fixed price (see Subsection 9.1.3).

The search for special offers will be evaluated in Section 9.1 in Chapter 9: *Computational Study*.

6.3 Reliability of Transfers

The reliability of transfers is an important facet of the quality of a connection. Especially when dealing with delayed scenarios, a higher probability of not missing a connecting train may be worth a lower score for the other quality criteria. To our best knowledge nobody has tried to capture this notion of reliability before, although we consider it a very important criterion. The number of interchanges is already included in the most common criteria, together with travel time and ticket cost (cf. Chapter 2.1). Consider choosing between two connections that only differ in the buffer time when changing trains. Think of the buffer time as the time to spare after reaching the platform of the connecting train.[iv] One connection has a buffer of 1 minute, the other 6 minutes. Intuitively, the larger buffer seems to result in a higher reliability of transfers.

In this section we will define the key values for a single interchange. Then we will discuss how to determine the score for a complete connection from these key values, and how to search optimizing this criterion.

6.3.1 Reliability Measure

Consider two otherwise equivalent connections a and b with 2 interchanges each. Connection a has 5 minutes buffer time for each interchange, connection b has 9 minutes buffer time for the first and 1 minute for the second interchange. Although the sum is identical, connection a seems somehow more secure. If any one of its trains is delayed by at most 5 minutes, there is no problem. But if the second train for connection b is only 2 minutes late, the connection breaks. It gets even more complicated if we compare connections with different numbers of interchanges. Connection a from above might be considered safer than a connection with just one train change and 0 minutes buffer.

6.3.1.1 Definition of the Buffer Time for a Single Interchange

To obtain a confidence measure for the reliability of transfers there are a number of factors to consider: the excess time when changing trains, empirical values for delays at the station, the number of passengers entering the connecting train / leaving the feeding train, the current situation at neighboring stations, condition of the tracks, ...

As most of these are not easy to observe, impossible to estimate, and/or simply not available beforehand, we opted to use the available *buffer time* to base our calculation on.

Apart from the arrival $arr_s(f)$ and departure time $dep_s(t)$ of the feeding train f and the connecting train t at station s we need the *change time* $ct_s(f,t)$ to define the buffer time. Time $ct_s(f,t)$ is the time needed to walk from train f to train t. It depends on the station layout (number of platforms, distances in the station) and the platforms the trains stop at (for more details see Section 1.1). In the basic case we can determine the buffer time

$$buf := dep_s(t) - arr_s(f) - ct_s(f,t).$$

Scenario with delays In a scenario with delay information additional values determine the buffer time. We have the minimum change time $minct(f,t)$ that is applicable if a train arrives

---

[iv]We will formally define the buffer time later.

late. In this case announcements in the train or even railway personnel guiding passengers can make it possible to change faster. The change time can often be decreased by up to two minutes. Furthermore, connecting trains may wait for the arrival of feeding trains according to a set of waiting rules (cf. Chapter 7.2.2). We can increase the buffer time by the number of additional minutes available, e.g. if t would wait for train f at station s up to $wt_s(t, f)$ minutes and is already x minutes late we have $wait_s^+(t, f) = \max\{wt_s(t, f) - x, 0\}$ additional minutes. If train t waits for train f, it departs not later than $dep_s^{sched}(t) + wt_s(t, f)$. The additional waiting time is zero if train t has a higher delay than $wt_s(t, f)$ on its own.

For an interchange i from train t to f with $\Delta := dep(t) - arr(f)$ for the (possibly delayed) event times, we now get the buffer time:

$$buf(i) := \begin{cases} \Delta - ct_s(f, t) + wait_s^+(t, f) & \text{if } ct_s(f, t) \geq \Delta \\ 0 + wait_s^+(t, f) & \text{if } minct_s(f, t) \leq \Delta < ct_s(f, t) \\ \bot & \text{if } \Delta < minct_s(f, t) \end{cases}$$

For the first case we simply apply the rules from above. When a train arrives too late to use change time $ct_s(f, t)$, we switch to using the minimum change time. In that case, we do not want to gain additional buffer time in our model by defining $buf(i)$ as $\Delta - minct_s(f, t) > 0$. Therefore, the buffer time is set to zero in the second interval. In the last case the interchange will break as the train would have to wait more than $wt_s(t, f)$ minutes to make the interchange possible (as train t arrived later than time $dep_{sched}(t) + wt_s(t, f) - minct_s(f, t)$).

6.3.1.2 Reliability Rating

We assume we have a buffer time for each of the interchanges of a connection and want to determine the reliability of transfers for the whole connection.

In his Bachelor thesis Kai Mehrungskötter [Meh07] investigated evaluation functions to determine the reliability of transfers $rel(c)$ for the whole connection c with interchanges $i_1, \ldots, i_k$:

Min Obtaining the reliability measure from the minimum over the buffer times of all interchanges $rel(c) := \min_j(buf(i_j))$ is not sufficient, e.g. a connection with two interchanges, with 1 and 20 minutes buffer, is regarded as equally reliable as a connection with 1 and 2 minutes buffer time.

Sum Defining the reliability $rel(c) := \sum_j(buf(i_j))$ as the sum of the buffer times is not a good measure, e.g. two interchanges with 3 minutes of buffer each are considered better than only one interchange with 5 minutes buffer.

Arith If we define the reliability $rel(c) := \frac{\sum_j(buf(i_j))}{k}$ as the average of the buffer times, it fixes the previous example, but as we disregard the number of interchanges and the distribution of buffer times, this is still not enough. For example, two interchanges with 1 and 9 or 4 and 6 as well as one interchange with 5 minutes buffer, all evaluate to the same result.

To overcome all these drawbacks we decided to calculate a probability factor $sec(i_j)$ for each interchange i_j and to determine the reliability as

$$rel(c) := \prod_{j=1}^{k}(sec(i_j)).$$

6.3.1.3 Reliability-Functions for an Interchange

Now we want to determine the security factor $sec(i_j)$ for a single interchange i_j with a buffer of $x = buf(i_j)$. We need some preliminary considerations. According to the schedule construction a railway company does not consider a buffer time of zero minutes as an endangered or impossible interchange. So we cannot set the security factor for zero minutes to 0% but have to choose a much higher value instead, e.g. $\eta = 60\%$. From the introductory example it is clear that a connection without interchanges should obtain the highest possible reliability measure of 100%. Connections with at least one interchange can obtain a reliability of at most $\mu < 1$, e.g. $\mu = 99\%$. On the other hand we do not want to impose a buffer of say at least 100 minutes to reach the highest possible reliability μ. Here we could choose $\theta = 45$ minutes (as within 60 minutes another train operates the same route for most frequencies).

With this consideration we can discuss the following examples:

linear With a linear function

$$sec(x) := \begin{cases} \frac{\mu-\eta}{\theta}x + \eta & : 0 \leq x \leq \theta \\ \mu & : otherwise \end{cases}$$

the increase of the buffer by δ minutes increases the security factor by $\frac{\mu-\eta}{\theta}\delta$. This is clearly not intended, as the increase in reliability from 0 to 5 minutes should be much higher than that from 30 to 35 minutes.

discrete For interval bounds $x_0 = 0, \ldots, x_n$ and $y_0 = \eta < y_1 < \ldots < y_n = \mu$ a discrete function

$$sec(x) := \begin{cases} y_j & : x_j \leq x < x_{j+1} \text{ for some } j \\ \mu & : x > x_n \end{cases}$$

requires too many intervals and guessing or fine-tuning too many y_j. Additionally, it is not strictly monotonically increasing, so a small change in buffer time either changes nothing or jumps from y_j to y_{j+1}.

6.3 Reliability of Transfers

Parameters		x	$sec(x)$	x	$sec(x)$	x	$sec(x)$
η	60%	0	60%	12	90%	19	95%
μ	99%	1	65%	13	91%	21	96%
θ	45min	4	75%	14	92%	24	97%
α	8	6	80%	15	93%	30	98%
		8	85%	17	94%	45	99%

Table 6.1: The parameters for the reliability function $sec(x)$ and sample values for some buffer times x.

piecewise linear For a piecewise linear function we need interval bounds and constant slopes a_j, with $a_0 > a_i > \ldots a_n$ in the intervals we again have to determine and adjust too many values for intervals and slopes.

exponential Addressing all the concerns from above we use an exponential function

$$sec(x) = \mu - e^{ln(\mu-\eta)-\frac{1}{\alpha}x}.$$

The formula evaluates to values in the range $[\eta, \mu]$, as we have

$$\lim_{x \to \infty} sec(x) = \lim_{x \to \infty} \mu - e^{ln(\mu-\eta)-\frac{1}{\alpha}x} = \mu - 0 = \mu$$

for large x, and for $x = 0$:

$$sec(0) = \mu - e^{(ln\mu-\eta)-\frac{1}{\alpha}0} = \mu - e^{ln(\mu-\eta)} = \mu - (\mu - \eta) = \eta.$$

We only have to fix the parameter α defining the steepness. A nice choice seems to be $\alpha = 8$, which results in the values given in Table 6.1, e.g. it gives us for our "long waiting time" θ a reliability of $sec(\theta) = \mu - 0.0014 (\approx \mu)$ which rounds to μ.

Thus, we selected the exponential function to calculate the reliability for a single interchange. Different sets of parameters have been evaluated in [Meh07] and we finally agreed on the parameters in Table 6.1 (left).

6.3.2 Good Measure = Good Additional Criterion?

Unfortunately, this measure cannot directly be used as an additional criterion. In Dijkstra's algorithm we have to sum non-negative integers for each of our criteria. The following problems arise from taking the reliability of interchanges as another dimension in our labels:

Maximization All other criteria have to be minimized, but we want to maximize the reliability. By simply minimizing the "unreliability" as 1 minus the reliability, or replacing all relevant smaller-than with larger-than operators (possible, since the criterion is bounded), we overcome this issue.

Multiplication Instead of adding the length of an edge to the length stored in the label we multiply. This can be fixed by using the group isomorphism from the multiplicative group of nonnegative real numbers to the additive group of real numbers provided by the logarithm. We may calculate the reliability rating $sec(c)$ after using an interchange i for connection $c' = c + i$ as
$$log(sec(c')) = log(sec(c)) + log(sec(i)).$$

Different signs of edge lengths In our graph model all train edges and stay-in-train edges do not influence the reliability rating. But the edges modeling train changes do. For the use of special interchange edges the constructions from above may directly be applied (as only one edge represents the interchange and the waiting time). However, we cannot do likewise for regular interchanges consisting of a leaving (or foot) edge followed by an arbitrary number of waiting edges and an entering edge. If we update the reliability after each used edge, we have the following developments:

- The rating drops significantly after leaving the train (leaving or foot edge), because we have an additional interchange (thus the rating is multiplied by η).

- The rating increases with each waiting edge used, as the buffer time increases.

History aware edge lengths Depending on the amount of time already spent waiting at a station, the increase from the same waiting edge varies. Looking at the values in Table 6.1 (middle and right) we see that 7 additional minutes of buffer nets us 20% when increasing the buffer from 1 to 8, whereas we only gain 5% from 12 to 19 minutes.

Example Consider the following situation (cf. Table 6.2): We have two labels a and b at some node, with buffer times 1 and 12 minutes, respectively. Both already have one earlier interchange, label a with a buffer of 12 minutes (rating 90%), and label b a buffer of 4 minutes (rating 75%). When we compare these two labels we have $sec(a) = 58.5\%$ and $sec(b) = 67.5\%$. Label b is better, regarding reliability. After using a waiting edge with a length of 7 minutes, the updated reliability rating is $sec(a') = 76.5\%$ and $sec(b') = 71.25\%$. This makes a' better than b. Sadly, we would not have created a' because label a was dominated. Note that all other criteria could have been identical for a and b and thus would be identical for a' and b' as well.

6.3 Reliability of Transfers

	label a				label b		
	this interchange		total	attainable	this interchange		total
	buffer	sec	sec	max sec	buffer	sec	sec
before e	1 min	65%	58.5%	89.1%	12 min	90%	67.50%
after e	8 min	85%	76.5%	89.1%	19 min	95%	71.25%

Table 6.2: Comparing the reliability of interchanges of two labels a and b with one previous interchange with a buffer of 12 minutes (rating 90%) for label a and a buffer of 4 minutes (rating 0.75%) for label b. Using total sec for both labels allows b to dominate a before using edge e. The modified version with comparison against the maximal attainable reliability of a does not allow domination.

Modified comparison

To overcome the last two problems, we have to modify the comparison of labels. When we ask whether label a is dominated by label b, we enter a case distinction:

1. At event nodes (i.e. after traveling or staying in a train or after an interchange is completed) we compare the values of a and b as usual.

2. On the change level, where the reliability might still improve due to additional waiting time, we use the current rating for label b and the *maximal attainable reliability* for label a. To obtain this value we multiply the reliability after the previous interchange (or 100% if no previous interchange exists) by μ.

In the previous example, label a would not have been dominated, because we now use $maxsec(a) = \mu \cdot 90\% = 89.1\%$ instead of $sec(a) = 65\% \cdot 90\% = 58.5\%$. The new score is better than the 67.5% of label b.

6.3.3 Refinements

After the implementation of the reliability measure as an additional criterion and the necessary adjustments in our label data structures and the methods for dominance testing, we were able to test our search for more reliable connections.

6.3.3.1 Discretization and Filtering

As the evaluation of the exponential function leads to floating point values, we have a huge set of possible values. So a solution set may contain a very large number of connections because of increased reliability of interchanges, but all of them only differ by an absolute value of say 2%. An increase of 0.1% at the expense of traveling 1 hour longer leads to a new Pareto optimum but is surely neither desired nor acceptable. To overcome these problems we did two things.

Discretization Firstly, we consider the reliability measure to be an integer between zero and one hundred, thus obtaining 100 equivalence classes. For more than one interchange we can get below our $\mu = 60\%$ for one interchange and arbitrarily close to zero, because all factors are at most 1.0, (e.g. 0.7^4 rounds to 24%).

Although 100 seems to be the natural choice, we can use this discretization step to speed up computation and observe a run time - quality tradeoff. For example, using only 1 equivalence class, we completely disable the search for connections with higher reliability of interchanges and if we change the number from 10 to 50, 100, or even 1000 classes, the number of investigated labels increases, as we will see in Section 9.9.1.

Advanced Dominance And secondly, we added the following conditions a label with longer travel time but higher reliability measure has to fulfill:

- the travel time increase may not exceed a certain threshold δ (e.g. 90 minutes)
- the travel time may not exceed twice the travel time of the other connection
- for each additional minute the reliability has to increase by at least 1%.

We implemented the third point only. Using reliability of interchanges as an optimization criterion in advanced Pareto dominance, we require a wage of δ_{sec} increased reliability per additional minute travel time (similar to the hourly wage for ticket cost already introduced in Chapter 2).

6.3.3.2 Limiting the Maximal Effective Reliability

When introducing the highest reliability rating μ of an interchange, we thought about using $\mu = 99\%$. However, discussions with practitioners made us wonder, whether a lower value, still above 90%, might actually improve the desired quality. We introduced the *maximal effective reliability* $\hat{\mu}$ and define $\theta(\hat{\mu}) = \min\{x | sec(x) \geq \hat{\mu}\}$ as the first minute x for which the reliability is higher than $\hat{\mu}$. For $\hat{\mu} \in [90\%, 99\%]$ the values $\theta(\hat{\mu})$ are given in Table 6.1. We now use the truncated reliability function

$$sec'(x) = \begin{cases} \mu - e^{ln(\mu - \eta) - \frac{1}{\alpha}x} & \text{if } x < \theta(\hat{\mu}) \\ \hat{\mu} & \text{otherwise.} \end{cases}$$

So for times below $\theta(\hat{\mu})$ we use the reliability function exactly as introduced in Section 6.3, for times greater or equal $\theta(\hat{\mu})$, we limit the reliability to $\hat{\mu}$.

Due to the exponential function in $sec'(\cdot)$, the increase of $\theta(\hat{\mu})$ in minutes per additional percent in $\hat{\mu}$ is not linear. In fact for $\hat{\mu} \in [90\%, 93\%]$ it is one minute, in $[93\%, 96\%]$ two minutes and 3, 6, and 15 minutes from 96% to 97%, 97% to 98%, and 98% to 99%, respectively (cf. Table 6.1).

6.3 Reliability of Transfers

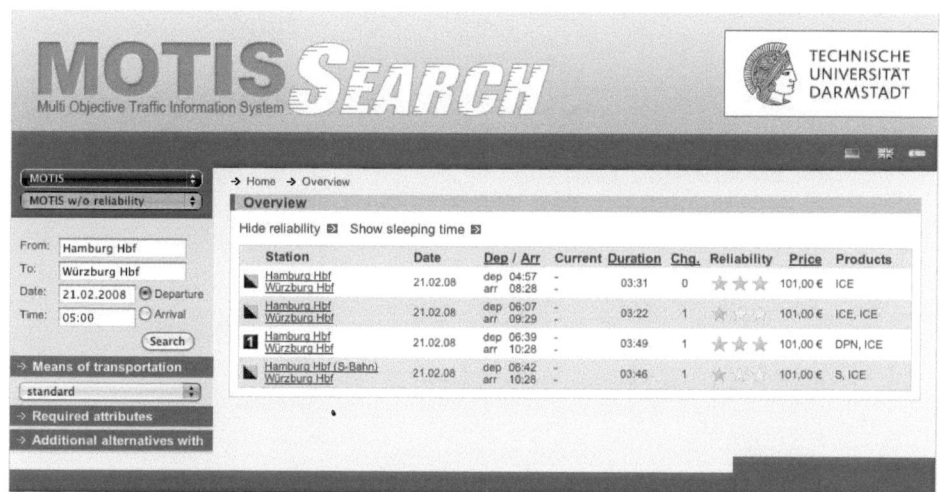

Figure 6.1: Comparison display of the search results determined by two servers, one with (blue) and the other without (yellow) reliability of interchanges as an optimization criterion.

After extensive regression tests and single case analysis we agreed on the value $\hat{\mu} = 96\%$. In our discussion with practitioners they appreciated the values for α, η, μ, and $\hat{\mu}$ (and especially the connections obtained when using this model). The investigation of the effect of changing $\hat{\mu}$ is presented in Section 9.9.2.

6.3.4 Example Result Set

In Figure 6.1 we see the results for an example query from Hamburg main station (Hbf) to Würzburg main station (Hbf). The screen-shot was taken from the multi-server display of our MOTIS Search GUI (introduced in Section 11.2). One server was configured with (blue #1), the other without (yellow #2) reliability of interchanges as an optimization criterion. Results marked with a square half yellow half blue were determined by both servers, the one with a blue square only by server #1. The reliability of interchanges score is visualized as intuitively understandable graphics, here stars for whole connections and clocks for individual interchanges; the more the better. One can easily observe that the additional result delivered by #1 increases the reliability of transfers, usually at the cost of only a few (here three) additional minutes of travel time. The third connection, obtained by server #1 only, departs three minutes earlier than the fourth and drastically increases the reliability rating. Both connections use ICE 583 from Hamburg Harburg to Würzburg Hbf (see Figure 6.2). The third connection uses a RB from Hamburg Hbf to Hamburg Harburg, whereas the fourth uses an S-Bahn from the S-Bahn station Hamburg Hbf (S-Bahn) of Hamburg Hbf to the S-Bahn

78   Chapter 6: Additional Criteria and Special Search Forms

Figure 6.2: Details for the third (upper) and fourth (lower) connections from the previous figure. The higher reliability of the upper connection is due to the higher buffer time in Hamburg-Harburg.

station Hamburg-Harburg(S) of Hamburg Harburg and a footpath with duration 10 minutes to the long distance station Hamburg Harburg. As the RB is much faster than the S-Bahn, the buffer time at Hamburg Harburg is increased by more than the three minutes the RB leaves earlier and the five minutes difference between the change time at Hamburg Harburg and the length of the footpath. A buffer increment of 16 minutes is achieved, thus the reliability score is significantly improved.

6.4 Sleeping Time in Night Trains

The search for attractive *night train connections* is fundamentally different from an ordinary search: the primary objective of a customer of a night train is to have a reasonably long sleeping period without interruptions from train changes. For most passengers it is also undesirable to reach the final destination too early in the morning. These objectives are in sharp contrast to standard information systems which focus on minimizing the total travel time.

In this section, we present and compare two new approaches to support queries for night train connections. These approaches have been integrated into our timetable information system MOTIS.

6.4 Sleeping Time in Night Trains

Our work on night trains has appeared in [GMS07]. An extended journal version has been accepted for publication in [GMS09].

6.4.1 Introduction and Motivation

Marketing campaigns of major railway companies praise the advantages of night trains: "By traveling at night you save paying for a hotel night, and you gain a full day of activities." Compared to traveling by plane, passengers can take more luggage with them, and they save the check-in procedures at airports and transfers from the airport to the city center.

At a first glance, it may seem surprising that the same railway companies put little effort into supporting potential customers in their search for attractive night train connections. To be applicable in practice, night train queries have to be answered more or less instantly (i.e., in very few seconds). Given the size of the search graph (about 2.5 million nodes), the challenge is to design an approach which runs in linear or even sublinear time for typical instances.

Current search engines support the search for night trains in one of two types. One is not all, the other is limited and supports only direct connections. It requires the user to already know the stations served by night trains from which he wants to start and at which he wants to leave the train. Of course, the search of direct connections is algorithmically very simple. The problem immediately becomes much more difficult if the starting point or the final destination are not served by a night train connection at all. Usually, there will be several night train stations in the neighborhood of the starting point and the destination of a planned journey. Thus, this section deals with the complex environment of a relatively dense network (like the railway network of central Europe), which offers many alternatives. The goal of this section is to introduce and to discuss several approaches for an effective night train search.

In general, we look for a connection consisting of three parts:

- one or more trains from the origin to the point of boarding a night train (called *feeder train*),
- a night train, and
- again one or more feeder trains from the station of disembarking the night train to the final destination.

The first or last of the parts may be missing.

The purpose of the initial feeder trains is to bring the customer on time (with a certain safety margin) to the night train. For the feeder trains (in the first and the third part), we aim for the fastest and most convenient connections with respect to the number of interchanges,

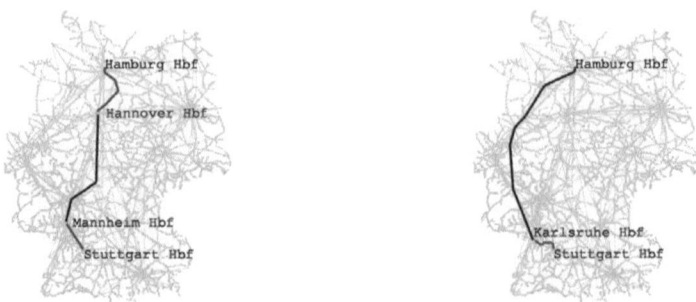

Figure 6.3: Alternative night train connections from Stuttgart to Hamburg.

whereas the night train section should have a minimum length of h hours. The parameter h can be set by the customer; a typical choice might be $h = 6$ hours.

Thus, the overall connection which we are looking for will typically not be the fastest possible, and that is why information servers which focus on fastest connections will fail to find and offer them. If there are several alternatives for the arrival time at the destination, the search engine should present all alternatives. Fig. 6.3 shows an example of a query from Stuttgart main station (Hbf) to Hamburg main station (Hbf) with two alternative night train connections. The first connection is faster with a total duration of 8h 23min, but requires two train changes and has a sleeping period of only 5h 19min. The second connection has a total duration of 9h 54min and only one train change, but offers an uninterrupted sleeping period of 8h 02min.

Our Contribution. We are not aware of any previous work on searching for night trains. Our first contribution in this section is a formal model which tries to capture the notion of attractive night train connections. Afterwards, we discuss how to model that a connection offers enough sleeping time and other aspects which should be considered.

Based on this formal model, we develop two general approaches for night train search. The first approach is an enumerative approach. It is based on the idea that there are only relatively few night trains which are candidates for a given query. This approach was explained and evaluated in more detail by our student Torsten Gunkel in [Gun07]. Our second approach considers sleeping time as an additional criterion in a multi-criteria search. Here, we extend a multi-criteria version of Dijkstra's algorithm to this additional criterion.

The basic versions of both general approaches are quite inefficient. Therefore, we have engineered them both. By using appropriate speed-up techniques, we achieve acceptable average runtimes of only a few seconds per query. In an extensive computational study we show that our fastest versions yield high quality solutions, much better than those that we can reach by standard methods.

6.4.2 Attractive Night Train Connections

6.4.2.1 Discussion of Objectives for Night Trains

How can we ensure that a connection offers enough sleeping time? From a modeling point of view, we could simply impose a lower bound on the sleeping time as a side constraint. Let us call this lower bound *minimum sleeping time* and denote its value by lb_{st}.

Unfortunately, the choice of some suitable constant lb_{st} is not obvious since different customers may have very different opinions on what they regard as sufficient sleeping time. But even if customers are allowed to choose this constant individually according to their personal preferences, any sharp border imposed by such a constant is questionable. If we choose lb_{st} too large we may miss valuable alternatives (which are just below the given value). In contrast, choosing the constant lb_{st} too small may lead to relatively short sleeping periods, since the search algorithm has no incentive to favor alternatives with longer sleeping periods.

However, to use the pure objective "maximize the sleeping time" is also questionable as it supports unnecessary, but costly detours. Thus, we have to balance the goal of maximizing the sleeping time with the usual goal of minimizing the overall travel time.

Therefore, we combine both ideas and propose the following model. We choose a fairly small lower bound on the minimum sleeping time, to distinguish night train connections which include a reasonable sleeping period from other connections which only partially use a night train.

Suppose we want to compare two connections c_1 and c_2 with total travel times $tt(c_1)$ and $tt(c_2)$ and sleeping times $st(c_1)$ and $st(c_2)$, respectively, with $st(c_1), st(c_2) > lb_{st}$. We suggest the following domination rules:

1. If connection c_1 is faster than c_2, then the increase in sleeping time $st(c_2) - st(c_1)$ should be at least as large as the increase in total travel time $tt(c_2) - tt(c_1)$. Otherwise, we consider c_2 as dominated by c_1 with respect to these two criteria.

2. We also impose an upper bound on the sleeping time ub_{st}. The idea is that sleeping times longer than this upper bound should not be considered as beneficial for the customer. Thus, instead of using the original sleeping time st, we use a *modified sleeping time* $mst := \min\{st, ub_{st}\}$ in our comparisons of connections.

6.4.2.2 Filtering Attractive Solutions

Trains are considered as *night trains* if they are officially labeled as such (and not just operate during the night). A connection is considered as a *night train connection* only if it includes a night train with a sleeping time of at least lb_{st} minutes.

This definition does only partially capture what passengers will consider as an *attractive* night train connection. Therefore, we propose applying additional constraints to remove undesired solutions from the set of found connections. In this subsection, we use the following additional rules:

- We remove all night train connections with an extremely long feeder section, since such connections usually imply a large detour. To this end, we use an upper bound on feeder lengths ub_{fe}.

- We also remove all connections which have more than two additional interchanges than some other night train connection as such connections are quite uncomfortable.

- From the remaining solutions, we filter out all dominated solutions, where we use modified sleeping time $mst := \min\{st, ub_{st}\}$ as explained above.

Since ticket costs depend very much on the chosen train category and the fare system is quite complicated, we do not consider ticket costs in this section for ease of exposition.

6.4.2.3 Size of Solution Set

While in general the number of Pareto optima can be exponentially large for multi-criteria shortest path problems [MW01, MW06], our application is more restrictive and can be bounded under quite reasonable assumptions.

Namely, it is an easy observation that the number of different k-tuples of Pareto optimal solution vectors (with k criteria) is polynomially bounded if the possible values in all but one criterion are polynomially bounded. Since the number of interchanges is polynomially bounded (in fact, in practice a small constant) and the number of possible sleeping times is also polynomial, we conclude that our application has only polynomially many different solution vectors.

Since we do not use ordinary Pareto dominance but relaxed Pareto dominance, the solution set can be larger, but only by constant factors if our relaxation allows only a constant increase on each criterion.

As several different paths may have the same solution vectors (and we also want to find these alternatives) this observation does not directly imply polynomiality of our approach. However, in night train search the number of alternative connections with identical objective values is empirically very small. This can be explained by the observation that the likelihood to have two connections with different night train sections but the same sleeping time is small, and that for some fixed night train the corresponding feeder sections have only very few interchanges.

6.4.3 Approaches for Night Train Search

In this section we describe two new approaches which we have developed for night train search.

6.4.3.1 Pre-Selection of Night Trains

We first present an enumerative approach. Its general idea is to select suitable night train sections first, and then to compute corresponding feeder sections. The main steps can be stated quite easily.

1. Iterate over all night trains of the train schedule which operate on the query day.
2. For each such train, determine all stations which may serve as entry point and all stations which may serve as exit points.
3. For each such pair, determine feeder sections to compose complete connections.
4. Let C be the collection of connections determined. Apply Pareto dominance to filter out all dominated connections from C. Return the result.

In the following we will first describe steps 2 and 3 in more detail. Afterwards, we will discuss how to speed up this general approach.

6.4.3.1.1 Selection of Entry and Exit Points.
Given a query and a particular night train, we have to select suitable pairs of entry and exit points to this train in Step 2. This has to be done with care to achieve a reasonable efficiency. Thus, in this phase we intend to reject as many pairs as possible without losing valuable solutions.

A station where a night train stops (and entering/leaving is allowed) qualifies as a possible entry or exit point if it is close, with respect to some distance metric, to the start or to the terminal station of the query, respectively.

To this end, two metrics can be used: Euclidean distance and lower bounds on the travel time for the feeder section. The advantage of Euclidean based bounds is that we can compute them in constant time. However, such bounds completely ignore the railway network and the train schedule. Two stations which are geographically close may be far from each other with respect to public transport. Estimates of the required travel time between two stations would allow us to make more accurate decisions. We propose using lower bound on the travel time as estimates. These bound can be computed quite efficiently.

As the length of required feeder sections depends very much on the given query, we do not use any fixed absolute bound to decide whether two stations are close enough to each other. Instead we propose using a query-dependent rejection rule which is visualized in Figure 6.4. A pair of entry and exit points is rejected for a query if the bound a on the feeder length from the start station to the entry point and the bound b on the feeder length from the exit point to the terminal station together exceed the bound c on the length of a direct connection between start and terminal station by some factor α, i.e., if

$$a + b > \alpha \cdot c.$$

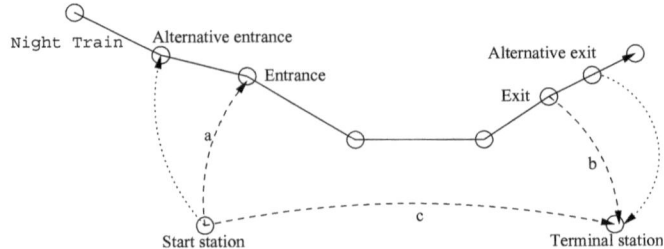

Figure 6.4: Selection of pairs of entry and exit points. Pairs are rejected if $a + b > \alpha \cdot c$, i.e., if they would induce too large a detour.

Our experiments revealed that setting $\alpha := 1$ is a suitable conservative choice.

Finally, we accept a pair of entry and exit stations only if the travel time of the corresponding night train between these two stations is above our lower bound on the sleeping time lb_{st}.

6.4.3.1.2 Computation of Feeders.
Given a pair of entry and exit points for a night train the next step is to compute feeder trains.

The entry point for the night train determines when we have to arrive at this particular station at the latest. Since we really want to reach the night train we incorporate some extra safety margin to this calculation. Then we can use an ordinary backward search (with the same safety margin for interchanges) from this station and the latest arrival time to the start station to find suitable feeder trains.[v] Likewise we perform an ordinary forward search from the exit point to the terminal station.

Since entry and exit points are likely to appear in several pairs, we have to make sure not to compute the same feeder sections several times. To avoid repeated calculations, we therefore introduced a caching mechanism which stores the results of each feeder search.

6.4.3.1.3 Pruning the Search Space.
A naive implementation of our enumerative approach would do the feeder computation in an arbitrary order for all selected pairs. Since the selection of pairs is done in a very conservative way, the resulting algorithm would be quite inefficient.

A more clever refinement of this approach uses a priority queue to determine the order of feeder computations. Our motivation is that already computed solutions can be used to prune the search space. The priority queue contains all pairs for which at least one feeder has not yet been computed. The key by which we order the entry and exit point pairs in the priority queue is an estimate of the travel time of the overall connection. This travel

---

[v]Ordinary search allows the replacement of start and terminal stations by equivalent meta-stations. The possibility for such a replacement has to be switched off for the entry and exit point as in our scenario we really have to arrive at the pre-selected station and not at some equivalent one.

time estimate is composed of the known length of the night train section plus estimates on the feeder lengths. When a particular feeder has been determined during the course of the algorithm, our estimates are updated for all elements in the priority queue where this feeder fits. In each iteration we select and remove the top element from the priority queue. For the corresponding pair we check whether it is already dominated by previously computed connections. If this is the case, we discard this pair. Otherwise, we compute one missing feeder. Afterwards, we either obtain a set of complete connections for this pair, or the other feeder section is still missing. In the latter case, we reinsert the pair into the priority queue with the updated key information.

6.4.3.2 Multi-Criteria Search with an Additional Criterion

The second approach, which we propose, adds sleeping time as a new criterion to the multi-criteria search for attractive connections. Form a software-engineering point of view the multi-criteria framework implemented in MOTIS is easily extendable to an additional criterion. In general, only two modifications are necessary.

1. We have to make sure that the labels representing partial connections keep track of the additional criterion.

2. The domination rules have to be adapted so that they effectively prune labels.

While the modification of labels is straightforward, finding good domination rules is much more difficult (and usually requires some experimental evaluation).

Pruning of labels during search by domination can only be done with the help of good and efficiently computable bounds, lower bounds for minimization and upper bounds for maximization, respectively. See Section 8.5 for details on lower bounds and Section 8.4 for an introduction of the speed-up technique *domination by labels at the terminal*.

Thus, for the maximization criterion sleeping time we need an upper bound. Given a partial connection, this bound should limit the maximum additional sleeping time this connection can accumulate en route to the terminal station. With the help of such an upper bound a label of a partial connection can be dominated with respect to the criterion sleeping time if the current sleeping time plus the additional sleeping time is smaller than the sleeping time of some known complete connection. Unfortunately, we do not know such upper bounds, except for trivial ones which are far too loose to help in pruning.

Since a Pareto search without pruning is hopeless (although the search space is polynomially bounded in practice [MW01, MW06], it is still far too large to achieve computation times of a few seconds), we have to use heuristic domination rules which cannot guarantee finding all attractive solutions.

We adapt the domination rules of MOTIS as follows: A complete connection c is only allowed to prune a partial connection p

- if p "has used and already left" a night train but did not reach at least lb_{st} sleeping time, or

- if p "has used and already left" a night train but did not reach more sleeping time than c, or

- if p is currently "in a night train", then c has to have sleeping time above the threshold lb_{st}, and the sleeping time of c has to be at least the sleeping time of p plus β times a lower bound on the remaining travel time for p (for some constant β), or

- if p contains no night train at all.

While the first two rules are still exact, the two others are aggressive heuristics.[vi]

If c is allowed to prune it still needs to be "relaxed Pareto smaller" with respect to the other criteria. For the comparison of labels belonging to the same node (i.e., partial connection against partial connection) nothing has to be changed.

We will evaluate both approaches to the search for night trains in Section 9.2 in Chapter 9: *Computational Study*.

[vi]Initial experiments showed that without these heuristics the average CPU time would be about one minute. This is clearly not acceptable for on-line use of information systems.

Chapter 7

Delays

The search for train connections in state-of-the-art commercial timetable information systems is based on a static schedule. Unfortunately, public transportation systems suffer from delays for various reasons. Thus, dynamic changes of the planned schedule have to be taken into account. A system that has access to delay information about trains (and uses this information within search queries) can provide valid alternatives in case a connection is not possible as planned due to a broken interchange. Additionally, it can be used to actively guide passengers as these alternatives may be presented before the passenger becomes stranded at a station due to an invalid transfer.

In this chapter, we present an approach which takes a stream of delay information and schedule changes on short notice (partial train cancellations, extra trains) into account. Primary delays of trains may cause a cascade of so-called secondary delays of other trains which have to wait according to certain policies for delays between connecting trains. We introduce the concept of a dependency graph to efficiently calculate and update all primary and secondary delays. This delay information is then incorporated into a time-expanded search graph which has to be updated dynamically. These update operations are quite complex, but turn out not to be time-critical in a fully realistic scenario.

We finally present a case study with data provided by Deutsche Bahn AG, showing that this approach has been successfully integrated into the multi-criteria timetable information system MOTIS and can handle massive delay data streams instantly.

Our early results on this subject have appeared in [FMS08]. The extended results presented here have been accepted for publishing in [MS09]. We want to thank our students Lennart Frede [Fre08] and Mohammad Keyhani [Key09] who contributed to the software design and implementation.

7.1 Introduction and Motivation

In recent years, the performance and quality of service of electronic timetable information systems has increased significantly. Unfortunately, not everything runs smoothly in scheduled traffic and delays are the norm rather than the exception.

Delays can have various causes: Disruptions in the operations flow, accidents, malfunctioning or damaged equipment, construction work, repair work, and extreme weather conditions like snow and ice, floods, and landslides, to name just a few. On a typical day of operation in Germany, an online system has to handle about 6 million forecast messages about (mostly small) changes with respect to the planned schedule and the latest prediction of the current situation. Note that this high number of changes also includes cases where delayed trains catch up some of their delay.

A system that incorporates up-to-date train status information (most importantly, information about future delays based on the current situation) can provide a user with valid timetable information in the presence of disturbances.

Such an on-line system can additionally be utilized to verify the current status of a journey.

- Journeys can either be still valid (i.e., they can be executed as planned),

- they can be affected such that the arrival at the destination is delayed, or

- they may no longer be possible.

In the latter case, a connecting train will be missed, either because the connecting train cannot wait for a delayed train, or the connecting train may have been canceled. In a delay situation, such status information is very helpful. In the positive case – all planned train changes are still possible – passengers can be reassured that they do not have to worry about missing their connecting train(s). To learn that one will arrive x minutes late with the planned sequence of trains may allow a customer to make arrangements, e.g. inform someone to pick one up later. In the unfortunate case that a connecting train will be missed, this information can now be obtained well before the connection breaks and the passenger is stranded at a station. Therefore, valid alternatives may be presented while there are still more options to react. This situation is clearly preferable to missing a connecting train and then using any information system (ticket machine, service counter) to request an alternative.

Up to now commercial systems do not take the current situation into account. Even though estimated arrival times may be accessible for a given connection, these times are not used actively during the search. Their recommendations may be impossible to use, as the proposed alternatives already suffer from delays and may even already be infeasible at the time they are delivered by the system.

7.1 Introduction and Motivation

From Static to Real-Time Timetable Information Systems.

Previous research on timetable information systems has focused on the static case, where the timetable is considered as fixed.

Here we start a new thread of research on dynamically changing timetable data as a consequence of disruptions. Our contribution is:

- the development of a first prototypal yet completely realistic timetable information system that incorporates current train status information into a multi-criteria search for attractive train connections. Modeling issues have been discussed in the literature on a theoretical level [DGWZ08] but no true-to-life system with real delay data has been studied and, to our knowledge, no such system that guarantees optimal results (with respect to even a single optimization criterion) exists. We provide results of implementing such a system for a real world scenario with no simplifying assumptions.

- We propose a system architecture intended for a multi-server environment, where the availability of search engines has to be guaranteed at all times. Our system consists of two main components, a *real-time information server* and one or several *search servers*. The real-time information server receives a massive stream of status messages about delayed trains. Its purpose is to integrate this information into the "planned schedule". Moreover, based on the received messages (primary delays) it has to compute all so-called secondary delays which result from trains waiting for each other according to certain waiting policies. The new overall status information is then sent to the search servers which incorporate all changes into their internal model. Search servers, in turn, are used to answer customer queries about train connections.

- Both servers require a specific graph model as the underlying basic data structure. We here introduce the concept of a *dependency graph* as a model to efficiently propagate primary delay information according to policies for delays in the real-time information server. Our dependency graph (introduced in Section 7.4) is similar to a simple time-expanded graph model with distinct nodes for each departure and arrival event in the entire schedule for the current and following days. This is a natural and efficient model, since every event has to store its own update information.

  For the search server we use a *search graph*. Here, we are free to use either the time-expanded or the time-dependent model. In this chapter, we have chosen to use the time-expanded model for the search graph, since MOTIS is based on this. Although update operations are quite complex in this model, it will turn out that they can be performed very efficiently, averaging $17\mu s$ per update message.

- To store a full timetable over a typical period of a year, static timetable systems are usually built on a compact data structure. For example, they identify the same events on different days of operation and use bitfields to specify valid days. This space saving technique does not work in a dynamic environment since the members of such an equivalence class of events have to be treated individually, as they will generally have different delays. We will show how a static time-expanded graph model can be extended to a dynamic graph model without undue increase in space consumption.

Related work. Independently of us, Delling et al. [DGWZ08] came up with ideas on how to regard delays in timetabling systems. In contrast to their work we do not primarily work on edge weights, but consider nodes with timestamps. The edge weight for time is the difference between head and tail node. Thus, it automatically updates with the timestamps of the nodes, whereas edge weights for transfers and cost do not change during the update procedures. This is important for the ability to do multi-criteria search. Due to a number of low-level optimizations we achieve a considerable speed-up over the preliminary work in Frede et al. [FMS08].

A related field of current research is disposition and delay management. Gatto et al. [GGJ+04, GJPS05] have studied the complexity of delay management for different scenarios and have developed efficient algorithms for certain special cases using dynamic programming and minimum cut computations. Various policies for delays have been discussed, for example by Ginkel and Schöbel [GS07]. Schöbel [Sch07] also proposed integer programming models for delay management. Stochastic models for the propagation of delays are studied, for example, by Meester and Muns [MM07]. Policies for delays in a stochastic context are treated in [APW02].

Overview. The remainder of this chapter is organized as follows. In Section 7.2, we will discuss primary and secondary delays. We introduce our system architecture in Section 7.3, and describe its two main components afterwards. First, we explain our dependency graph model and the propagation algorithm for delays (in Section 7.4). Then, we present the update of the search graph (in Section 7.5). A major issue for a real system, the correct treatment of days of operation, will be discussed in Section 7.6. Next, we provide our experimental results in Section 7.7. Finally, we conclude and give an outlook.

7.2 Up-To-Date Status Information

7.2.1 Primary Delay Information

The input stream of status messages mainly consists of reports that a certain train departed or arrived at some station at time τ either on time or delayed by x minutes. In case of a delay, such a message is followed by further messages about predicted arrival and departure times for all upcoming stations on the train route.

Additionally, there can be information about additional trains (specified by a list of departure and arrival times at stations plus category, attribute and name information). Furthermore, we have (partial) train cancellations, which include a list of departure and arrival times of the canceled stops (either all stops of the train or from some intermediate station to the last station).

Moreover, we have manual decisions by the transport management. They are of the form: "Change from train t to t' will be possible" or "will not be possible". In the first case it is guaranteed that train t' will wait as long as necessary to receive passengers from train t. In the latter case the connection is definitively going to break although the current prediction might still indicate otherwise. This information may depend on local knowledge, e.g. that not enough tracks are available to wait or that additional delays are likely to occur, or may be based on global considerations about the overall traffic flow. We call messages of this type *connection status decisions*.

7.2.2 Secondary Delays

Secondary delays occur when trains have to wait for other delayed trains. Two simple, but extreme examples for policies for delays are:

- *never wait*

  In this policy, no secondary delays occur at all in our model. This causes many broken connections and in the late evening it may imply that customers do not arrive at their destination on the same travel day. However, nobody will be delayed who is not in a delayed train.

- *always wait as long as necessary*

  In this strategy, there are no broken connections at all, but massive delays are caused for many people, especially for those whose trains wait and have no delay on their own.

Both of these policies seem to be unacceptable in practice. Therefore, train companies usually apply a more sophisticated rule system specifying which trains have to wait for others and for how long. For example, the federal German railroad company, Deutsche Bahn AG, employs a complex set of rules, dependent on train type and local specifics.

In essence, this works as follows: There is a set of rules describing the maximum amount of time a train t may be delayed to wait for passengers from a feeding train f. Basically, these rules depend on train categories and stations. But there are also more involved rules: e.g. if t is the last train of the day in its direction, the waiting time is increased. Or during peak hours, when trains operate more frequently, the waiting time may be decreased.

The *waiting time* $wt_s(t, f)$ is the maximum delay acceptable for train t at station s waiting for a feeding train f. Let $dep_s^{sched}(t)$ and $dep_s(t)$ be the departure time according to the schedule and the new departure time of train t at station s, respectively. Furthermore, $arr_s(t)$ is the arrival time of a train and $minct_s(f, t)$ the *minimum change time* needed to change from train f to train t at station s. Note that in a delayed scenario the change time can be reduced, as guides may be available that show changing passengers the way to their connecting train. Train t waits for train f at station s if

$$arr_s(f) + minct_s(f, t) \leq dep_s^{sched}(t) + wt_s(t, f).$$

In this case, train t will incur a secondary delay. Its new departure time is determined by the following equation

$$dep_s(t) = \begin{cases} arr_s(f) + minct_s(f, t) & \text{if } t \text{ waits} \\ dep_s^{sched}(t) & \text{otherwise.} \end{cases}$$

In case of several delayed feeding trains, the new departure time will be determined as the maximum over these values.

During day-to-day operations these rules are always applied automatically. If the required waiting time of a train lies within the bounds defined by the rule set, trains will wait. Otherwise they will not. All exceptions from these rules have to be given as connection status decisions.

7.3 System Architecture

Our system consists of two main components (see Figure 7.1 for a sketch). One part is responsible for the propagation of delays from the status information and for the calculation of secondary delays, while the other component handles connection queries. The core of the first part, our *real-time information server*, is a *dependency graph* which models all the dependencies between different trains and between the stops of the same train. It is used to compute secondary delays (in Section 7.4 we introduce the dependency graph and propagation algorithm in detail). The dependency graph stores the obtained information needed to update the search servers and transmits this information in a suitable format to them. The search servers in turn update their internal graph representation whenever they receive these changes. This decoupling of dependency and search graph allows us to use any graph model for the search graph.

In a distributed scenario this architecture can be realized with one server running as the real-time information server that continuously receives new status information and broadcasts it. We will present some details in the following subsection. Load balancing can schedule the update phases for each server. If this is done in a round-robin fashion, the availability of service is guaranteed.

7.3 System Architecture

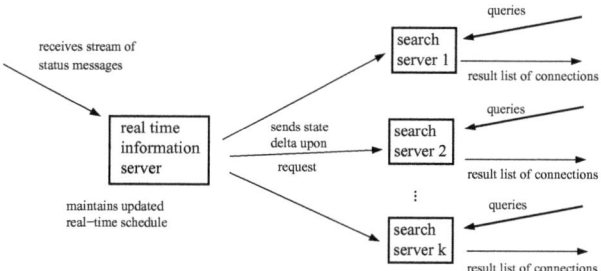

Figure 7.1: Sketch of the system architecture.

Multi-Server Approach

The *search server* mainly consists of a search graph, an update component for the search graph, and a query algorithm.

In a multi-server environment, updates of a search server are either triggered by a load balancer or an internal clock after a maximum amount of time without update. The data it receives (called *state delta* for the remainder of this work) consists of lists of changed departure and arrival times as well as meta-information about additional and canceled trains and connection status decisions. Subsequently, it adjusts the search graph accordingly and thereafter the graph looks exactly as if it were constructed from a schedule with all these updated departure and arrival times. Thus, the search algorithm does not need to know whether it is working on a graph with updated times or not.

The *real-time information server* receives all the up-to-date status information, uses its internal *dependency graph* to compute updated departure and arrival times (cf. Section 7.4) and stores these and the meta-information in a data structure UDS (*update data structure*). UDS maintains for every event with a changed timestamp a 3-tuple consisting of (1) a reference to the event itself, (2) the latest updated timestamp of this event, and (3) the release time when the last update of this event took place. Whenever a search server requests an update, it receives all events with a release time later than the last update of that server. If the timestamp of an event (or node in the graph model) changes, we call the necessary update a *(node) shift*.

For a true multi-server architecture with multiple search servers we basically have two update scenarios:

- An additional search server joins in and has to be initialized to the current time: We iterate over all existing event entries in UDS and transmit all those with times differing from the scheduled time.

- A search server has answered a number of queries and now enters update mode: We could simply transmit all events with release time greater than the last update time of the search server (referenced as *iterator version*). As this requires iterating over all stored events even to calculate a small delta, we can do so more efficiently utilizing a map (referenced as *map version*).

In the map version a map of all changed events and their previous event times is maintained for each search server individually. Whenever a new event time is released, we look for that event in the map. Only if it is not already present, we store the event itself and its event time before the last change. This is the current timestamp of the event in the search server. To answer an update request we simply return all events in this map, whose new event time differs from the event time in the map (and thus the time in the current server), and clear the map afterwards. Using this technique we not only save iterating over all entries to determine the set of changed events (our state delta) but also avoid transmitting events that have been changed more than once and do not require a shift, since their new event time is the same as in the last update.

Our UDS data structure enables us to transmit only consistent state deltas on demand. Thereby, we can decrease both the time spent in communication and updating the graphs (e.g. if between two update phases more than one information for a single event is processed in the dependency graph, it is not required to transmit the intermediate state and adjust the graph accordingly).

7.4 Dependency Graph

7.4.1 Graph Model

Our *dependency graph* (see Figure 7.2) models the dependencies between different trains and between the stops of the same train. Its node set consists of four types of nodes:

- departure nodes,
- arrival nodes,
- forecast nodes, and
- schedule nodes.

For each event, there are three nodes, an event node (either departure or arrival), a schedule node, and a forecast node. Each node has a timestamp which can dynamically change. The timestamps of departure and arrival nodes reflect the current situation, i.e. the expected departure or arrival time subject to all delay information known up to this point. Schedule nodes are marked with the planned time of an arrival or departure event, whereas the timestamp of a forecast node is the current external prediction for its departure or arrival time.

7.4 Dependency Graph

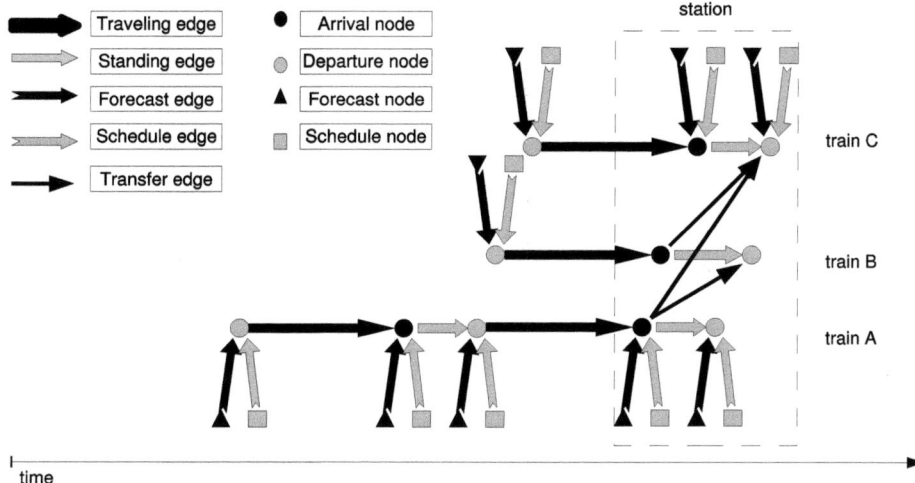

Figure 7.2: Illustration of the dependency graph model.

The nodes are connected by five different types of edges. The purpose of an edge is to model a constraint on the timestamp of its head node. Each edge $e = (v, w)$ has two attributes. One attribute is a Boolean value, signifying whether this edge is currently active or not. The other attribute $\tau(e)$ denotes a point in time which basically can be interpreted as a lower bound on the timestamp of its head node w, provided that the edge is currently active.

- *Schedule edges* connect schedule nodes to departure or arrival nodes. They carry the planned time for the corresponding event of the head node (according to the published schedule). Edges leading to departure nodes are always active, since a train will never depart prior to the published schedule.

- *Forecast edges* connect forecast nodes to departure or arrival nodes. They represent the time stored in the associated forecast node. If no forecast for the node exists, the edge is inactive.

- *Standing edges* connect arrival events at a certain station to the following departure event of the same train.

  They model the condition that the arrival time of train t at station s plus its minimum standing time $stand_s(t)$ must be respected before the train can depart (to allow for boarding and disembarkment of passengers). Thus, for a standing edge e, we set $\tau(e) = arr_s(t) + stand_s(t)$. Standing edges are always active.

- *Traveling edges* connect a departure node of some train t at a certain station s to the very next arrival node of this train at station s'. Let $dep_s(t)$ denote the departure time of train t at station s and $tt(s, s', t)$ the travel time for train t between these two stations. Then, for edge $e = (s, s')$, we set $\tau(e) = dep_s(t) + tt(s, s', t)$. These edges are only active if the train currently has a secondary delay (otherwise the schedule or forecast edges provide the necessary conditions for its head node).

  Due to various, mostly unknown factors determining the travel time of trains in a delayed scenario, e.g. speed of train, condition of the track, track usage (by other trains and freight trains that are not in the available schedule), used engines with acceleration/deceleration profiles, signals along the track etc. we assume for simplicity that $tt(s, s', t)$ is the time given in the planned schedule. However, if a more sophisticated, but efficiently computable oracle for $tt(s, s', t)$ taking the mentioned factors into account were available, it could be used without changing our model.

- *Transfer edges* connect arrival nodes to departure nodes of other trains at the same station, if there is a planned transfer between these trains. Thus, if f is a potential feeder train for train t at station s, we set $\tau(e) = wait_s(t, f)$, where

$$wait_s(t, f) = \begin{cases} arr_s(f) + minct_s(f, t) & \text{if } t \text{ waits for } f \\ 0 & \text{otherwise} \end{cases}$$

(cf. Section 7.2.2) if we respect the waiting rules. Recall that t waits for f only if the following inequality holds

$$arr_s(f) + minct_s(f, t) - dep_s^{sched}(t) \leq wt_s(t, f)$$

or if we have an explicit connection status decision that t will wait.

By default these edges are active. In case of an explicit connection status decision "will not wait" we mark the edge in the dependency graph as not active and ignore it in the computation.

For an "always wait" or "never wait" scenario we may simply always set $\tau(e)$ to the resulting delayed departure time or to zero, respectively.

7.4.2 Computation on the Dependency Graph

The current timestamp for each departure or arrival node can now be defined recursively as the maximum over all deciding factors: For a departure of train t at station s with feeders $f_1, \ldots, f_n$ we have $dep_s(t) =$

$$\max\{dep_s^{sched}(t), dep_s^{for}(t), arr_s(t) + stand_s(t), max_{i=1}^{n}\{wait_s(t, f_i)\}\}.$$

7.4 Dependency Graph

For an arrival we have

$$arr_s(t) = \max\left\{arr_s^{sched}(t), arr_s^{for}(t), dep_{s'}(t) + tt(s', s, t)\right\}$$

with the previous stop of train t at station s'. Inactive edges do not contribute to the maximum in the preceding two equations.

If we have a status message that a train has finally departed or arrived at some given time dep^{fin} resp. arr^{fin}, we do no longer compute the maximum as described above. Instead we use this value for future computations involving the node.

We maintain a priority queue (ordered by increasing timestamps) of all nodes whose timestamps have changed since the last computation was finished. Whenever we have new forecast messages, we update the timestamps of the forecast nodes and, if they have changed, insert them into the queue. For a connection status decision we modify the corresponding transfer edge and update its head node. If its timestamp changes, it is inserted into the queue. As long as the queue is not empty, we extract a node from the queue and update the timestamps of the dependent nodes (which have an incoming edge from this node). If the timestamp of a node has changed in this process, we add it to the queue as well.

For each node we keep track of the edge e_{max} which currently determines the maximum so that we do not need to recompute our maxima over all incoming edges every time a timestamp changes. Only if $\tau(e_{max})$ was decreased or $\tau(e)$ for some $e \neq e_{max}$ increases above $\tau(e_{max})$, the maximum has to be recomputed. The other possible cases are:

- If $\tau(e)$ decreases and $e \neq e_{max}$, nothing needs to be done.
- If $\tau(e)$ increases and $e \neq e_{max}$ but $\tau(e) < \tau(e_{max})$, nothing needs to be done.
- If $\tau(e)$ increases and $e = e_{max}$, the new maximum is again determined by e_{max} and the new value is given by the new $\tau(e_{max})$.

When the queue is empty, all new timestamps have been computed and the nodes with changed timestamps can be sent to the search graph update routine or, in the multi server architecture, to the UDS data structure.

A note on the implementation. For ease of exposition we have introduced all kinds of nodes and edges in the dependency graph as being real nodes and edges. Of course, in our implementation we do not use a node and an edge to encode nothing more than a single timestamp for schedule and forecast times. Only arrival and departure nodes are real nodes with entering and leaving edges plus two integer variables representing the scheduled and forecast time. The latter is set to some predefined value to specify "no real-time information available (yet)". An arrival node has a container of leaving transfer edges, one entering traveling edge and one leaving standing edge. Analogously, a departure node has a container of entering transfer edges, one entering standing edge and one leaving traveling edge. Iterators over incoming dependencies and markers for the current input determining the timestamp of the node (the incoming edge, schedule time, or forecast time with maximum timestamp) have to be able to traverse resp. point to the different representations. We deemed the much more elegant version of the update routines - pretending the existence of nodes and edges for schedule and forecast times - better suited for presentation.

7.5 Updating the Search Graph

The Dynamic Model

The static time-expanded graph model (as introduced in Chapter 4 and refined in Section 5.1) has been slightly adapted for the dynamic scenario. Compared to the standard search graph we have to store additional information, namely status decisions, a second timestamp for each node to report actual and scheduled time in query results, additional strings containing reasons for the delays, and the like. Moreover, we need a slightly different representation of trains with identical schedules on multiple days. We defer details of this modification to Section 7.6.

The Update Process

The update in the search graph does not simply consist of setting new timestamps for nodes (primary and secondary delays), insertions (additional trains) and deletions (cancellations) of nodes and resorting lists of nodes afterwards. All the edges modeling the changing of trains at the affected stations have to be recomputed respecting the changed timestamps, additional and deleted nodes, and connection status information. The following adjustments are required on the change level (see Figure 7.3):

- Updating the leaving edges pointing to the first node reachable after a train change.
- Updating the nodes reachable from a change node via entering edges.
- Inserting additional change nodes or unhooking them from the chain of waiting edges at times where a new event is the only one or the only event is moved away or canceled.
- Recalculating special-interchange edges from resp. to arrival resp. departure nodes with a changed timestamp (either remove, adjust or insert special-interchange edges).

The result of the update phase is a graph that looks and behaves exactly as if it was constructed from a schedule describing the current situation. Additionally, it contains information about the original schedule and reasons for the delays.

Next, we give two examples for updating the search graph. In Figure 7.3 (left) it is possible to change from train t to all trains departing not earlier than t'' using leaving edge g, any number of consecutive waiting edges and an entering edge (e.g. h to enter t''). A

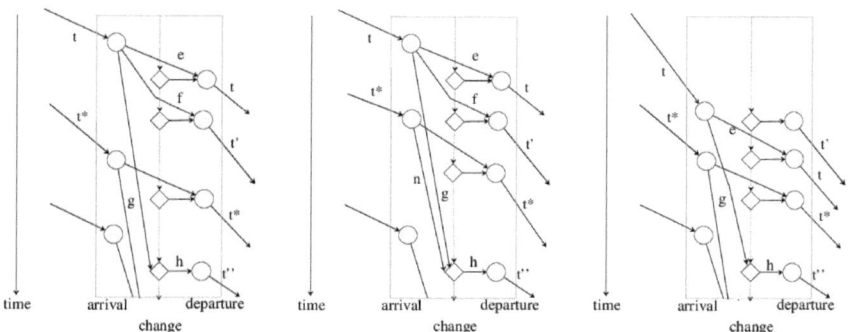

Figure 7.3: The change level at a station (left) and necessary changes if train t^* arrives earlier (middle) or train t arrives later (right).

change to train t' on the same platform is also feasible using special-interchange edge f and, of course, to stay in train t via stay-in-train edge e. However, it is impossible to change to train t^* although it departs later than t', because it requires more time to reach it.

Suppose train t^* manages to get rid of some previous delay and now arrives and departs earlier than previously predicted (see Figure 7.3, middle part). In the new situation it is now possible, to change from t^* to train t'' using the new leaving edge n and the existing entering edge h.

In our second example let train t arrive delayed as depicted in Figure 7.3 (right). As it now departs after t', it is not only impossible to change to t' (special-interchange edge f is deleted), but also the departure nodes for the departures of t' and t are in reverse order. Therefore, the waiting edges have to be re-linked.

7.6 Traffic Days

A common simplification in theoretical work on timetable information systems is the assumption that trains operate periodically. Often even a periodicity of one hour is used. In real schedules, however, there is a considerable difference between peak hours, late evenings and "quiet" nights. For our timetable server MOTIS we take time modulo a single day in order to have a better manageable graph size as opposed to full time expansion. Recall that traveling edges carry traffic day flags (stored in bitfields) to model the days of operation, e.g. trains operating only on weekdays, or weekends, different schedules for school days and non school-days, trains operating on public holidays according to the weekend schedule etc.

In our scenario with delay information we have to take care of multiple traffic days as well. To be able to supply the customer with updated information we need to model not only "today" (the current day) but also tomorrow as some connections might pass the midnight border (have a so-called *"night jump"*), especially if we query with a departure in the afternoon or evening. Resulting alternative journeys, requested after a delay on a journey, may even end on the next day due to delays, although no night jump was present in the original connection.

Therefore, we chose a schedule length of two days. In our time-expanded graph we represent all the trains operating today and tomorrow. However, trains that have the same schedule on both days can no longer be represented just once with two traffic day flags set. To be able to shift today's train without affecting the version of tomorrow, thus not incorrectly cloning delays, or vice versa, we need two distinct versions of such trains.

7.6.1 Memory Consumption Issues

The simplest version to attain separate nodes for today's and tomorrow's events is to use full time expansion on all our schedule days and not take time modulo 1440 and use traffic day flags on the train edges. Unfortunately, this would not only increase the number of event nodes and edges as well as the change edges, it would also significantly increase the number of change nodes and waiting edges. Whereas there is no way to avoid the increase for the former type of nodes and edges, we found a way to keep the size of the rest the same: We only use full time expansion for departure and arrival events and link all events to a change level with only one node per necessary timestamp, regardless of the day of that event, i.e. the number of change nodes and waiting edges remains the same, only the number of adjacent edges to the change nodes increases. Three different models for the search graph arise.

- Model (A) is the static model where the same events on two subsequent days are represented only once but two traffic day flags are set.

- Model (B) treats each arrival and departure event individually and uses the sparse change level implementation as described above.

- Model (C) also treats each arrival and departure event individually but uses full change level expansion.

Note that in the dependency graph we opted for full time expansion. There is no change level with waiting edges and all the change representation is between the trains themselves and only necessary to decide whether trains wait for others or not and compute the resulting changes. In this model a source delay propagation may or may not delay events on the following day. There is no need for case distinctions due to day changes.

Test data. To study the effect of these models on the space consumption, we use the train schedule of Germany in 2008. The schedule contains 68,300 trains for the whole year with over 5,000 distinct bitfields for the days of operation. We look at the graphs prepared for two subsequent days, either two weekdays, Wednesday and Thursday (We & Th) with 38,600 trains with distinct schedules or for Sunday and Monday (Su & Mo) with 46,600 trains with distinct schedules.

7.6 Traffic Days

	model	unit	event nodes	tr/std edges	change nodes	change edges	wait edges	total nodes	total edges
We & Th	(A)	(in k)	988	950	459	988	459	1,447	2,397
We & Th	(B)	(in k)	1,956	1,878	459	1,954	459	2,415	4,291
We & Th	(C)	(in k)	1,956	1,878	912	1,954	912	2,868	4,744
increase	(A → B)	(in %)	98.0	97.7	0.0	97.8	0.0	66.9	79.0
increase	(A → C)	(in %)	98.0	97.7	98.7	97.8	98.7	98.2	97.9
Su & Mo	(A)	(in k)	1,181	1,134	498	1,180	498	1,679	2,812
Su & Mo	(B)	(in k)	1,702	1,634	498	1,701	498	2,200	3,833
Su & Mo	(C)	(in k)	1,702	1,634	798	1,701	798	2,500	4,133
increase	(A → B)	(in %)	44.1	44.1	0.0	44.2	0.0	31.0	36.3
increase	(A → C)	(in %)	44.1	44.1	60.2	44.2	60.2	48.9	47.0

Table 7.1: Sizes of the search graph for two days, Wednesday and Thursday resp. Sunday and Monday and the increase when changing between the models (A), (B), and (C).

Comparison of models. In Table 7.1, we compare our three different models for the search graph. For the more homogeneous case of two weekdays version (C) requires double the amount of space while for our variant (B) we manage to increase the number of nodes by two thirds and the number of edges by four fifths. The tremendous increase of (C) is due to the large number of trains operating identically each weekday. If we look at the graph for Sunday and Monday the increase is much smaller as many of the trains operate either on Monday or on Sunday, therefore the increase in nodes and edges for the trains is below 50%. Still our model improves the additional required memory space from nearly one half to about one third.

During the actual search for train connections, variant (B) has a slight running time overhead in comparison with full time expansion (C). This overhead turns out to be negligible if a look-ahead in the search process categorizes entering edges as not allowed if they lead to a departure node for a train not operating on the required day.

7.6.2 Moving from One Day to the Next

At midnight we have to change the current day for our real-time information server as well as the search servers. Now, information about yesterday is no longer relevant as tomorrow becomes today and we need to load the "new tomorrow".

The real-time information server loads the dependency graph for tomorrow and "forgets" yesterday. With the fully time-expanded model there is no hassle in doing so. Note that we still have to keep yesterday's events that are delayed to today and have not happened yet, but nothing more about yesterday is needed any longer. Thus, we can delete all information about yesterday's events in the data structure. With our prototype, this whole procedure is finished in less than 35 seconds for the complete German timetable.

The search servers need a longer update phase than usual as they have to be restarted with the now current day and the following day. Afterwards, they request an update for a new server (exactly as described for a new server in Section 7.3). In this update they receive all information for today currently available. These updates typically take less than ten seconds. Together with the restart time of about 20 seconds a single search server is down for about half a minute. Even a server that has not yet changed days can still be updated after midnight and produce correct search results, as only the information about the next day is missing, not the current day. So there is no problem with the last server updating at say 01:00 a.m. Since midnight is not a peak hour for timetable information systems a number of servers might change days concurrently without compromising the availability of service. In summary, within a multi-server solution down-times of individual servers can easily be hidden from the customer.

7.7 Evaluation of the Prototype

We implemented the dependency graph and the update algorithm described in Section 7.4 and extended our time table information system MOTIS to support updating the search graph (cf. Section 7.5). Although these update operations are quite costly, we give a proof of concept and show that they can be performed sufficiently fast for a system with real-time capabilities.

Our computational study uses the German train schedule of 2008. During each operating day all trains that pass various trigger points (stations and important points on tracks) generate status messages. There are roughly 5000 stations and 1500 additional trigger points. Whenever a train generates a status message on its way, new predictions for the departure and arrival times of all its future stops are computed and fed into a data base. German railways Deutsche Bahn AG provided delay and forecast data from this data base for a number of operation days. The simulation results for these days look rather similar without too much fluctuation neither in the properties of the messages nor in the resulting computational effort.

In the following subsection, we present results for a standard operating day with an average delay profile. We tested various waiting profiles with an implementation that broadcasts the update information as soon as it becomes available. In the succeeding subsection we will present first results for the multi-server architecture (as described in Section 7.3) and test different update intervals. All experiments were run on 2 cores of an Intel Xeon 2.6 GHz with 8GB of RAM under Ubuntu 8.04 in a Virtual Machine (VMWare ESXi 3.5.0). Our code was compiled with gcc V.4.3 with compile option 02.

As no system with the capabilities of our prototype exists, we cannot compare our results to others. To ensure the correctness of our approach we used automated regression tests continuously checking the status of a large number of connections and determining alternatives, and collected meta-information about the encountered delays in the process. Furthermore, we intensively investigated isolated test cases (e.g. explicit search for trains known to be de-

search graph	
event nodes	0.99 mil
change nodes	0.46 mil
edges	2.40 mil

dependency graph	
events	0.97 mil
standing edges	0.45 mil
traveling edges	0.49 mil

Table 7.2: Properties of the search graph (left) and dependency graph (right) modeling a single day of the schedule.

layed, searches for trains departing next to a delay, searches for which the off-line optimum was affected by a delay).

7.7.1 Overall Performance and Waiting Profiles

To test our system, we used five sets of waiting profiles. Basically, the train categories were divided into five classes: high speed trains, night trains, regional trains, urban trains, and class "all others." Waiting times are then defined between the different classes as follows:

- *standard* High speed trains wait for each other 3 minutes, other trains wait for high speed trains, night trains, and trains of class "all others" 5 minutes, night trains wait for high speed and other night trains 10 minutes, and 5 minutes for class "all others."

- *half* All times of scenario standard are halved.

- *double* All times of scenario standard are doubled.

- *all5* All times of scenario standard are set to five minutes, and in addition regional trains wait 5 minutes for all but urban trains.

- *all10* All times of the previous scenario are doubled.

It is important to keep in mind that the last two policies are far from reality and are intended to strain the system beyond the limits it was designed to handle.

Our dependency graph model assumes that we know at each station which pairs of trains potentially have to wait for each other, i.e., which transfer edges are present. In our implementation we use the pragmatic rule, that if the difference between the departure event of train t_1 and the arrival event of another train t_2 at the same station does not exceed a parameter δ, then there is a transfer edge between these two events.

For each of our waiting profiles we tested different maximum distances (in minutes) of feeding and connecting trains $\delta \in \{5, 15, 30, 45, 60\}$, and compare them to a variant without waiting for other trains (policy *no wait*). In this reference scenario it is still necessary to propagate delays in the dependency graph to correctly update the train runs. Thus, the same computations as with policies for delays is carried out, only the terms for feeding trains are always zero.

transfer edges	5min	15min	30min	45min	60min
std / half / double	7.1k	54.7k	123.8k	207.8k	267.8k
all5 / all 10	14.6k	168.3k	399.6k	665.4k	874.3k

Table 7.3: The number of transfer edges depending on the waiting policy and the maximum allowed time difference δ between feeding and connecting train.

We constructed search and dependency graphs from the real schedule consisting of 36,700 trains operating on the selected day. There are 8,817 stations in the data. The number of nodes and edges in both graphs are given in Table 7.2. The number of standing and traveling edges are in one-to-one correspondence to the stay-in-train and traveling edges of the search graph. The number of transfer edges depends on the waiting policy and parameter δ and can be found in Table 7.3. Note that, whether a transfer edge exists or not, depends on the classes that wait for each other and not on the actual number of minutes they wait. Therefore, the number of edges are identical for the policies *half*, *standard*, and *double* as well as for the policies *all5* and *all10*. There is a monotonous growth in the number of transfer edges depending on the parameter δ. Additionally, the number of these edges increases as more trains wait for other trains because of additional rules.

In Table 7.4, we give the results for our test runs for the different policies and values of δ. Running times are averages over 25 test runs. For the chosen simulation day we have a large stream of real forecast messages. Whenever a complete sequence of messages for a train has arrived, we send them to the dependency graph for processing. 336,840 sequences are handled. In total we had 6,340,480 forecast messages, 562,209 messages of the type "this train is now here" and 4,926 connection status decisions. Of all forecast messages 2,701,277 forecasts are identical to the last message already processed for the corresponding nodes. The remaining messages either trigger computations in the dependency graph or match the current timestamp of the node. The latter require neither shifting of nodes nor a propagation in the dependency graph. The resulting number of node shifts is given in the seventh column of Table 7.4. Depending on the policy we have a different number of nodes that were shifted and stations that have at least one delayed event (last two columns of the table).

The key figures for the computational efficiency (required CPU times in seconds, operation counts for the number of touched stations and node shifts in multiples of thousand) increase when changing to policies for which trains wait longer or more trains have to wait. Increasing δ yields a higher effect the more trains wait. The overall small impact of changing δ is due to the majority of delays being rather small. We notice a significant growth in all key criteria when increasing δ from 5 to 15. All policies behave rather similarly for $\delta = 5$, whereas the differences between the realistic policies and the extreme versions and even from *all5* to *all10* for higher values of δ are apparent.

Amongst the plausible policies there is only a 16% difference in the number of moved nodes. It little more than doubles going to policy *all5* and even increases by a factor of 3.8

7.7 Evaluation of the Prototype

Instance policy	δ in min	Computation time for				Node shifts in k	With delay	
		SG in s	DG in s	IO in s	total in s		nodes in k	stations
no wait	-	59.8	6.4	39.4	105.6	3,410	396.2	5,385
half	5	59.1	6.2	40.0	105.3	3,432	396.6	5,397
	15	60.7	6.4	39.7	106.8	3,525	400.1	5,483
	30	60.8	6.4	40.4	107.7	3,535	400.4	5,494
	45	61.2	6.5	40.0	107.8	3,539	400.6	5,494
	60	62.3	6.8	39.7	108.8	3,540	400.7	5,496
standard	5	59.1	6.2	39.3	104.6	3,443	396.8	5,408
	15	62.6	6.5	39.5	108.5	3,614	402.5	5,532
	30	63.4	6.7	40.1	110.2	3,636	403.2	5,541
	45	63.6	6.8	39.9	110.2	3,646	403.6	5,541
	60	63.6	6.7	40.3	110.7	3,651	403.7	5,545
double	5	58.9	6.3	39.7	104.9	3,447	396.8	5,419
	15	66.4	6.6	40.4	113.4	3,835	406.2	5,590
	30	67.9	6.9	40.5	115.3	3,908	407.5	5,639
	45	69.4	7.2	40.1	116.7	3,945	408.0	5,642
	60	69.0	7.3	39.9	116.2	3,959	408.1	5,642
all5	5	60.7	6.4	40.3	107.4	3,623	403.5	5,588
	15	123.1	11.5	40.0	174.6	7,603	440.5	6,051
	30	124.9	13.0	40.4	178.3	7,670	442.8	6,064
	45	124.9	14.7	40.6	180.2	7,687	443.4	6,064
	60	126.0	16.5	40.4	182.9	7,689	443.7	6,070
all10	5	60.7	6.4	40.4	107.5	3,651	404.0	5,608
	15	193.8	19.0	39.8	252.6	13,052	457.9	6,118
	30	195.2	21.6	40.9	257.7	13,231	463.0	6,145
	45	198.0	24.6	40.6	263.2	13,346	464.4	6,148
	60	200.7	27.3	40.7	268.7	13,466	465.3	6,162

Table 7.4: Computation time for the whole day (propagation in the dependency graph (DG) and update of the search graph (SG), IO and total) and key figures (in multiples of thousand) for the executed node shifts in the search graph and the number of nodes and stations with changed status information with respect to different policies for delays.

towards policy *all10*. Roughly 40 seconds of our simulation time are spent extracting and preprocessing the messages from the forecast stream. This IO time is obviously independent of the test scenario. The increase in running time spent in the search graph update is no more than 3 seconds for $δ > 5$ for all policies except *all10* with 7 seconds and differs by at most 10 seconds or 17% among the realistic scenarios. The running time scales with the number of shifts. An increase of factor 1.9 resp. 3.4 of node shifts results in a factor of 1.8 resp. 3.3 in running time (compare policies *double* to *all5* and *all10* with $δ = 60$). The time spent in the dependency graph differs by at most 1 second (about 16%) for realistic scenarios and stays below 30 seconds even for the most extreme policy.

Even for the most extreme scenario a whole day can be simulated in less than 5 minutes. The overall simulation time for realistic policies lies around 2 minutes. For the policy *standard* with $\delta = 45$, we require on average $17\mu s$ reconstruction work in the search graph per executed node shift. By incident, the overall runtime per computed message is also $17\mu s$.

Worst-case considerations (based on policy standard with $\delta=45$)

The highest number of messages received per minute is 15,627 resulting in 29,632 node shifts and a computation time of 0.66 seconds for this minute.

However, the largest amount of reconstruction work occurred in a minute with 5,808 messages. It required 172,432 node shifts and took 2.38 seconds; this is the worst case minute which we observed in the simulation. Thus, at our current performance we could easily handle 25 times the load without a need for event buffering. This clearly qualifies for live performance.

7.7.2 Multi-Server Performance

As we have seen in the previous subsection most of the time is spent in reconstructing the search graph. Applying sophisticated software engineering the update process has been sped up considerably. Additionally, a big potential lies in doing less reconstruction work. In a real-time environment it is not necessary to update multiple times per minute as soon as new information is available (as we did in the previous subsection). It clearly suffices to update each minute. Depending on the load balancing scheme, update cycles of 2 or 3 minutes still produce results of high quality.

To be able to compare the numbers to the previous section we tested the two servers as introduced in Section 7.3 "in line", i.e. one waited for the other to finish computation before continuing its own work. We use our waiting profile "standard" with $\delta = 45$ for all versions. The *baseline* version does not use the UDS and immediately updates the search graph. The version *split* additionally inserts and retrieves events into/from the UDS. Our code spends about 47 seconds on extracting and preprocessing the messages from the forecast stream and propagation in the dependency graph. Pushing all the events through the UDS data structure in the split architecture only requires an additional 7.2 seconds.

As we do not see a need for update intervals shorter than one minute, we now read all incoming messages for a particular minute and calculate the resulting changed event times in the dependency graph. These are transmitted to the data structure UDS in our real-time information server part. Meanwhile the search graph requests an update every 1, 2, 3, 4, or 5 minutes, using either the *iterator* or *map* version. The results can be found in Table 7.5. The numbers are averages over 25 runs.

By sending the state delta of the last x minutes as a batch job to the search graph we save a lot of reconstruction work due to mutually interacting messages arriving between two

Instance		Transmissions		Computation time			
Version	interval in min	needed in k	unnec-essary in k	SG in s	UDS ins in s	UDS ext in s	total in s
baseline	-	3646	0	63.5	0.0	0.0	110.3
split	-	3646	0	63.7	3.7	3.5	117.7
iterator	1	3143	0	53.9	3.1	55.6	159.0
	2	2809	149	45.5	2.9	29.3	124.4
	3	2447	284	38.3	2.9	20.4	108.2
	4	2177	360	33.3	2.8	15.8	98.6
	5	1954	404	29.3	2.8	13.1	91.4
map	1	3143	0	54.3	4.9	2.1	107.4
	2	2809	0	45.4	4.9	1.9	98.5
	3	2447	0	38.3	4.8	1.8	91.2
	4	2177	0	33.4	4.7	1.7	86.3
	5	1954	0	29.2	4.7	1.5	81.7

Table 7.5: The number of transmitted events, node shifts and execution time for simulating the whole day. We compare versions with and without two server architecture using an iterator or a map to determine the relevant events (cf. Section 7.3) for different update intervals.

subsequent updates, e.g. oscillating forecasts for trains, or reconstruction is done for a train but later it is shifted again due to a changed arrival time of one of its feeding trains.

With increasing interval size the number of messages to transmit significantly decreases. The resulting time required for updating the search graph is sped up by nearly 10 seconds when changing from immediate update to an interval of one minute. The increase of the interval size by one additional minute within the range of [1-5] reduces the execution time by a few seconds.

The *iterator* version of detecting events to transmit (cf. Section 7.3) only uses the release time information and cannot detect that an event does not require shifting, therefore it transmits 149k to 404k (depending on the update interval) of these irrelevant messages demanding a node "shift" to the node's current position. On the other hand, the *map* version only transmits events with changed timestamp, even if the release time is newer, therefore we do not have unnecessary transmissions. As shifts to the same position are never executed we only have the unnecessary transmission and no extra work, as we can see with the identical runtimes for the search graph update (column SG).

Inserting the information (column UDS ins) about changed event times into the UDS takes between 2.8 and 3.7 seconds, depending on the number of insertions (and thus the interval size). For the *map* version the bookkeeping requires an additional 1.8 to 2.0 seconds for the whole day. While the extraction (column UDS ext) using the *map* version requires 1.5 to 2.1 seconds, iterating for each update over all stored events to find the relevant new information in the *iterator* version is very costly and takes 13.1 to 55.6 seconds. Obviously, these times do not depend on the number of transmissions but on the number of iterations, as we observe that the extraction time is inversely proportional to the interval size.

The improvement in runtime of 3 seconds (from 110.3 to 107.4 seconds), when changing from the baseline version to the split version with an interval of one minute, does not seem like much. However, it enabled us to do load balancing and handle updates on demand with our multi-server approach. The update time for the search servers consists of the time for receiving events from the UDS plus the time for the search graph update. Therefore, instead of taking 110.3 seconds to read messages, propagate delays and update the search in our baseline version, we only need 56.4 seconds in the split architecture for keeping the search graph up-to-date. Thus, we gain more than 50 seconds of available computation time per search server (about half the time required by the baseline version that does all the work on its own). Together with the initial startup phase and the first update with all relevant information for today depending on yesterday's data of about half a minute (cf. Subsection 7.6.2) a search server is only busy with startup and updating for 60 to 90 seconds

Figure 7.4: CoCoAS example: Alternatives for a broken connection from Kaiserslautern to Mönchengladbach. The upper two alternatives arrive less than 10 minutes after the original arrival time but are delayed themselves. The lower two arrive half an hour later than the original connection.

per day. This means that each search server can use 99.9% of its time for answering search queries.

The real-time information server spends about 47 seconds for reading messages and propagation in the dependency graph and additional 3 seconds storing the data. For each registered server (in our tests just one) it takes 2 seconds maintaining the map of relevant events and 2 seconds to extract and transmit those events. Thus, we have by far enough time to update a multitude of search servers.

7.8 A New Service for Travelers

A true real-time timetable information system as demonstrated by our prototype opens the door for a new service to passengers who want a system that supports them until they have reached their destination. The provider of such a service would constantly check the validity of planned connections, and in case of necessary changes due to delays inform the affected passenger. The service would propose new alternative connections by sending messages to a mobile phone or an email address.

In Figure 7.4 we see four alternatives for a broken connection from Kaiserslautern to Mönchengladbach. Two arrive delayed and 11 or 12 minutes later than the broken connection. The other two arrive as scheduled but about 20 minutes later than the delayed alternatives. The four alternatives were determined using CoCoAS (Connection Controller and Alternatives System), our implementation of this service. The system will be introduced in Section 11.3.

7.9 Conclusions and Future Work

We have built a first prototype which can be used for efficient off-line simulation with massive streams of delay and forecast messages for typical days of operation within Germany. Using the presented multi-server solution, the correct handling of all necessary updates is so fast that each search server can use almost all of its time for answering search queries. Stress tests with extreme policies for delays showed that the update time scales linearly with the amount of work. So even for cases of major disruptions we expect a sufficient performance of such a multi-server solution. Compared to typical stream profiles, we are able to handle about 25 times as much reconstruction work.

It remains an interesting task to implement a live feed of delay messages for our timetable information system and actually test real-time performance of the resulting system. Since update operations in the time-dependent graph model are somewhat easier than in the time-expanded graph model, we also plan to integrate the update information from our dependency graph into a multi-criteria time-dependent search approach developed in our group (see Chapter 10).

Chapter 8

Speed-Up Techniques

Introduction

Speeding up shortest path search is a very active field due to the importance of shortest paths themselves in route-planing (cars, trucks, trains, airlines), as a modeling tool for many optimization problems (e.g. scheduling) and as a subroutine for important techniques (most prominently network flows). The biggest progress has been made in the field of route-planning on road-networks, where query times in milliseconds for whole Western Europe are possible (usually at the cost of long preprocessing), a part of the development there has been summarized in [SS07a].

This chapter is not intended to give a complete overview of these techniques. Instead, we will start with the introduction of basic concepts and main characteristics of many of the approaches. In the process we will point out the challenges we are facing when we try to adapt certain techniques to our scenario. The main part of this chapter will deal with details about adapted and specially tailored techniques for the search for advanced Pareto optimal connections in dynamically changing time-expanded graphs for time table information. Towards the end of the chapter we will outline how all our techniques harmonize with dynamic graph updates due to delay information. Afterwards, we present all the changes to the graph model and the algorithm resulting from the speed-up techniques. The chapter will end with further thoughts on speed-up techniques for the future

8.1 Speeding up Dijkstra's Algorithm

Most of the approaches discussed in the literature differ from our scenario in at least one of the following areas.

- Time Dependency of the network
  Road networks are usually modeled without time-dependency. Recently, some time-dependent edges have been added to model traffic jams or slower traffic during rush-

hours. Our networks, however, do not only have some time-dependent edges but are inherently time-dependent as modeled in our time-expanded graph (cf. Chapter 4).

- Static networks vs. dynamically changing networks

  As seen in the previous chapter, a lot of changes to the graph have to be performed when incorporating delay messages. These messages appear in rapid succession making long update cycles infeasible.

- Single point of departure vs. departure interval

  Shortest-path search on railway networks has been dominated for years by solving the earliest arrival problem only, i.e. given a point and time of departure the earliest possible arrival at another station is to be determined. Even if the classical pre-trip scenario is considered, a single point in time as the possible starting moment is typically assumed. We explicitly want to optimize over an interval of possible departure times.

- Single-criterion vs. multi-criteria

  Only very little effort has been put into determining the set of all Pareto optimal solutions. Recall from Chapter 2 that we actually want to compute all attractive alternatives based on the concept of advanced Pareto optimality. Due to the departure intervals we employ a relaxation on travel time based on the difference in the departure or arrival times of connections. This requires even more connections to be inspected.

Due to the last two points we almost always have more than a single optimal path which makes preprocessing more involved.

8.1.1 Early Termination

Dijkstra's algorithm solves the *one-to-all* version of the shortest path problem. When querying for a pair (s, t), the shortest paths and distances to other nodes is of no importance. In the worst case it may happen that t is the very last node to be labeled permanently. However, in most graphs and for most searches this is very unlikely. Therefore, the attention may be restricted to a (hopefully small) subset of nodes instead of calculating the distances for all nodes. The algorithm safely terminates once node t is removed from the priority queue and labeled permanently and thus a shortest path has been computed (cf. Figure 8.1 (left)).

Towards our Scenario In multi-criteria search, and when considering multiple start nodes (departure intervals), there are many optimal paths. Hence, the search may not be stopped after the first (or a certain number) of optimal paths have been computed. However, the labels at the terminal station may be used to dominate partial connections at other nodes due to the transitivity of the smaller relation. For details on the technique *domination by labels at the terminal* see Section 8.4.

8.1 Speeding up Dijkstra's Algorithm

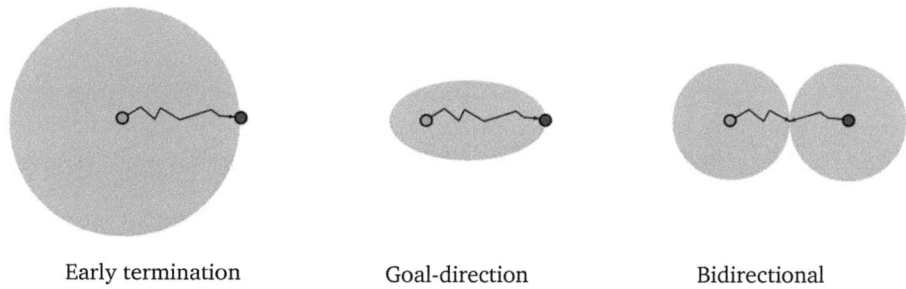

Early termination Goal-direction Bidirectional

Figure 8.1: Schematic visualization for the speed up-techniques early termination, goal-direction, and bidirectional search.

8.1.2 Goal-Direction / Lower Bounding

Goal-Direction is a strategy to help the search reach its target faster. Instead of extracting the node or label with the currently shortest distance from the priority queue, the algorithm selects the most promising one. This is done by modifying the edge lengths using a potential function $\lambda(\cdot)$ that is a *lower bound* on the distance from a node to the target (cf. Figure 8.1 (middle)). This modification shortens edges in the "right direction" and lengthens those that bring you farther away from the terminal. These lower bounds are often obtained from geographical information (e.g. coordinates).

Precomputing and storing better lower bounds for all nodes to all others requires preprocessing and has quadratic memory consumption. Instead of computing lower bounds for all nodes, a small set of *landmarks* ([GH05]) can be used. For each node the distance to all landmarks and between all of the landmarks are precomputed. Applied in conjunction with the triangle inequality these landmarks are a substitute for lower bounds. If chosen wisely, only a few of these landmarks result in really good lower bounds. Landmarks that lie "behind" the terminals seem to work well, as well as sets of landmarks with large distances between the individual landmarks.

Another approach is to partition the graph and determine the distances between clusters (Precomputed Cluster Distances (PCD) [MSM06]). However, these distances cannot be used for goal-direction (modified edge lengths may become negative). But they give upper and lower bounds for pruning and can be computed efficiently using many to many routing.

Towards our Scenario Our approach is to compute good lower bounds for all nodes in a preprocessing step before each single search without the need to store those results for all possible source/terminal pairs, for details we refer to Section 8.5. This can be done for all our criteria in a reasonable amount of time.

8.1.3 Priority Queues

Details on the implementation and effects on the performance of different priority queues have already been mentioned in Chapter 3. There are no issues when utilizing priority queues in our scenario, details on priority queues (different types, the smaller relation, and a heuristic reducing the number of insert and extract operations on the priority queue) will be given in Section 8.8.

8.1.4 Reach Based

The concept of the *reach* of a vertex ([Gut04, GKW07]) encodes the lengths to either end of all shortest paths on which the vertex lies. The reach of a node v with respect to a single shortest path P from s to t, reach(v, P), is defined as the minimum over the length of the sub-path from s to v and from v to t. For the set $\mathcal{P}$ of all shortest path in the graph, we have the reach of v as the maximum over all reach(v, P) with $P \in \mathcal{P}$ and v on P. In order to have a high reach, a node has to be on shortest paths that extend a long distance in both directions. Dijkstra's algorithm does not need to scan a node whose reach is smaller than its distance to the source or terminal, as it cannot be part of a shortest path.

To correctly determine reaches, the all pairs-shortest paths problem has to be solved, which may take months for interesting graph sizes. Bounding techniques and bootstrapping produce reliable estimates for the reach of a node within acceptable time frames.

Towards our Scenario Remember from Section 8.1.2 that we have lower bounds for the distances from all nodes to the target. If such a lower bound for a node is already higher than the distance from source to target, this node may be ignored, similarly to the idea of *reach*. This insight is the basis for our pruning techniques introduced in Section 8.5.5.

8.1.5 Bidirectional Search

Two searches are run simultaneously, one forward search from the source and one backward search from the target. Once the search spaces meet, the shortest path can be obtained from the search frontiers. On road networks with nearly circular search spaces, a speedup of factor two is expected, since one circle with the radius of the shortest path has twice the area of two circles with half the radius (cf. Figure 8.1 (right)).

This technique can not only be combined with most of the other techniques, it is also essential for many of the hierarchical approaches.

Towards our Scenario In time-expanded and time-dependent networks the time (or interval) of arrival is not known beforehand. Under certain conditions guessing the right time might be possible. In our scenario with search intervals, determining the arrival interval leads to rather large intervals, e.g. by shifting the start of the departure interval by a lower bound on the travel time and the end of the departure interval by some upper bound. Moreover, analogously to early termination, we are not finished once the search space of forward and backward searches meet. Therefore, we did not realize bidirectional search. See Section 8.13.1 for ideas on bidirectional search in our scenario as part of future work.

Bidirectional lower bounding The combination of goal-direction and bidirectional search is not as trivial as it might seem. Depending on the lower bounds, forward and backward searches may use different lengths on the same edges. Consequently, it is not clear whether the shortest path is indeed found when they meet. With certain conditions on the lower bounds this is possible (e.g. using lower bounds obtained in the same way for forward and backward searches).

8.1.6 Arc Flags and Geometric Containers

These techniques basically store the set of all nodes for an edge that are reachable on a shortest path starting with the edge. Due to the fact that all sub-paths of shortest paths are shortest paths as well. An edge only needs to be considered if the target is contained in the set of that edge. Storing explicit sets requires too much space, thus two main approaches to tackle this problem have been studied:

- *Geometric containers.* Geometric information about the nodes reachable on a shortest path is used to design containers for those sets. Depending on the type of container more or less nodes not in the set are included as well. The following different containers have been proposed, angular sectors (two angles relative to the edge) [SWW00], bounding boxes (axes parallel rectangles), rectangles (edge parallel), circles, ellipses etc. and intersections of objects. A comprehensive study can be found in the dissertation of Willhalm [Wil05]. Bounding boxes work extremely well. Complicated objects containing fewer nodes that are not in the set are usually too expensive to evaluate. Preprocessing requires growing a shortest path tree from each node.

- *Arc flags.* The graph is partitioned into r regions and for each edge r bits mark the regions in which target nodes of shortest paths are [Lau04, KMS07] (see Figure 8.2 (left) for an example). This approach seems to work best for non-trivial partitions. Extensions like multi-level partitions (kd-trees) reduce the memory requirements of finer partitions with more regions [MSS$^+$05]. For this approach single-source shortest path searches from all boundary nodes of regions are executed in the preprocessing phase.

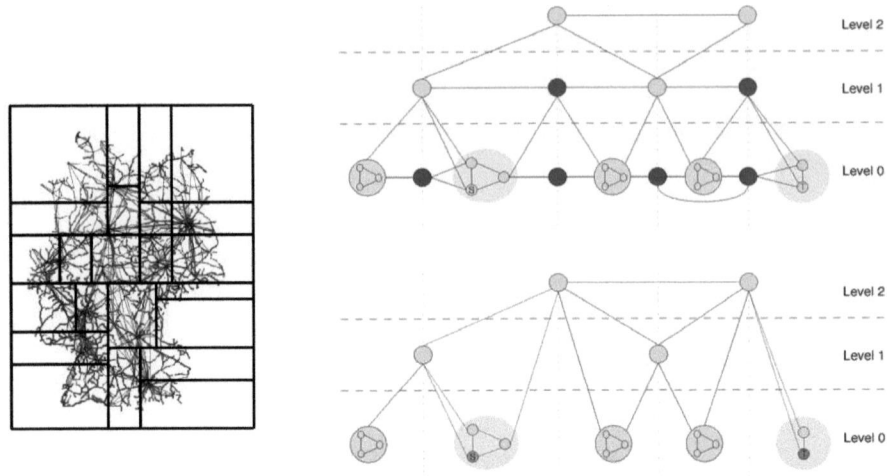

Figure 8.2: Schematic view of a graph partitioning for arc flags (left) and a multi-level overlay graph (right). In the upper right image the layered graph is shown, in the lower right image the effective subgraph for a shortest path search from s to t consists of the red edges only.

Towards our Scenario In the multi-criteria case there is not only one shortest path but several optimal paths starting at one node. The shortest-path tree becomes an optimal-path subgraph (with parallel edges). Every reasonable partitioning will not be able to separate nodes belonging to the same station. Thus, lots of nodes, namely all departures at each of the stations will have to be considered at region borders. Updating this optimal-path subgraph in the presence of delay information is costly.

8.1.7 Hierarchical Techniques

Multi-Level Techniques. A hierarchical coarsening results in a much smaller subgraph for searching that still contains the shortest path. A separating set of nodes is selected and lifted to a higher level. On this level, shortcuts representing the shortest paths between the nodes are introduced. Choosing suitable separators improves the effectiveness. A single-pair version of Dijkstra's algorithm only considers the components containing source and target, and the shortcuts on the higher levels. Iterating this process yields a hierarchy of *overlay graphs* ([SWW00, SWZ02, Hol08, HSW08]). Graphs on higher levels become rather dense, as shortcuts between nearly all pairs of nodes are inserted.

See Figure 8.2 (right) for an example with three levels. On the lowest level (the original graph) only the components containing s and t are drawn in detail. The small graph in the other regions may represent much larger components. The dark nodes on Level 0 separate

8.1 Speeding up Dijkstra's Algorithm

the graph into five components. We see the edges between those components and the lifted nodes on Level 1. The edges on Level 1 represent shortest paths between the nodes on that level. This construction process is repeated with the selection of the dark nodes on Level 1. In the lower picture, the edges forming the relevant subgraph for the search from s to t are red. The search never even enters the other three components on Level 0 and the component between the selected nodes on Level 1.

Most of the more involved variants rely on bidirectional search to improve search speed. For the following improved hierarchical approaches bidirectional search is essential:

For *Highway Hierarchies* a definition of local neighborhood separates nodes. "Highways" are introduced between nodes that are not in the neighborhood. The construction iterates contraction of unimportant (low degree) nodes and addition of shortcut edges [SS06, Sch08]. Technique *Highway Node Routing* no longer requires separators and works by stalling searches in non-promising lower regions in a hierarchy of overlay graphs [SS07b]. *Contraction Hierarchies* use one level per node and store only edges from unimportant to important nodes. Searches are a simple bidirectional Dijkstra on the resulting graph [GSSD08].

Distance Tables For any hierarchical technique this approach computes and stores information about all pairs-shortest paths on a small enough graph on some level (in $\mathcal{O}(\sqrt{n})$). Once a query reaches this level, shortest-path computation can be done as a lookup on this level. Technique *transit node routing* uses a distance table for important (transit) nodes (e.g. highway ramps) and additionally precomputes the shortest paths to all remaining nodes on the same level [BFSS07]. Interestingly, selecting nodes categorized as important by other techniques as transit nodes seems to work best. Preprocessing times are huge.

Towards our Scenario Most techniques (basically all except the classical multi-level overlay graph technique) require bidirectional search. Growing shortest path trees is an auxiliary step. Issues with both of these concepts in our scenario have already been discussed (cf. the end of the previous section for details on shortest-path trees that become optimal-path subgraphs and Section 8.1.5 for bidirectional search).

8.1.8 Combinations

Various combinations of the different techniques have been evaluated, e.g. different hierarchical and goal-directed speed-up techniques in [HSWW05, BDS+08]. Technique ALT, for example, combines landmarks and bidirectional search and adds shortcuts to reduce reaches [GKW06]. A nice overview can be found in [DSSW09]. We want to highlight SHARC (shortcuts and arc-flags ([BD09, Del08a]) which combines the ideas of contraction and arc-flags. It builds a contraction based hierarchy and sets arc-flags such that removed edges on a level are only feasible at the beginning and end of a search on that level. This construction allows *unidirectional* search.

8.1.9 Steps Towards Our Scenario

Dynamically Changing Graphs Incorporating delay information requires updating the search graph. For most of the speed-up techniques with heavy preprocessing the precomputed data has to be rebuild which is usually not feasible in a real-time environment. Techniques that are robust to graph changes often decrease in their performance after some update steps. A notable exception is the fully dynamic data structure for shortest path problems in [FR01]. Updating a shortest-path tree after the change of one single edge weight requires recomputation from scratch [DI04]. Dynamic approaches have been proven to be useful [DI06] but have not been evaluated for such complex scenarios and work only for much smaller graphs. Landmarks based approaches (ALT) have been adapted [DW07] and, additionally, first results for arc-flags exist [BDD09]. The technique of highway-node routing allows updating the cost of edges with only minimal time overhead per edge [SS07b]. However, the last three were again specifically designed for road-networks. Delling et al. presented a model different from ours to regard delays in timetabling systems [DGWZ08], changing edge weights rather than moving event nodes as in our model (cf. Chapter 7).

Search on Graphs with Time Dependency As mentioned in the introduction and throughout this section, most of these techniques were developed for road-networks and support no dependency on time at all. Even the concept of time-dependent edge lengths due to rush-hours or traffic jams (as e.g. for time-dependent SHARC [Del08b] and contraction hierarchies [BDSV09]) is inherently easier than a whole time-expanded or time-dependent graph. Delling et al. observed that the adaption of speed-up techniques to time-expanded graphs is not as easy as one might think [DPW08] and they did not even consider departure intervals. An overview on time-dependent routing can be found in [DW09b].

Multi-Criteria Search The investigation of shortest-path search has not been focused on multi-criteria approaches. Previous and related work [Han79, Mar84, BSS89] has already been mentioned in Chapter 3 when we introduced multi-criteria search. Müller-Hannemann and Weihe [MW01, MW06] observed that the number of optima is bounded by a small constant in our scenario. In conjunction with speed-up techniques there is a recent result from Delling and Wagner on a Pareto version of SHARC (for road networks) [DW09a].

Multi-Criteria Search with Time Dependency There is not much previous work in this field: The publications [CH66, KW93, HRT06] concentrate on other applications than timetable information. The most recent publication by Berger et al. in which they try to develop

Number of	
trains	68073
footpaths	425
attribute combinations	951

node type	(in k)
arrival	801.8
departure	801.8
change-departure	556.6
nodes total	2160.2

edge type	(in k)
train	801.8
stay-in-train	733.7
entering	796.7
leaving	795.7
waiting	556.6
special-interchange	20.2
edges total	3704.7

Table 8.1: Number of trains, stations, edges, and nodes for our schedule.

speed-up techniques for multi-criteria timetable information is even entitled "Accelerating Time-Dependent Multi-Criteria Timetable Information is Harder Than Expected" [BDGM09].

Speeding up Our Search Algorithm

In spite of the problems and challenges illustrated in the previous section, we developed and adapted some techniques for our scenario. We did not investigate preprocessing heavy techniques and those requiring bidirectional search for two reasons: a) as a consequence of the inability to produce the correct intervals for bidirectional search. And b) because of the expensive preprocessing to calculate optimal-path subgraphs. Updating those due to delay information is very costly and thus renders real-time updates impossible.

For the remainder of this chapter we will present the speed-up techniques to be investigated for MOTIS. Major contributors to these ideas and implementations were Matthias Müller-Hannemann, Peter Jung [Jun06], and Daniel Mäurer [Mäu09].

Search Graph For the sizes of auxiliary graphs and the motivation of some of the techniques we will refer to either absolute figures or relate to a certain search graph. It was constructed from the schedule of German Railways (Deutsche Bahn AG) for 2008. It encompasses all German long distance and local trains. Its key criteria are presented in Table 8.1.

8.2 Multi-Criteria Approach

Compared to single criteria optimization the Pareto approach is costly. Aiming to find even more attractive alternatives with relaxation, increases the computational effort required even further. However, discarding undesired alternatives by means of advanced Pareto dominance drastically speeds up the search without sacrificing quality, since according to our definition of advanced Pareto dominance all interesting alternatives will be found.

We will also experiment with different parameter sets, namely our *least common parameter set* or a customer specific one for e.g. a businessman, as presented as one way to apply advanced Pareto Dominance at the end of Chapter 2.

8.3 Goal-Directed Search

The strategy *goal-direction* [HNR68, GH05] is based on a real valued function $\lambda : V \to \mathbf{R}_+$. $\lambda(v)$ is a lower bound on the minimal distance from v to t for any $v \in V$. For all $(v,w) \in E$ the values $\lambda(v)$ and $\lambda(w)$ must additionally satisfy the condition $\lambda(v) - \lambda(w) \leq \ell(v,w)$. The modified length $\ell'((v,w))$ is then:

$$\ell'(v,w) := \ell(v,w) - \lambda(v) + \lambda(w) \geq 0.$$

It can be shown that the shortest paths with respect to the length function $\ell'(\cdot)$ are identical with the shortest paths with respect to the original length function $\ell(\cdot)$. Hence, we may alternately compute a shortest path with respect to $l'(\cdot)$.

Lemma 8.1. *Once t is extracted from the priority queue in goal-directed search, a shortest (s-t)-path is found.*

Proof. We use the notation $\lfloor P \rfloor_x = \{s, \ldots, x\}$ for the sub-path from s to x of any path $P = \{s, \ldots, x, \ldots, v\}$.

Let $P^* = \{s = u_0, \ldots, u_z = t\}$ be a shortest $(s\text{-}t)$-path. Suppose the algorithm extracted t from the priority queue and found path $P = \{s = v_o, \ldots, v_k = t\}$ with $\ell(P) > \ell(P^*)$. The modified length of path P is:

$$\begin{aligned}
\ell'(P) &= \sum_{i=0}^{k-1} \ell'((v_i, v_{i+1})) \\
&= \sum_{i=0}^{k-1} \Big(\ell((v_i, v_{i+1})) - \lambda(v_i) + \lambda(v_{i+1}) \Big) \\
&= \sum_{i=0}^{k-1} \ell((v_i, v_{i+1})) - \sum_{i=0}^{k-1} \lambda(v_i) + \sum_{i=1}^{k} \lambda(v_i) \\
&= \ell(P) - \lambda(v_0) + \underbrace{\lambda(v_k)}_{\lambda(t)=0} \\
&= \ell(P) - \lambda(s).
\end{aligned}$$

Since $\ell(\lfloor P^* \rfloor_{u_i}) + \lambda(u_i) \leq \ell(P^*) < \ell(P)$ we have

$$d(u_i) = \ell'(\lfloor P^* \rfloor_{u_i}) = \ell(\lfloor P^* \rfloor_{u_i}) - \lambda(s) + \lambda(u_i) < \ell(P) - \lambda(s) = \ell'(P)$$

8.3 Goal-Directed Search

for all u_i on P^*. Therefore t can not be extracted from the priority queue before all u_i have been computed. Then the value of $d(t)$ has been updated to

$$d(t) = \ell'(\lfloor P^* \rfloor_{u_{z-1}}) + \big(\ell'((u_{z-1}, t))\big) = \ell'(P^*)$$

and $p(t)$ is set to u_{z-1}. Thus the shortest path P^* is found. □

Hence, the algorithm may terminate once t is extracted from the priority queue.

If the $\lambda(v)$-values are just any estimation of the distance from v to t the property $\ell'(\cdot) \geq 0$ will not hold. Suppose we have an edge $(v, t) \in E$ with length $\ell((v, t)) = k$ and a distance estimation $\lambda(v) = k + c$ for some $c > 0$. Clearly this estimation is too high. The modified length of edge (v, t) is $\ell'((v, t)) = k - (k + c) + 0 = -c < 0$.

Roughly speaking, the tighter the lower bounds $\lambda(\cdot)$ are, the larger the speed-up effect will be. Using the trivial lower bounds $\lambda \equiv 0$ clearly does not provide any speed-up whatsoever. If the $\lambda(v)$ values are the exact length of a shortest path from all nodes $v \in V$ to the target t, all shortest paths will have a modified length of zero. The algorithm will not extract any node from the priority queue except those on the shortest path from s to t that is computed.

Goal-Direction and Dial's Data Structure

Using goal-direction in combination with Dial's data structure the maximum difference between labels in the queue may exceed the maximum edge length C:

Suppose a shortest path P to the terminal with $\ell'(P) = \ell(P) - \lambda(s) < C/2$ exists, because the lower bounds are tight. Furthermore, there is a very long edge $e = (s, v)$ with length $\ell(e) = C - \epsilon$ to a node v. Let v be farther away from t than s with $\lambda(v) = \lambda(s) + C - \epsilon_2$ for $\epsilon_2 < \epsilon$ and $\epsilon + \epsilon_2 < C/2$.

Thus, the path P_v at v has a modified distance value

$$\ell'(P_v) = \ell'(s, v) = \ell(s, v) + \lambda(v) - \lambda(s) = \underbrace{C - \epsilon}_{\ell(s,v)} + \underbrace{\lambda(s) + C - \epsilon_2}_{\geq \lambda(v)} - \lambda(s) = 2C - (\epsilon + \epsilon_2).$$

Due to its large distance value the label at v will stay in the priority queue very long, even until path P reaches the terminal. The difference in the distance values for the labels at v and t exceeds C, since $\ell'(P_v) = 2C - (\epsilon + \epsilon_2) > C + C/2$ and $\ell'(P) < C/2$.

This problem may be overcome by using some upper bound U on the path length instead of C. This increases the worst case running time, but for our application the upper bound[i] is easy to obtain. Employing this modification still results in excellent runtimes for Dial's data structure (as we will see in Section 9.8.1).

---

[i]For searches within Germany an upper bound of 36 hours on the travel time is quite pessimistic.

Goal-Direction in Multi-Criteria Search

In the single-criterion case the search can be terminated once the first (and optimal) label at the target station is removed from the priority queue (see Section 8.3). If *all* Pareto optimal solutions have to be computed this speed-up approach *may* not be used.

However, if we are interested in item 4 of the variants of multi-criteria optimization (see page 35): finding some lexicographically interesting path(s), goal-direction may be used to speed up searching. For example looking for a path that minimizes $\ell_i(\cdot)$ at a first place and minimizes $\ell_j(\cdot)$ over all paths that minimize $\ell_i(\cdot)$ at a second place.

Let us first consider the bi-criteria case. Formally, the following strategy computes every path P with

- $\nexists P' : \ell_i(P') < \ell_i(P)$ and

- $\nexists P^* : \ell_i(P) = \ell_i(P^*)$ and $\ell_j(P) > \ell_j(P^*)$.

We use two-dimensional labels storing the modified length regarding criterion i and the length for criterion j: $(\ell'_i(P), \ell_j(P))$ instead of $\ell(P)$ in each label. The modified ith length of edge $(v, w) \in E$ reads:

$$\ell'_i(v, w) := \ell_i(v, w) - \lambda(v) + \lambda(w) \geq 0,$$

$\lambda(v)$ being a lower bound on the distance from v to t with respect to the length function $\ell_i(\cdot)$ only (compare Section 8.3). Any implementation of a priority queue as discussed in Section 3.3 may be utilized with the following definition of addition

$$(a_1, a_2) + (b_1, b_2) = (a_1 + a_2, b_1 + b_2)$$

and smaller relation on pairs:

$$(a_1, a_2) <^* (b_1, b_2) \Leftrightarrow (a_1 < b_1) \vee \big((a_1 = b_1) \wedge (a_2 < b_2)\big)$$

The first label at t removed from the priority queue minimizes $\ell_i(\cdot)$, since goal-direction was used. The path P found has minimal $\ell_j(\cdot)$-value over all paths as for all other paths P' of same $\ell_i(\cdot)$-value $\ell_j(P') \geq \ell_j(P)$.

This is a goal-directed version of the approach considering labels of the form $(\ell_i(P), \ell_j(P))$ and the same smaller function. That approach minimizes $\ell_i(P)$ due to the properties of Dijkstra's algorithm.

This strategy can easily be adapted to handle any "ranking" in the distance functions, i.e. given a permutation $\sigma : \{1, \ldots k\} \to \{1, \ldots k\}$ the algorithm may find paths satisfying the following

1. P minimizes $\ell_{\sigma(1)}$

2. P minimizes $\ell_{\sigma(2)}$ over all paths minimizing $\ell_{\sigma(1)}$ (item 1)

3. P minimizes $\ell_{\sigma(2)}$ over all paths fulfilling item 1 and item 2

...

k. P minimizes $\ell_{\sigma(k)}$ over all paths fulfilling items 1. to $(k-1)$.

The algorithm uses the same k-dimensional distance labels as in the standard case. Goal-direction for the criterion $\sigma(1)$ can be applied. The smaller relation for the priority queue simply has to be modified to:

$$(a_{\sigma(1)},\ldots,a_{\sigma(k)}) <_k^* (b_{\sigma(1)},\ldots,b_{\sigma(k)}) \Leftrightarrow$$
$$\left(a_{\sigma(1)} < b_{\sigma(1)}\right) \vee \left((a_{\sigma(1)} = b_{\sigma(1)}) \wedge (a_{\sigma(2)} < b_{\sigma(2)})\right) \vee$$
$$\left((a_{\sigma(1)} = b_{\sigma(1)}) \wedge (a_{\sigma(2)} = b_{\sigma(2)}) \wedge (a_{\sigma(3)} < b_{\sigma(3)})\right) \vee \ldots$$

Note that the algorithm still computes *all* optimal paths if it is not terminated once the first label at t is removed from the priority queue.

Goal-direction alone will not speed-up the search for all optimal paths. However, together with the strategy introduced in the following section it significantly reduces computation times, as it improves the performance of the that technique.

8.4 Domination by Labels at the Terminal

Recall that early termination is not possible in the multi-criteria scenario. However, once a first result has been found, the search can profit from it. Relying on Fact 3.19 (all subpaths of Pareto optimal paths are also Pareto optimal), we can narrow the search horizon by discarding all intermediate labels which are dominated by any labels already created at the terminal.

The correctness of the strategy follows from the fact and the observation, that any edge added to a path does not reduce the travel time, number of interchanges or the cost. When using the maximal attainable reliability of interchanges (cf. Section 6.3.2) this also works for the reliability criterion. Therefore all labels dominated in such a fashion may be dropped. (Essentially the same trick has been used to speed up the single criterion Dijkstra algorithm for the one source many targets case [MS01]). See also [MW01, MW06].

If lower bounds $\lambda_i(v)$ on the cost $\ell_i(\hat{P})$ of a v-t-path $\hat{P}$ are known, labels $(P, \ell(P))$ that satisfy

$$(\ell_1(P^*),\ldots,\ell_k(P^*)) <_k (\ell_1(P) + \lambda_1(P),\ldots,\ell_k(P) + \lambda_k(P))$$

compared to a label $(P^*, \ell(P^*))$ at the target, can also be discarded. Even lower bounds for only some and not all of the length functions $\ell_i(\cdot)$ can reduce the number of labels significantly. If lower bounds for some criterion i are unknown or too expensive to calculate, they can always be replaced by the trivial lower bounds $\lambda_i \equiv 0$. Together with *goal-direction* this strategy works even better, since via goal-direction labels at the target are generated very early in the search process. This results in a considerable speed-up.

8.5 Lower bounds

Lower bounds can be used to improve the search speed and limit the number of nodes and stations visited. Two approaches, namely goal-direction (Section 8.3) and domination by labels at the terminal (Section 8.4) have already been mentioned from a more theoretical point of view.

In this section we will first show how to calculate lower bounds for the criteria travel time, ticket cost, number of interchanges, and reliability of interchanges and afterwards how exactly they are used to speed up the search process via the aforementioned methods and a pruning technique.

Note that for storing the lower bound to one station from all other stations we need memory space quadratic in the number of stations. Saving the pruning status of each station for each possible pair of source and terminal station would even require cubic space.

8.5.1 The Station Graph for Lower Bounds

Let us first consider lower bounds for the criterion travel time: Regarding space efficiency, it is not reasonable to store a precomputed lower bound for every pair of stations. Thus, these values must be computable "on the fly" during the search. One easy approach for calculating a lower bound on the remaining travel-time is to calculate the straight-line distance from the station $S(n)$ of node n to the target station Ω and divide this value by the fastest travel speed of all trains in the data, as used for example by Schulz, Wagner and Weihe [SWW00]. Empirical testing revealed that this method leads only to a small speed-up since the bounds are too weak.

Our idea, giving tighter lower bounds, uses the *station graph*. This graph consists of one node per station and we insert an edge from station A to B if there is a direct connection between those stations The minimum travel time over all such connections (not considering traffic days) defines the travel time of the edge. We simply reverse all edges in the *station graph* and use one Dijkstra-search on the *station graph* starting at the target station Ω at the beginning of each search. Thus we get a lower bound on the travel time to Ω for *every* station or the information that no connection to Ω exists.

8.5 Lower bounds

Name	Time exp.	Intervals	Interval-width	Nodes	Edges
simple	-	-	-	8,820	22,537
sixhours	✓	4	6h	35,280	113,896
rushhours	✓	4	var	35,280	117,762
fourhours	✓	6	4h	52,920	163,835

Table 8.2: Sizes of the station graphs for lower bounds on travel time or ticket cost, standard version (standard), with fixed interval sizes (sixhours / fourhours) or variable interval sizes for the two rush hours and the times in between (rushhours).

Ticket Cost

The same type of graph can be used to obtain lower bounds for fares. Instead of taking the fastest direct connection between two stations we use the cheapest connection (or rather an estimate derived from the length and train class cf. Section 6.2.2) and store its cost on the edges. Now one Dijkstra-search gives us lower bounds on the ticket cost to Ω for every station which we can reach Ω from.

Expanded Station Graph

If we use time expansion on the station graph (to some degree) we might be able to calculate tighter lower bounds. A station is now represented by a number of k nodes n_S^i, each representing an interval $I_i = [\tau_i, \tau_{i+1})$ in time with $\tau_{k+1} = \tau_1$. The intervals cover the whole day, i.e. $\bigcup_{i=1}^{k} I_i = [0, 1440)$. Now, we have an edge between stations S and R connecting n_S^i and n_R^j if a train departs in interval I_i at station S and arrives in interval I_j at station R. Its length is the fastest travel time over all trains sharing that property. Additionally, an edge connects nodes n_S^i and n_S^{i+1} ($1 \leq i \leq k$) representing waiting from the latest arrival in interval I_i to the first departure in interval I_{i+1}. Its length is the time difference between those two events.

These lower bounds are tighter but more costly: The computation of the bounds is more involved as we have a bigger graph with multiple start labels since the arrival time at the terminal is not known in advance. During the search we are no longer querying the lower bound for a station but for an interval at a station.

We used the following four graphs in our computational study

standard Standard station graph without time expansion

sixhours Four nodes per station with an interval width of 6 hours each

fourhours Six nodes per station with an interval width of 4 hours each

rushhours Four nodes per station, two for the morning and afternoon rush hours and two for the times in between

The sizes of these graphs can be found in Table 8.2.

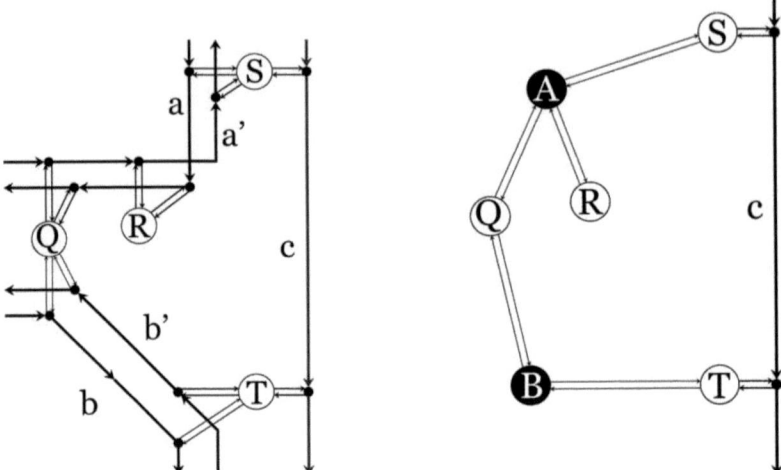

Figure 8.3: Example section of an interchange station graph with four stations (white nodes Q,R,S,T) and five routes, route nodes are solid black (left). Same example with contraction of bidirectional routes (all except c) to single event nodes (right).

8.5.2 Interchange Graph

To obtain lower bounds for the number of interchanges, a graph representing train changes is required. The easiest way to obtain such a graph from the search graph is to contract all the change nodes (including all waiting edges) at a station to a single *station node* and each pair of arrival and departure nodes of train t at station S to an *event node* for t at S (removing the stay-in-train edge). We assign edge weights of zero to all edges except *entering edges*. A backward Dijkstra-search from the terminal Ω may label all stations S with the minimum number of trains required to get from S to Ω. This number minus one is, of course, the minimum number of train changes required.

Unfortunately, this graph is nearly as big as the original graph and the computation of the bounds is very slow. Instead of trains we can use *routes*. Every train is represented in exactly one route with the same sequence of stations. As there are many more trains than routes, the graph size significantly reduces (cf. Table 8.3).

In Figure 8.3 (left) we see an example. It is possible to get from Station S to station T with one train (namely train c). On the other hand, to get from station T to S two trains are required (trains b' and a').

Contracting Bidirectional Routes If a train route is available in forward and backward direction for a list of stations $(S_1, \ldots, S_k)$, it is possible to reach any of the S_i from station S_j ($i \neq j$) using only one train. We may contract all event nodes in forward and backward

8.5 Lower bounds

	Routes total	Standard routes	Bidirectional routes	Nodes	Edges
Trains	68,073	68,073	-	810,622	2,414,433
Routes	7,267	7,267	-	105,048	281,842
Unified routes	4,946	2,625	2,321	75,648	168,874

Table 8.3: Sizes of the interchange station graph using trains (Trains) or routes without (Routes) and with (Unified routes) contraction of bidirectional routes.

direction on such a bidirectional route to a single event node (see Figure 8.3 (right)). For a bidirectional route serving k stations we need only half the number of entering and leaving edges. We have 1 node plus $2k$ edges instead of $2k$ nodes plus $6k - 2$ edges ($k - 1$ train edges and k leaving as well as k entering edges in either direction). This construction saves 28% of the nodes and 40% of the edges (cf. Table 8.3).

Reliability of Interchanges

The lower bound on the number of interchanges can also be used to determine an upper bound (as we maximize this criterion) on the reliability score of a connection. In Section 6.3 we have set the highest reliability factor for an interchange $\mu := 96\%$. So an upper bound for reliability of the remainder of a connection is μ^{ic} for the lower bound on the number of interchanges ic. In case the destination is reachable without an additional interchange this evaluates to the neutral factor $1 = \mu^0$. However, this upper bound seems not really tight (in fact for 4 additional interchanges we have a factor of $\mu^4 = 85\%$ only).

8.5.3 Domination by Labels at the Terminal

The technique to dominate labels by labels at the terminal (cf. Section 8.4) is implemented as follows. We use these lower bounds on the cost of a path from node v to station Ω for the criteria:

time: bound from the station graph with time as edge cost

interchanges: bound from the interchange graph

fare: bound from the station graph with ticket cost as edge cost

reliability of transfers: the highest reliability factor for an interchange $\mu := 96\%$ to the power of the bound for the number of interchanges (from the interchange graph)

We maintain a list of relaxed Pareto optimal labels at the terminal station Ω. Every new label is checked against each label in this list. If the values of the label plus the lower bounds are dominated by any label in the list, there is no need to further regard the new one. It is discarded and not inserted into the priority queue.

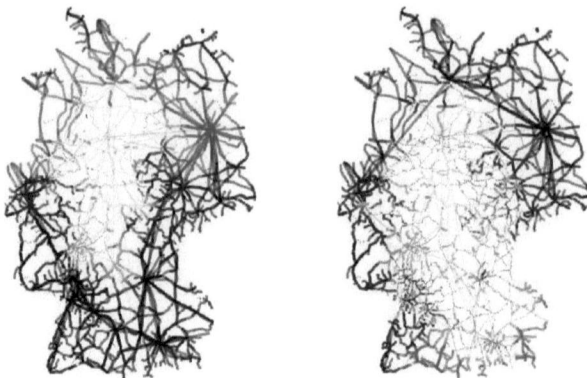

Figure 8.4: Pruning results using the station graph. Colored regions are pruned according to different techniques: too far from the terminal / the source, using triangle inequalities, and using biconnected components (left: Fulda to Hannover / right: Nürnberg to Kassel).

8.5.4 Usage in Goal-Directed Search

Travel time is our relevant criterion for goal-direction. We use already accumulated travel time and a lower bound on the remaining travel time to the target station. The lower bound is computed via the station graph (see Section 8.5.1). For details we refer to Section 8.8.1. Although the search cannot be terminated once the first label at the target station Ω is extracted from the priority queue using goal-direction, labels at Ω are generated fairly early in the search process, thus improving the efficiency of the strategy "domination by labels at the terminal" from the previous subsection.

8.5.5 Limiting the Search Horizon

We can use the lower bounds determined using the station graphs and the interchange graph to further improve the processing time. By labeling stations as unnecessary for our search we can prohibit the creation of labels and inspection of edges at these stations. In Figure 8.4 we can see the results of the pruning steps introduced in the following.

The basic idea is to use the lower bound β on the distance from source to target and label all stations unnecessary that have a lower bound of more than $f(\beta)$ for some suitable function $f(\cdot)$. For example, for travel time the function could be $f_{tt}: x \to 2x$ or for the number of interchanges $f_{ic}: x \to x + 4$. This technique is similar to the concept *reach* (introduced in Section 8.1.4).

Bidirectional Station Graph Dijkstra It is not mandatory to limit oneself to only the distance to the terminal. If we are willing to perform an additional search to determine the

8.5 Lower bounds

Figure 8.5: Biconnected components for a search from Chemnitz (S) to Arnsberg (T). All colored regions are considered in biconnected component pruning. Only the two big regions containing source and target are considered during the search.

distance β_s from the source, we can discard even more stations. Namely the ones we deem too far away from the source as well.

With two distances at our disposal it is possible to prune additional stations by our *triangles* heuristic: those with a sum of distances to source and to target over the threshold $dist_s + dist_t > g(\min\{\beta, \beta_s\})$ for some $g(\cdot)$ with e.g. $g(x) = 1.4 f(x)$ for all x.

Pruning Biconnected Components of the Graph A careful inspection of the resulting graphs with some regions removed by pruning led to the discovery of dead ends and even articulation points in these graphs. It is not at all sensible to head into dead ends or cross articulation points, unless the destination is in that component. Otherwise, the only way to continue is to turn back and, in case of articulation points, cross them again. During dominance testing this is discovered, but not before the station is visited for the second time. To prevent that we employ the following approach:

After using all (or some) of the above mentioned pruning techniques, we calculate the biconnected components of the resulting graph. Then we perform a BFS from the component containing the source to the component containing the target. All stations in components not touched by this search can safely be ignored, since it is unrewarding to pass the same station more than once.

In Figure 8.5 we see the biconnected components for a search from Chemnitz (S) to Arnsberg (S). The colored regions are left to be explored after using our bidirectional Dijkstra on the station graph with the *triangles* heuristic. Each component has a different color than its neighboring components. The BFS only visits the big components containing the source S and the target T. All stations in other components are discarded.

8.6 Skipping Nodes in the Graph or Search

In this section we will present techniques to reduce the number of nodes that are visited during the search. Most of these techniques modify the graph structure, either decreasing the overall number of nodes and edges or the number of nodes and edges on the paths.

8.6.1 Chaining Change-Arrival / Change-Departure Nodes

We do not need a copy of each arrival or departure event on the change level. For every departure time at a station only one change-departure node is required. This single node is connected to all departures at that point in time (observed in [MSW02]) We already save 30.6% of the change nodes and waiting edges (see Table 8.1 on Page 119).

The existence of a arrival and d departure nodes on the change level results in $2 \cdot (a + d)$ waiting edges, $a + d$ for forward and backward search each (see Figure 8.6 (left)). In forward search there is no need to consider arrival events except the ones that are extracted from the priority queue (inserted as the target of a feasible train edge). Therefore, we can unhook the change-arrival nodes from the change level and arrange the change nodes in two cycles, one by linking the departure change nodes with waiting edges according to increasing time values (for forward search) and the other by linking arrival change nodes ordered by decreasing time value (see Figure 8.6 (right), showing the edges for forward search only). This construction technique does not reduce the number of nodes. Applying this construction we only need d waiting edges for forward search and a for backward search. Thus, we save half of the edges and operations on the change level.

8.6.2 Skipping Departure Nodes

In our graph model, departure nodes have exactly one outgoing edge, namely the train edge. So whenever a label at a departure node survives dominance testing, it is entered into the priority queue. Later, it is extracted, and its outgoing train edge is inspected and, if the check does not fail, the label at the arrival node is created, tested, and potentially inserted into the priority queue.

As we have already decided to use the train as soon as the label at the departure node has passed testing, we may immediately check the train edge and upon success create the label at the arrival node without ever inserting and extracting the label at the departure node. Because our search only terminates once the priority queue is empty, we would have extracted these labels anyway. Since we normally insert about one third of the labels at departure nodes, we expect to save one third of the operations on the priority queue.

Note that this is done during computation opposed to changing the graph for the other speed-up techniques in this section. Of course, this can be done analogously for arrival nodes in backward search.

8.6 Skipping Nodes in the Graph or Search

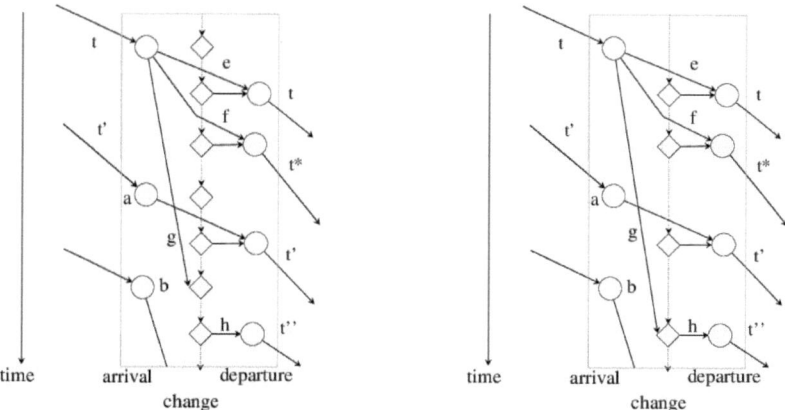

Figure 8.6: Time expanded model with change-departure and change-arrival nodes chained (left) and the extension to skip change-arrival nodes in forward search (right).

8.6.3 Bypassing Departure Nodes

The natural evolution of the technique in the preceding subsection is to eliminate departure nodes from the graph altogether (the same idea can be found in [DPW08] under the designation "Omitting Departure Nodes"). For this construction we introduce new edge types that model entering a train, staying in a train, or a special interchange together with using the train up to its next stop. This way we can bypass all the departure nodes and remove them from the graph. These bypass edges represent entering edges, stay-in-train edges or special-interchange edges and the succeeding train edges. They connect the arrival or change-arrival tail nodes of the other edge types to the head node of the train edge and replace the edges from the original model.

In Figure 8.7 we see an example with two bypassed departure nodes. The entering and stay-in-train edges before the upper train edge towards S_2 and the entering, stay-in-train, and special-interchange edge before the lower train edge towards S_3 have been transformed into bypass edges of the appropriate type and redirected to the arrival of their respective train edge. The leaving edges are not affected. In this example, we only need five bypass edges instead of seven edges adjacent to the departure nodes (five incoming edges plus two train edges).

In Table 8.4 we can see the reduction of the graph size., We save all the train edges and departure nodes, whereas of the combinations of an edge type with a train edge we have exactly the same number as the edge type in the original model. Note that the edges now carry more information, e.g. an entering edge originally only consisted of its two adjacent

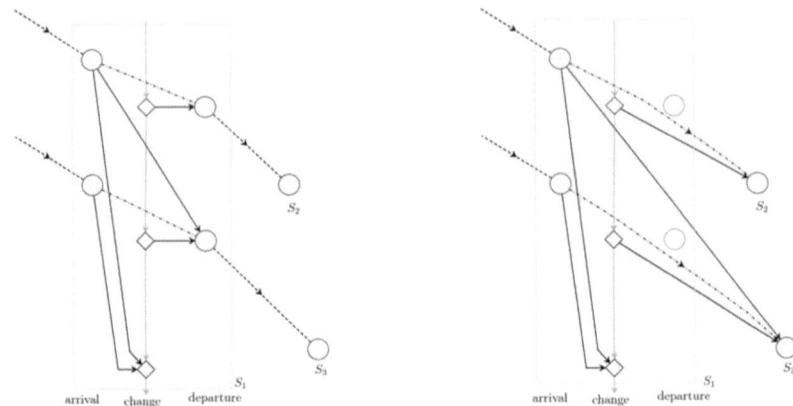

Figure 8.7: Example for bypassing departure nodes. From the left to the right figure, two departure nodes at station S_1 have been removed from the graph.

nodes and now has to store all train information. The technique *connection infos* from Section 5.3.2 now becomes even more important as there are not only a number of (subsequent) train edges without a change in train number, category, attributes etc. but also instead of one train edge we have at least two edges (bypass edges for entering edge or stay-in-train edge plus following train edge, maybe additional ones for special-interchange edges) that have to store this information from the same original train edge.

We did not test additional removals (arrival, change nodes). Delling et al. observed in [DPW08] that these removals actually increase query times because the overall graph size grows, due to a tremendous increase in the number of edges and only a moderate decrease in the number of nodes.

Again, this can be done analogously for arrival nodes in backward search.

	nodes (in k)					edges (in k)		
	dep	arr	change	sum	saved	train	total	saved
org	802	802	557	2,160	0%	802	3,705	0%
bypass	0	802	557	1,358	37.1%	0	2,902	21.6%

Table 8.4: Number of edges and nodes saved using the "bypass" heuristic.

8.7 Important Station Heuristics

Imagine a small station S served by only two routes, one from A to B and the other from B to A. Traveling in a train from A to B it does not make sense to exit at station S and either

8.7 Important Station Heuristics

take a later train in the same direction, much less a train in the opposite direction. This simple observation was the starting point for the *important station heuristic*. The important station heuristic allows leaving a train only at important stations determined using one of the following measurements.

Routes The size of a station measured in the number of routes passing the station is one way of deciding the importance of a station.

Neighbors Only stations, where a route begins or ends or two routes meet (for the first time) or separate might be considered important. A similar idea has been used by [BDGM09]. For routes to meet or separate a station has to have at least 3 neighbors. Consequently, one possibility to decide for a station whether it is important or not is the number of neighbors. Requiring more than 3 neighbors picks more important hub stations.

The resulting share of important stations for selected threshold values is given in Table 8.5. Note that even for the smallest sensible value of 3 for the neighbors heuristic we already have more than two thirds of the stations categorized as unimportant.

8.7.1 Skipping Nodes at Unimportant Stations

The idea of skipping departure nodes (cf. Section 8.6.2) may be adapted for the important station heuristic as well. Whenever an arrival at an unimportant station is processed, its stay-in-train edge is the only allowed edge (unless we are at the target station). Instead of inserting the arrival into the priority queue, we immediately process the target node of that edge. Like in the original *skip departure nodes* heuristic, the label at this departure node is not inserted into the priority queue, as well. Instead, the next arrival is processed immediately. Should this arrival occur at an unimportant station, it and the next departure are treated likewise, and so on. So after entering a train, the next label inserted into the priority queue is the first label of this train at an important station or the terminal.

Variant			Routes			Neighbors		
Threshold			R5	R10	R15	N3	N4	N5
Important Stations	in %		60.2	35.2	21.3	29.6	15.9	9.2
Average number of		N/F	1.0	1.0	1.0	1.0	1.0	1.0
shortcuts per node		A	8.7	7.1	5.9	5.1	3.8	3.1

Table 8.5: The share of important stations as determined by the important stations heuristic using the neighbors (N) or routes (R) variant and the number of shortcuts when connecting each departure to the final stop of the train (F), the next (N) or all subsequent (A) important stations.

8.7.2 Shortcuts in the Graph

Starting from the concept of important stations we want to add shortcuts to the graph that bypass stations which are not important. With this technique we want to decrease the number of visited stations before the terminal is reached. Instead of joining two edges to one (as in the case of bypassing departure nodes), we are now interested in bypassing whole sections of a train. Let us first give an example (see Figure 8.8): Train t serves five stations A,B,C,D, and E. Stations C and E are *important*.

Our first concept is to add shortcuts to the next important station (*scnext*). Thus, we have shortcuts (A,C) and (B,C) to station C and shortcuts (C,E) and (D,E) to station E (left figure). Alternatively, we could add shortcuts from each station to all succeeding important stations (*scall*). To this end, we add shortcuts (A,C), (B,C), and (C,E) as before and additionally the shortcuts (A,E) and (B,E) from before important station C to E (right figure).

Simply adding these edges is not enough, of course. If we ignore the parallel edges for the time being, we now have 4 paths in (*scnext*), instead of one from A to E; in (*scall*) even 6 paths. Therefore, we have to slightly modify the search, namely the decision whether an edge is feasible or not. Additionally to the standard test for traffic days, categories, attributes etc. we use the following:

Shortcut edges are always allowed, except when they bypass the terminal or a station from which the terminal is reachable via a foot path. On the other hand, train edges are not allowed during the search in general, only if a shortcut has been blocked that starts with this train edge.

In our example let station D be our target and our current node the departure at station A. In mode (*scnext*) we are allowed to take shortcut edge (A,C), but not train edge (A,B). No label at station B is created. We use the stay-in-train edge at C and are not allowed to use the shortcut (C,E) since it bypasses terminal D. The failed feasibility check of the shortcut enables us to use train edge (C,D) and we arrive at our destination.

In variant (*scall*) we even disallow stay-in-train edges (as long as the departure after the edge has no feasible train edges) to prevent exploring the same train section more than once. The previous example would work like described for variant (*scnext*) except that we disallow shortcuts (A,E) and (B,E) as well.

But if our terminal were E, we would not allow the stay-in-train edge at C and thus not explore both of the two paths from A to E (shortcut (A,E) and the two shortcuts (A,C) and (C,E) with the stay-in-train edge at C) which both model going from A to E in train t. Of course we still have to create an arrival at C and explore other ways to get from C to E since C is an important station.

The last station of a train is always important to guarantee capturing all stations of each train. The other important stations may be determined for example using the important

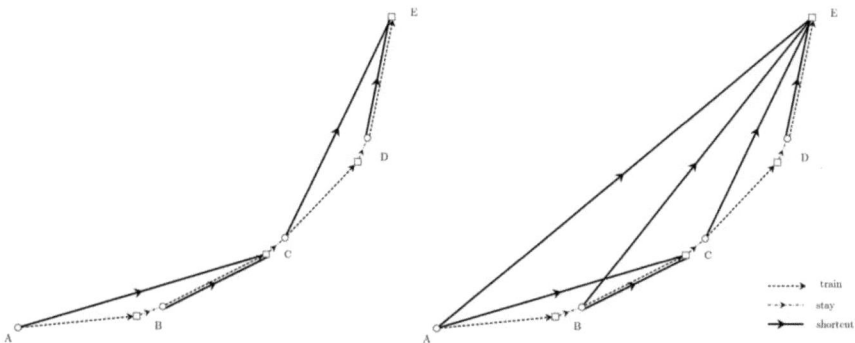

Figure 8.8: A train with additional shortcuts to its important stations C and E. Shortcuts are introduced either from each node to the next important station (left) or to all subsequent important stations (right).

station heuristics presented earlier (in Section 8.7).

We propose the following three variants:

scfinal Shortcuts from all nodes to the final stop of the train,

scnext Shortcuts to the next important station, and

scall Shortcuts to all succeeding important stations.

The number of shortcuts depending on the small station heuristic and the variant of the shortcut heuristic can be found in in Table 8.5 on Page 133. While for *scfinal* and *scnext* each departure node receives one shortcut edge (either to the final or next important station), the number of shortcuts for *scall* lies between 3.1 and 8.7 for our sample values.

8.8 The Priority Queue

In this section we will introduce the employed data types for our priority queues, discuss the binary relation (or for Dial's data structure: the function) used to order elements in these queues, and present two techniques related to priority queues that might improve the search speed.

8.8.1 Smaller Relation for Priority Queues

In multi-criteria search the smaller relation $<'$ used for domination (either standard, relaxed or advanced Pareto) cannot be used for sorting labels, as for many pairs of labels x, y neither

$x <' y$ nor $y <' x$ holds, although $x \neq y$. Therefore, we need to define a smaller relation for the priority queue.

This smaller relation may either be a *lexicographic smaller* for a certain ranking of the criteria, (e.g. time, number of interchanges, reliability of transfers, and price in that sequence of priority) or a smaller on a *weighted sum* of some of the criteria. The *lexicographic smaller* leads to a version that is closest to the classical *label-setting* version of the algorithm. However, since all labels at a node (and not only the smallest) have to be evaluated and processed in a multi-criteria approach anyway, using exactly that smaller relation is not essential for the correctness. Actually, we apply a *label-correcting* scheme.

The lexicographic ordering is formulated and implemented straightforwardly. The relevant value for comparisons for the smaller relation on *weighted sums* may be based on:

one dominant criterion e.g. travel time so far,

goal-direction e.g. travel time so far plus lower bound, or

goal-direction plus other criterion e.g. travel time so far plus lower bound plus weighted number of interchanges, or

any of the above plus some tie-breaking rule e.g. travel time so far plus lower bound plus weighted number of interchanges and some rule to be applied if the difference between the relevant values is zero.

Let S_A denote the last station of connection A and $lb_{time}(S)$ the lower bound on the remaining travel time from S to the terminal Ω (cf. Section 8.5.1). Then

$$\texttt{value}(A) = time_A + \theta \cdot lb_{time}(S_A) + \gamma \cdot (ic_A)$$

describes one promising way to calculate the relevant value for connection A with travel time $time_A$ and number of interchanges ic_A. For $\theta = 0$ and $\gamma = 0$ we have the first variant. The second is used if we set $\theta = 1$ and $\gamma = 0$. To additionally involve the number of interchanges, we set $\theta = 1$ and $\gamma > 0$, resulting in the third variant. Should we encounter ties in any of these variants, we may use the FIFO principle to break them. Interestingly, Dial's data structure (as introduced in 3.3.4) automatically breaks ties this way, as it uses FIFO-queues to store labels with the same values.

8.8.2 Different Priority Queue Types

The smaller relation from the previous subsection will be used to test four different priority queue types:

- Dial's data structure ([Dia69], cf. Section 3.3.4).

- Binary Heap (cf. 3.3)

- k–heap with $k = 4$ (cf. 3.3)

- Pairing Heap ([FSST86])

For the heaps the smaller relation

$$\texttt{smaller}(A, B) : time_A + \theta \cdot lb_{time}(S_A) + \gamma \cdot ic_A < time_B + \theta \cdot lb_{time}(S_B) + \gamma \cdot ic_B$$

and for Dial's data structure $\texttt{value}(A) = time_A + \theta \cdot lb_{time}(S_A) + \gamma \cdot ic_A$ is used to order the labels.

For the heaps we may additionally use the FIFO principle to break ties or let the details of the restructuring methods decide, what happens to labels scoring the same value.

8.8.3 Reordering the PQ

A nice idea to speed up multi-criteria Pareto search is based on the following insight for bi-criteria search. We look at the exemplary case of the criteria travel time and number of interchanges with goal-direction for travel time.

Assume the first Pareto optimal solution P_1 has been found with cost (tt_1, ic_1). We were using goal-direction, hence no faster connection exists. In fact, all Pareto optimal connections P_i with cost (tt_i, ic_i) have the properties $tt_i \geq tt_1$ and $ic_i \leq ic_1$. Therefore, it does not make sense to test partial connections with more interchanges than ic_1 as they cannot lead to optimal connections.

For the remaining part of the search we can safely discard all labels that lead to connections with more than ic_1 interchanges. Furthermore, we can reorder the priority queue according to our second criterion number of interchanges (using lexicographic search, breaking ties by favoring faster connections). All further connections have at most ic_1 interchanges (otherwise the labels were discarded). Once the priority queue is empty, all Pareto optimal connections have been found. Without discarding labels leading to connection with more than ic_1 interchanges, the search can be terminated as soon as the first label with more than ic_1 interchanges is extracted from the queue.

In our scenario, ordering the priority queue according to other criteria than time and number of interchanges (i.e. ticket cost or reliability of transfers) does not seem useful. Besides, it is not at all clear how to adapt this technique to not simply finding the Pareto optimal connections but the relaxed or advanced Pareto optimal ones. Although we may not stop early or discard labels, reordering after the first solution will produce a good solution with the least possible number of interchanges fairly early in the search, so there is hope that we may nonetheless profit from reordering the queue, especially for the technique *domination by labels at the terminal*.

8.8.4 Avoid Inserting Minimum Labels

There are many edges of relatively short length: Entering edges have duration zero. Most waiting edges are only one or two minutes long. Furthermore, Many high-speed train edges on a shortest path increase the travel time by nearly the same amount as they reduce the bound on the remaining travel time. Thus, the labels at head and tail have values (cf. Section 8.8.1) close to each other when using goal-direction. Whenever a label is created after such an edge, it is highly likely that the label will be the new minimum element min_{PQ} in the priority queue. Instead of inserting and extracting these elements into/from the priority queue, we keep an additional FIFO queue that stores those elements x for which $min_{PQ} \not< x$ holds. During the execution of the algorithm we first empty the FIFO queue before taking the next element from the priority queue.

8.9 Edge-Blocking

In this section we will introduce a framework of heuristics we will call *edge-blocking*. Whenever we call method `checkEdge` for some label and edge we use information stored during this search to decide whether an edge is allowed or not. Every time we create a new label after a successful edge inspection, we update the information pool used in our decision process.

8.9.1 Mass Transportation Heuristic

This heuristic tries to avoid using multiple alternatives of highly frequent means of transportation like busses, trams, subways, and the like (mass transportation) to get from some station to another. After the arrival with say a high-speed train t at station S we face different tram lines with differing terminal stations (therefore they are in different routes and not covered by the routes heuristic introduced in Section 8.9.2). Many of these tram lines may meet again at some hub station. Usually, which tram is used between two stations is immaterial, especially if they do not differ in travel time. Assume we have left train t at S and arrived in S' via mass transportation. Having thus already reached the change level at S' after mass transportation, leaving a means of mass transportation reaching S' later in the search process does not create interesting alternatives unless we get from S to S' faster, with less interchanges or with any better label than we reached S' in the first place. Especially taking the next means of mass transportation of the same line to arrive at S' is only favorable if reliability of interchanges is among the optimization criteria.

Consequently, whenever we leave such a highly frequent means of transportation at some station, we store the last used train edge describing a non mass transportation part of the journey and the label in a list at the station. In checkEdge calls we will not allow leaving mass transportation after exactly the same previous non mass transportation edge in case the new label is not better than the information associated with the other label. Note that the algorithm usually does not compare labels at a station that do not belong to the same node.

We implemented three variants of this heuristic. They all only differ in the definition of whether another exit is allowed for the new label or not:

mass transport changes only if it has used less interchanges between means of mass transportation to get to this station,

travel time only if it has used less travel time to get to this station, and

advanced Pareto dominance only if it is not advanced Pareto dominated by any other label that has left a means of mass transportation at this station.

This heuristic was motivated by the observation that many searches requiring high computational effort explore several possibilities of using mass transportation (cf. Section 9.13).

8.9.2 Route Blocking

We are interested in finding all Pareto optima and have an interval of starting points, therefore we may not simply allow only one train edge to each of the neighboring stations of one node (a technique Delling et al. call "node blocking" in [DPW08]). However, we developed an adaption of that technique. Think of a *reference item* as either a label created at an arrival or a train arriving at a station S. For each such reference item we only allow a subset of the trains available at S. We restrict the choice to just the very next train of each route at the station.

To realize this heuristic we create an entry at a station S for each reference item with a list of all routes that are available at S. When we now use a train belonging to a route we mark this route as no longer permitted for the corresponding item. In subsequent checkEdge calls we only select from routes that are marked as still permitted for the corresponding arrival label.

We implemented three versions of this heuristic, each maintaining the set of already used and therefore not eligible routes according to different strategies. Every route is eligible at most once for each *reference item*, either of the following:

station A route may only be used once per station, all connections arriving later at the station may only pick one of the remaining routes.

arriving train edge All connections arriving later with the same train may only pick one of the remaining routes.

arrival label Each different connection reaching the station may continue using any of the routes at that station.

Note that the first variant is an implementation for comparison to the "node blocking" approach. We do not expect useful quality from this crude version of the heuristic.

8.9.3 Shortcut Blocking

The same mechanics can be used to implement the search using shortcuts (cf. Section 8.7.2). Whenever a shortcut edge fails the feasibility check as it bypasses the terminal, we mark the first train edge of the shortcut as feasible. Train edges are only allowed if they have been marked as feasible for a shortcut edge at the same tail node during the current iteration over the leaving edges of that node.

For the variant *scall* the routines get somewhat more involved, as train edges can be part of multiple shortcuts and stay-in-train edges have to be checked as well, but it still fits within the framework.

8.10 Bitonic Search

A simple heuristic, intuitively used on road networks, is to look for *bitonic paths*. It is motivated by the idea to first take urban and regional roads to get to the nearest national roads, then using them to reach highways and once you leave the highways you take again national roads to bring you close to your target and regional and urban roads to the target. Usually, no trip contains a regional road in between two highway segments. For train networks we can group the trains into four groups:

1. urban services (bus, streetcar, etc.)
2. local trains (IR, RE, RB, etc.)
3. long-distance trains like IC and EC
4. high speed trains (ICE, TGV, Thalys, etc.)

Each connection has a sequence of means of transportation (or products) π_i, $i = 1, \ldots, n$ each in group $g(\pi_i)$. A connection is bitonic if

$$\exists j : g(\pi_i) \leq g(\pi_{i+1}) \text{ for } 1 \leq i \leq j \text{ and } g(\pi_i) \geq g(\pi_{i+1}) \text{ for } j < i < n.$$

Müller-Hannemann and Weihe tested Pareto optimal paths in their train graph model using two criteria: travel time and fares. They stated in [MW01, MW06] that 84% of all paths were indeed bitonic.

The heuristic *bitonic* records for each partial connection, whether the sequence of products has already started to descend. Initially, ascending and descending in the hierarchy of groups is allowed. Once a search has started descending for a partial connection, it may never ascend again for all extensions of the connection.

8.11 Speed-Up Techniques and Graph Updates

Delays and information about additional and canceled trains (cf. Chapter 7) require constantly updating the search graph. In this section we will take a backward glance at the speedup techniques introduced earlier in this chapter and will see how well they harmonize with these kinds of updates.

Lower Bounds: Station Graphs, Interchange Graphs and Goal-Direction
Delays and train cancellation or additional trains may require updating the auxiliary graphs for the computation of lower bounds. If a train has a delay at its departure and manages to cancel out/compensate for it, the minimum travel time between two stations may decrease. Additional or canceled trains may require changes to both the station graphs and the interchange graph. Trains traveling slower can safely be ignored, as the lower bounds stay valid, nonetheless, we may increase the fastest travel time if needed. Updating the auxiliary graphs is mostly limited to recomputing the values for a few edges and rarely changing anything at all. This is another advantage of actually computing the bounds in a preprocessing step before each search instead of preprocessing and storing all the values.

Modifications Bypass and Shortcuts All edges that have replaced or represent multiple edges in techniques *bypass departure nodes* (cf. Section 8.6.3) and *shortcuts* (from Section 8.7.2) connect regular nodes to regular nodes and, in the latter case, know the represented edges. After shifting nodes, the length of the bypass and shortcut edges automatically adjusts, as edge lengths are determined according to the time stamps of the head and tail nodes of an edge. Whenever an edge needs to be deleted, the corresponding bypass and shortcut edges are easy to determine. Adding new trains may require computing this type of edges for that train in a straightforward way. Note that our shortcuts only represent sections of trains and no train changes, thus they exist as long as all their train edges exist. No special treatment according to broken train changes due to delays is required.

Techniques avoid and skip The techniques *avoid inserting minimum labels* (cf. Section 8.8.4) and *skip departure nodes* (see Section 8.6.2) only modify the processing of labels (by not inserting some of them into the priority queue), so they are immune to graph updates.

Heuristics Bitonic Search and Edge-Blocking: Mass Transportation
As long as the train classes of all train edges in the schedule are available, dynamic graph changes do not concern these heuristics.

Heuristic Route Blocking This heuristic only requires updating the route information according to additional and canceled trains.

Heuristic Important Stations Although additional and canceled trains may change the number of trains at a station, neither the topology of the network changes (to determine importance from the number of neighbors) nor the number of routes is significantly affected (to determine the importance from the number of routes).

8.12 MOTIS Algorithm with Speed-Up Techniques

In this section, we present the adjustments and extension to the graph and algorithm according to the speed-up techniques introduced throughout this chapter.

8.12.1 Changes to the Graph

The following changes affect the final graph model as introduced in Chapter 5:

- Chaining change-arrival and change-departure nodes in separate change levels (cf. Section 8.6.1).
- Additional shortcut edges are inserted (cf. Section 8.7.2).
- Departure nodes are bypassed, these nodes are removed from the graph (cf. Section 8.6.3).

8.12.2 Changes to the Algorithm

In Figure 8 we give a pseudocode description of the MOTIS algorithm with speed-up techniques. The algorithm looks nearly identical to the version presented in Section 5.4 without those techniques. The differences are highlighted in light gray in the following list of details influencing certain steps and method calls.

createStartLabels() in pre-trip search labels for all nodes in the start interval, maybe at metas and stations reachable via footpaths as well, respecting attribute NotIn,
in on-trip search either at one arrival node or one change-departure node.

8.12 MOTIS Algorithm with Speed-Up Techniques

Input: a timetable graph and a query
Output: a set of advanced Pareto optimal labels at the terminal
foreach *node* v **do**
  $\quad$ labelListAt(v) := $\emptyset$;
PriorityQueue pq := $\emptyset$;
createStartLabels();

while ! pq.*isEmpty*() **do**
♭ $\quad$ Label label := pq.extractLabel();
  $\quad$ **foreach** *outgoing edge* e=(v,w) *of* v=label.*getNode*() **do**
    $\quad\quad$ **if** *isInfeasible*(e) **then** continue; // ignore this edge
    $\quad\quad$ Label newLabel := createLabel(label, e);
    $\quad\quad$ **if** *isDominated*(newLabel) **then** continue;
    $\quad\quad$ // newLabel is not dominated
    $\quad\quad$ **if** *isTerminalReached*(newLabel) **then**
      $\quad\quad\quad$ terminalList.insert(newLabel);
    $\quad\quad$ **else**
      $\quad\quad\quad$ metaData.update(newLabel);
      $\quad\quad\quad$ labelListAt(w).insert(newLabel);
      $\quad\quad\quad$ labelListAt(w).removeLabelsDominatedBy(newLabel);
      $\quad\quad\quad$ pq.insert(newLabel);
filterList(terminalList);

Algorithm 8: Pseudocode for the MOTIS algorithm with speed-up techniques.

pq.insert/extract(·) depending on priority queue type (Section 8.8.2), lower bounds (Section 8.5) and smaller relation (Section 8.8.1) used in goal-direction (Section 8.3), heuristics *avoid inserting minimum labels* (separate queue for those, cf. Section 8.8.4), and for heuristic *skip departure* (Section 8.6.2):

- at departure nodes, do not perform pq.insert(newLabel)
- instead goto line ♭
- there, execute label := newLabel instead of label := pq.extractLabel()

outgoing edge e=(v,w) all leaving edges, for arrival nodes additionally the foot edges stored for this station

isInfeasible(e) whether edge *e* is infeasible due to traffic days, attribute requirements, train class restrictions, or heuristics: *bitonic search* (Section 8.10), *mass transportation* (Section 8.9.1), *route blocking* (Section 8.9.2), *shortcut blocking* (Section 8.9.3) for shortcuts (either only shortcut or regular edges, cf. Section 8.7.2), or the head node is infeasible due to pruning techniques (Section 8.5.5) or the *important station heuristic* (Section 8.7)

isDominated (newLabel) test against other labels at the same node and labels at the terminal (Section 8.4), for the latter using lower bounds (Section 8.5)

isTerminalReached(·) if leaving allowed (attribute NotOut) at a node belonging to the terminal station (or any of the meta replacements)

metaData.update(·) for edge blocking heuristics: *mass transportation* (Section 8.9.1), *route blocking* (Section 8.9.2) or *shortcuts* (Section 8.9.3)

terminalList.insert(newLabel) label is stored for technique *domination by labels at the terminal* (Section 8.4)

filterList(terminalList) after a final evaluation of the complete connections represented by the labels in terminalList remove dominated labels

8.13 Further Thoughts on Speed-Up Techniques

8.13.1 Ideas for Bidirectional Search

To implement bidirectional search for the multi-criteria case on time-expanded (or time-dependent) networks assume we have somehow guessed the correct arrival interval. A label at a node that already has at least one label from the opposite search direction is stored and its leaving edges are not explored. Connections are constructed from the new label and all the labels from the other direction. These connections are used for *domination by labels at the terminal*. The search to determine all optimal paths continues until the queues for both directions are empty. Instead of guessing the correct arrival interval let us consider the following examples:

- empty arrival interval: the single-directed search is executed

- arrival interval too small: some of the shortest path from source to terminal are found only in forward direction (namely those arriving outside the assumed arrival interval) and we waste some speedup potential

- arrival interval too big: some additional paths from the terminal to the source are found, but they do not start in the departure interval. We have wasted search time

For the latter case we may employ an additional bounding technique discarding labels that will arrive later than the end of the departure interval.

A promising way of determining the arrival interval might be shifting the start of the departure interval by a lower bound on the travel time and the end of the departure interval by some upper bound. Note that good lower bounds are already present as part of our original algorithm. Upper bounds on the other hand are always hard to obtain. The better our estimation of the arrival interval, the more improvement we would expect.

8.13.2 Adapting Multi-Criteria SHARC

The *unidirectional* speed-up technique SHARC seems to be a prime candidate for adaption to our scenario. It has already been extended to cover multiple criteria [DW09a] and time-dependency in road-networks [Del08b]. Recently, it has been extended to multi-criteria timetable information in time-dependent graphs modeling train schedules [BDGM09]. We plan to apply their results to our time-expanded graph and advanced Pareto dominance approach. We hope to advance the techniques of arc-flag computation, graph partitioning, and contraction in our scenario.

Chapter 9

Computational Study

In this chapter, we will present an extensive computational study. We will start with the search for special offers and for night trains. These two were conducted based on the concept of relaxed Pareto optimality (see the history of the algorithm in Section 5.6). In the remainder of the chapter we will present an in-depth analysis of various aspects of our algorithm and the concept of advanced Pareto optimality.

In the section about special offers (Section 9.1) we will search for connections respecting the criteria travel time, number of interchanges, and ticket cost. For ticket cost we will look at regular fares and two contingent based fares, either fixed price or reduced price, simultaneously (as introduced in Section 6.2)

We will evaluate our two approaches for the search for night trains, our enumerative approach and sleeping time as an additional criterion (from Section 6.4) in Section 9.2. We will compare their performance and quality to the standard version without the capability of searching for night trains.

The importance of the criterion reliability of interchanges is much higher than that of these two other criteria or special search forms. Especially in a scenario with information about delayed trains available (cf. Chapter 7), the most important criteria are travel time, number of interchanges, and reliability of interchanges. Therefore, this criterion has become an integral part of the system and will be evaluated from Section 9.3 sec:compsetup onwards together with our three principle criteria travel time, number of interchanges, and ticket cost (without special offers) in the advanced Pareto optimality approach. in the computational study in Chapter 9 in Section 9.9 and when toggling the individual criteria in Section 9.5.2.2.. After a short overview of the testing environment and measurements for speed and quality, we will look at the influence of the different concepts of domination and the combinations of criteria. Then, speedup techniques without quality loss (lower bounds, priority queue types, goal-direction, basic modifications to the graph and the number of labels entered into the priority queue) and later heuristics that may fail to find all optimal connections (bitonic search, edge blocking heuristics: mass transportation and route blocking, the important station heuristic, and shortcuts, as well as combinations) will be thoroughly examined.

9.1 Computational Study on Special Offers

In this section, we will evaluate our approach to the search for special offers, fixed price and reduced price tickets subject to availability of contingents on high-speed edges as introduced in Section 6.2.

9.1.1 Computational Setup

9.1.1.1 Test Cases

We took the train schedule of trains within Germany from 2003. For our experiments, we used a snapshot of about 5,000 real customer queries of Deutsche Bahn AG falling within the week January 13-19, 2003. For all queries, we searched for valid connections within a two-hours time interval. This schedule and the derived time-expanded graph have sizes as shown in Table 9.1.

Ticket contingents exist for high-speed trains (like ICE, Thalys, TGV, IC, EC) or night trains. Each train t has a certain capacity $cap(t)$ (depending on the train type). We do not have access to real pre-booking data for trains. Therefore, we simulate the booking status for each train.

A random number of passengers uses each train with contingent restrictions. This number is based on the train class and some other criteria (number of stops, importance of the served stations, etc.). For each of the passengers a random station for entering and leaving the train is chosen evenly distributed from the stations the train visits. We then set thresholds $x_A(t)$ for the number of passengers required to exhaust the contingent on a train edge of train t according to the desired level of availability $A = x\%$. A travel edge which may have a contingent restriction is called *contingent edge*. For two availabilities A, A' with $A < A'$ we require $x_A(t) \geq x_{A'}(t)$ for all trains t. So the contingent edges that are not available for some availability A are not available for every availability $A^* < A$.

We consider the following scenarios for the availability of contingents: C10, C20, C40, C60, C80 and C100, where Cx has an availability of $A = x\%$ on the contingent edges. For comparison we also include the numbers for the search for regular fares (denoted by MOTIS).

number of	
stations	8,861
trains	45,370
high-speed trains	1,006
nodes	1,427,726
edges	2,395,703

Table 9.1: Size of the time-expanded graph.

9.1 Computational Study on Special Offers

Scenario	Runtime average in ms	PQ extracts average	Number of Pareto Optima	relaxed
MOTIS	1,702	169,114	3.93	7.26
C10	1,889	176,861	4.22	8.05
C20	1,839	175,221	4.13	7.92
C40	1,776	170,976	3.90	7.73
C60	1,734	167,114	3.67	7.46
C80	1,676	161,446	3.43	7.32
C100	1,605	155,219	3.19	7.06

Table 9.2: Computational results for simultaneous search for several tariff types (minimum of regular fare, contingent-restricted special offer and contingent-restricted 50% discount).

For all queries, we assume the same type of passenger, namely a single adult booking early enough to get a 50% discount if a contingent is available. The fixed price for special offers is assumed to be 29 Euros.

9.1.1.2 Computational Environment

All computations are executed on a standard Intel P4 processor with 3.2 GHz and 4 GB main memory running under Suse Linux 9.2. Our C++ code has been compiled with g++ 3.x and compile option -O3.

9.1.2 Searching for Multiple Tariffs

In the following, we compare computational results for running our code with regular fares only (this version is called MOTIS in the following) and a simultaneous search of several tariff types for different scenarios of available contingents. In the simultaneous search, we finally select the relaxed Pareto optimal connections where the fare is taken as the minimum of the regular fare, a contingent-restricted special offer and a contingent-restricted 50% discount on the regular fare if the contingent is available. Table 9.2 summarizes the key figures obtained in our experiment. In the first column of numbers we present the average CPU time in milliseconds for a single query. The average CPU time lies within the relatively small range of $1.6s$ and $1.9s$ for all scenarios.

As CPU times are very hardware-dependent, we prefer to add representative operations counts for the performance evaluation of algorithms. Previous studies [MS07] indicated that a suitable parameter for operation counts of a multi-criteria version of Dijkstra's algorithm is the number of extract minimum operations from the priority queue. This parameter is highly correlated with the CPU time for the corresponding query. Therefore, we display in the second column of numbers in Table 9.2 also the average number of these extract operations.

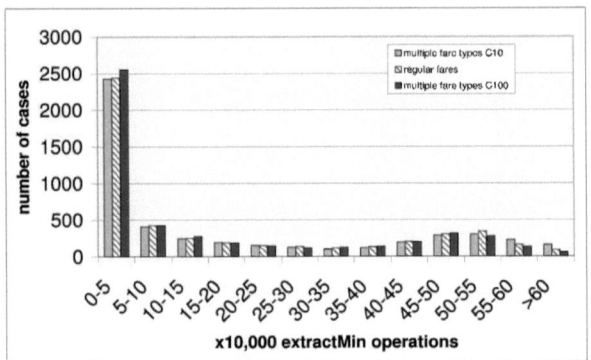

Figure 9.1: Histogram showing the distribution of the number of extract operations from the priority queue. We compare MOTIS (search only for regular fares) with a new version which simultaneously searches for a mixture of fare types.

The computational effort increases with decreasing availability of contingents mainly due to two reasons: On the one hand, very few available contingent edges force the algorithm to take longer detours to find cheap contingent prices. On the other hand, a high availability of contingent edges leads to many cheap connections. These help in dominance. There are actually less connections to explore to find cheap alternatives. If about half or more of the contingent edges are available, the contingent version has less operations than the version MOTIS not considering different tariffs.

We note that dominance rules are faster to evaluate if only regular fares are considered (case MOTIS) as less connections are mutually incomparable, see Subsection 6.2.3.1. Therefore, the workload per extract minimum operation is smaller in this version. For all versions using contingent information the correlation between runtime and number of extract min operations is plain to see.

In Figure 9.1, we show a histogram on the distribution of extract minimum operations. Case MOTIS mostly lies between the easiest (C100) and most difficult (C10) contingent scenario. The overall distribution looks very similar for all versions of our algorithm. It turns out that about half of all test cases require less than 50,000 extract operations. Such queries are very easy and take only a few milliseconds.

The two remaining columns of Table 9.2 display the average number of true Pareto optima and the number of relaxed Pareto optima, respectively.

MOTIS offers about 7-8 attractive connections on average, i.e. about four additional connections in comparison to standard Pareto filtering. The more contingents are available, the smaller is the number of Pareto optima, since more fast connections have a cheaper price.

9.1 Computational Study on Special Offers

Scenario	Runtime average in ms	Calls to SFPC	Fixed Price conn. from FTTD	Fixed Price conn. from SFPD	Certificates no fixed price conn. exists	Non high-speed total	Non high-speed too expensive
C10	204	3641	82	317	2790	1811	373
C20	153	3502	221	841	2224	1714	321
C40	111	3101	622	1490	288	2450	256
C60	90	2579	1144	1742	194	1920	216
C80	70	1534	2189	1275	59	1477	171
C100	45	0	3723	-	0	1277	152

Table 9.3: Results for the fast search for fixed price connections. Either a fixed price connection was found (by FTTD or SFPD), a certificate that no fixed price connection exists was computed, or a non high-speed connection was found which is cheaper than the fixed price in most cases.

Figure 9.2 shows the distribution of the number of Pareto optima and relaxed Pareto optima over the test cases for MOTIS and the most difficult contingent version C10.

9.1.3 Fast Search for Fixed Price Connections

We also evaluated the results of the preprocessing phase with our test set. In this experiment, we have run the subroutines "fastest travel time Dijkstra" (FTTD) and our "specialized fixed price Dijkstra" (SFPD). Recall that the purpose of these routines is to find either a fixed price connection, a suitable connection for dominance testing or a certificate, that no fixed price connection exists.

Table 9.3 shows the average runtime, the number of calls to the SFPD, the number of different types of connections and the number of certificates that no fixed price connection exists. The connections are either fixed price connections found by either of the algorithms

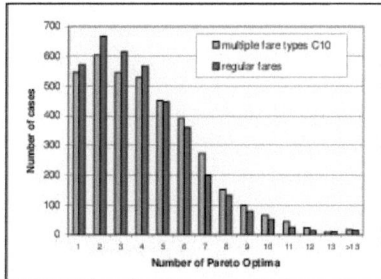
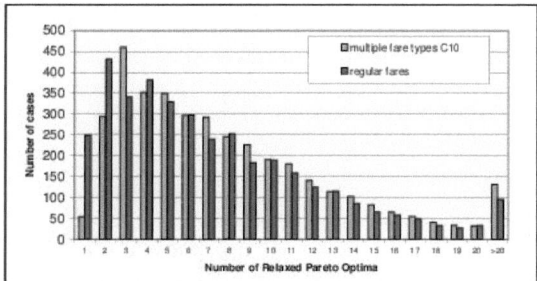

Figure 9.2: Histogram showing the distribution of the number of Pareto optima and relaxed Pareto optima.

a non-high-speed connection was more expensive than the fixed price. These cases are the only ones, where we have neither a connection to use in dominance testing (either a fixed price connection or a connection without high-speed train that is faster than any fixed price connection) nor the knowledge that no fixed price connection exists. This only happens in 152 to 373 cases, which is 3.04% to 7.5% of the cases, depending on the availability of contingent edges. This is acceptable for a heuristic that runs in at most a fifth of a second on average.

Not surprisingly the total number of fixed price connections increases with the availability of contingents. With decreasing availability the runtime, the number of calls to the SFPD, and the number of certificates that no fixed price connection exists increase. As the availability of contingent edges increases, the number of fixed price connections determined by the FTTD increases and the number of calls to the SFPD decreases, therefore the runtime improves. The number of fixed price connections SFPD determines increases with the availability but decreases if many fixed price connections have already been found by FTTD.

Fixed price search in MOTIS becomes harder the less contingent edges are available (as more detours have to be investigated).

Fortunately, with decreasing availability of contingents we can turn off the tariff option fixed price search in the multi-criteria search due to the preprocessing phase for a significantly increasing number of queries.

9.2 Computational Study on Night Train Search

Our two approaches to the search for night trains (introduced in Section 6.4), either as a specialized search for night trains only or modeling sleeping time as an additional criterion for multi-criteria optimization will be evaluated in this section.

Figure 9.3: The railway network of Germany. All night train routes are highlighted.

9.2.1 Computational Setup

9.2.1.1 Test Cases

We took the train schedule of trains within Germany of July 2007; the night train routes are shown in Figure 9.3. For our experiments, we used a snapshot of about 25,000 real customer queries of Deutsche Bahn AG. From these we selected and processed only those 1771 queries where the straight line distance between the start and terminal stations was at least 350 km. For all other queries the distance is likely to be too short to allow for a reasonable night train connection.

Among the 1771 queries, we have 347 queries which possess a direct night train connection and 937 require only one feeder. The remaining 487 queries need two feeders. The used schedule and the derived time-expanded graph have sizes as shown in Table 9.4.

number of	
stations	8,916
trains	56,994
night trains	229
nodes	2,400,534
edges	3,715,557

Table 9.4: Key parameters of the schedule and the corresponding graph.

9.2.1.2 Specific Definition of Attractive Solutions

We have chosen the following constants to specify our notion of attractive night train connections as introduced in Section 6.4.2.

- A connection is considered as a *night train connection* only if it includes a night train with a sleeping time of at least $lb_{st} = 240$ minutes.
- We limit the maximal travel time of some feeder section also to $ub_{fe} := 240$ minutes.
- In our definition of the modified sleeping time $mst := \min\{st, ub_{st}\}$ (as introduced in Section 6.4.2) we have chosen the upper bound as $ub_{st} = 420$ minutes.

9.2.1.3 Computational Environment

All computations are executed on an AMD Athlon(tm) 64 X2 dual core processor 4600+ with 2.4 GHz and 4 GB main memory running under Suse Linux 10.2. Our C++ code has been compiled with g++ 4.1.2 and compile option -O3.

We compare the following variants:

- Algorithm A: our standard MOTIS version which was designed to find all attractive train connections with respect to travel time minimization and minimizing the number of train interchanges. MOTIS requires a time interval specifying when the connection has to start. To use MOTIS for a night train search, we set this start interval to a period between 6:00 pm on the traffic day and 2:00 am on the following day. For our comparison with other variants, we considered only night train connections.

- Algorithm B: the enumerative approach of pre-selecting night trains as described in Section 6.4.3.1.

- Algorithm C: a heuristic version of Algorithm B. We replace the multi-criteria search for feeders by a single-criterion search with respect to travel time. The latter is much more efficient, but may lead to additional interchanges. The idea behind this variant is that feeder connections should in general not be very complicated.

- Algorithm D: the multi-criteria version of MOTIS with sleeping time as an additional criterion as described in Section 6.4.3.2.

9.2.2 Experiments

9.2.2.1 Experiment 1.

In our first experiment we want to study the basic question: How often is it necessary to use a specialized night train search to find any suitable night train connection?

To answer this question we compared Algorithm A with all other variants; see Table 9.5. Algorithm A (standard MOTIS) does not find any true night train connection in 370 out of 1771 test cases (20.89%), whereas Algorithms B and C always found at least one reasonable night train connection. This already shows that a specialized night train search can offer much more to customers. Our version of Algorithm D (MOTIS with one additional criterion) fails to find a night train connection in 41 cases (2.3%). This is due to our heuristic version of domination rules.

Algorithm	# connections	Runtime	# failures	
A (standard MOTIS)	2334	1.87s	370	20.75 %
B (pre-selection+feeder)	4223	14.20s	0	0 %
C (pre-selection+fast feeder)	3939	3.72s	0	0 %
D (MOTIS with additional criterion)	3196	2.34s	41	2.3 %

Table 9.5: The total number of connections found, average runtime in seconds, and the number of failures for all variants.

9.2.2.2 Experiment 2.

Comparing the four tested variants, what is their impact on the quality of the identified connections?

The qualitative comparison of the result sets, meaning the found connections, in a multi-objective search space can be done in several ways. A first, but only rough, indicator is the size of the solution set after filtering out dominated solutions. The largest set of connections is delivered by Algorithm B (4223 solutions over all instances), followed by Algorithm C (3939 solutions) and Algorithm D (3196 solutions). Algorithm A delivers only 2334 solutions.

Next we studied which algorithmic variant was able to find the most attractive connection. For this comparison we introduced after intensive discussions with practitioners a quality measure which allows us to rank the solutions for each query a posteriori.

Given a connection c with travel time $tt(c)$ in minutes, modified sleeping time $mst(c)$ also in minutes, and number of interchanges $ic(c)$, we measure the cost of c by the function

$$q(c) := tt - mst + k \cdot ic,$$

where we set the constant $k := 20$ and $ub_{st} = 480$ minutes. The smaller the cost value, the better we regard the quality of the corresponding connection. Our cost function can be interpreted as follows: We have to pay for each minute of travel time. This cost can be reduced by the sleeping time up to our upper bound ub_{st}. An interchange is counted as 20 minutes extra travel time. We now rank the solutions as follows: A direct night train connection has always first rank. All other connections are ranked according to increasing cost. We have experimented with different constants in our cost function. It turned out that the ranking of our algorithms is quite robust against changes of these constants.

With respect to this ranking of solutions, we now compared the quality of the first rank solutions against each other. Table 9.6 shows how often the first ranked solutions have strictly better quality, how often they match, and how often they are strictly worse. Standard MOTIS (without explicit night train search, Algorithm A) turns out to be clearly inferior to our new approaches. In fact, the results found by Algorithm B prove the existence of better alternatives in 889 out of 1771 cases, i.e., in about 50%.

The enumerative approach (Algorithm B) and its heuristic version (Algorithm C) behave quite similarly. We observe that the quality of Algorithm C is only slightly worse than that of Algorithm B (of course, Algorithm C can never beat Algorithm B). This confirms our intuition that the feeder parts of night train connections are usually not too complicated, and are therefore also found by the heuristic. In roughly 70% of the test cases, the enumerative approaches (Algorithm B or C) and the multi-criteria version of MOTIS (Algorithm D) deliver the same quality for the best solution. In the remaining cases, Algorithms B/C "win" about twice (2.5 and 2.1 times, respectively) as often as Algorithm D.

9.2.2.3 Experiment 3.

Is there a trade-off between computational efficiency and quality of the solutions?

See Table 9.5 for the average CPU times for all variants. Standard MOTIS (with an exceptionally long query interval of 8 hours) is the fastest variant with only 1.87 seconds, but fails too often to find a night train connection. Algorithm B which gives the overall best quality is about four times slower than Algorithm C. Since the quality delivered by Algorithm C comes close to that of Algorithm B, it will usually not be worthwhile to use the more expensive Algorithm B. Algorithm D is 37% faster than Algorithm C, but its quality is also somewhat poorer. Thus depending on what is more important either Algorithm D or Algorithm C should be used.

A vs. B	# cases
A wins	134
B wins	889
both match	748

B vs. C	# cases
B wins	46
C wins	0
both match	1725

C vs. D	# cases
C wins	385
D wins	181
both match	1205

A vs. D	# cases
A wins	3
D wins	625
both match	1143

B vs. D	# cases
B wins	389
D wins	155
both match	1227

Table 9.6: Pairwise comparison of the first ranked solutions.

9.2.2.4 Experiment 4.

To gain more insight into the behavior of Algorithms B and C we did some operation counting. The following numbers always represent averages.

From the set of all possible entry and exit points, 1719 have been rejected since they are not served on the query date, from the remaining 1605 entry points 1144 have been rejected because of our distance criterion, and 1205 pairs were removed because of insufficient sleeping time. It is worth noting that 405 additional feeder computations have been avoided by our caching mechanism. We had to calculate 111 feeder sections for each query. This explains why it was crucial to speed up Algorithm B by a more efficient feeder computation.

9.3 Computational Studies with Advanced Dominance

From now on, we will study the criteria travel time, number of interchanges, reliability of interchanges (as introduced in Section 6.3) and ticket cost (using regular fares as modeled in Section 6.2.2 only, no special offers) under the the concept of *advanced Pareto dominance*.

The results from the preceeding two sections were based on relaxed Pareto dominance due to the development stage of our algorithm at that time (cf. Section 5.6 on the history of MOTIS). We have seen that both types of searches have neither issues with quality nor with query times. The additional criteria can be modeled analogously in advanced Pareto dominance and the incomparability of results can be exploited, as well. Basically, advanced Pareto dominance removes unattractive solutions already during the search. Since it is faster (as we will see in the following sections), no runtime problems are to be expected. Thus, we did not repeat all the experiments.

The preprocessing step of searching for connections obtaining a fixed price or the certificate that no such connections exist takes about 100ms (cf. Section 9.1.3). This is only a small part in a search lasting almost 2 seconds. However, employing advanced Pareto dominance searches become much faster and this search would take up about 20% of the run-time. As the search respecting all criteria is much faster anyway, the benefit of the preprocessing step diminishes. Recall that it was only used to deactivate the search for fixed price connections. Consequently, it should be disabled in combination with advanced Pareto dominance.

During the following computational studies we will compare these results with new results on relaxed Pareto dominance. It will turn out that those match up quite nicely.

9.4 Computational Setup

9.4.1 Testing Environment

Hard- and Software
All experiments were run on 2 cores of an Intel Xeon 2.6 GHz with 4GB of RAM under Ubuntu 8.04 in a Virtual Machine (VMWare ESXi 3.5.0). Our code was compiled with gcc V.4.3 with compile option O2.

Search Graph
The search graph was already used in the previous chapter. It was constructed from the schedule of the federal German railway company (Deutsche Bahn AG) for 2008. It encompasses all German long distance and local trains. The key figures were presented in Tables 8.1.

Test Set
We use 5,000 real customer queries taken from the requests to the Internet portal of Deutsche

Bahn AG as available on http://www.bahn.de. Each of the queries has an interval of 3 hours. The set contains queries for short, medium, and long journeys and the stations are wide spread over Germany. Source or terminal are regional stations, medium-sized stations, or big hub stations with queries either between the same or different categories of stations.

9.4.2 Measures and Test Procedures

9.4.2.1 Performance Measurement

Runtimes heavily depend on the used machines and optimization of the code. Rather than on runtime only, we want to concentrate on the number of created labels and extractions from the priority queue, our *significant operations*. These are our key criteria to compare the performance of different variants and parameterizations of our algorithm. As runtime scales similarly to the numbers of created and extracted labels, the significant operations are a good indicator for computational complexity and runtime. Therefore, we decided to present the average numbers of created and extracted labels as well as the runtime averages, whenever talking about performance.

For runtimes we took the average over 10 runs to control for variations due to background processes, IO etc. The algorithm is deterministic, so the numbers of all significant operations do not vary between the individual runs. For our reference version (see below) the runtime average of a single run was at most 1.77ms higher and at most 1.79ms lower than the average of 412,14ms over all ten runs. This deviation of at most 0.43% in any direction in case of runtimes is small enough to have high confidence in our runtime statements.

9.4.2.2 Quality Measurement

Some of our speedup techniques are heuristics. Therefore, we need a measurement for the quality of the computed sets of results. Instead of using some score based approach for quality, we decided to measure the loss of quality in relation to other test runs (e.g. heuristics turned *on* or *off* or different parameterizations).

When comparing the quality of two versions, say *base* (B) and *heuristic* (H), we look at the set of calculated connections for each of the queries individually. To counteract the effect of significantly different quality (e.g. a heuristic only determines connections dominated by connections of (B)) and result sets of varying sizes (one result set is much larger but contains many worse connections) we first take the union of the results determined by (B) and (H). Afterwards, we apply filtering to the resulting set and remove duplicates. As both versions may have computed results of different quality, this filtering may remove results from the union. In most cases the applied rules for filtering are those relevant for the reference version, unless stated otherwise. The number of *surviving* connections for each version is the number of connections determined by that version remaining in the filtered union. Note that connections determined by both versions are counted as survivors for both. The quality loss for this query of (H) is then defined as the difference between the survivors of (H) minus the survivors of (B).

Think of an example for bi-criteria search with travel time and number of interchanges without relaxation. While (H) determined the results (100min, 3), (130min, 2), and (145min, 1), version (B) delivers connections (100min, 3) and (125min, 1). The filtered union of the results only contains the connections (125min, 1) and (100min, 3). Thus, (B) has a quality loss of zero, since it found all optimal connections. Meanwhile (H) found only one of the optimal connections (in the union). Consequently, it has a quality loss of one. Note that the number of suboptimal connections is not important. If a version had determined 10 connections that are not optimal (in the union) for the example above, it would not loose 10 connections in quality. It would have a quality loss of two, as it did not find any of the two optimal connections.

Summing up the quality loss over all queries gives us the total quality loss in connections. Normalized over the number of connections determined for all queries we get our first quality criterion, the *quality loss in connections* (Q_{conn}) in percent.

Two versions with nearly identical quality loss in connections may have totally different distributions of the lost optima. One may have lost quality for one quarter of the queries, whereas the other may have lost quality for each tenth query only. To cover the affected queries we have a second quality criterion, the *queries with worse quality* (Q_{query}), i.e. the number of queries for which (H) determined less survivors as (B), normalized over the number of queries.

Whenever we want to compare the quality of two or more variants, we select one base variant and determine the loss of quality in connections and queries in relation to that variant. For ease of exposition we will talk about loosing x% of the optimal connections or missing optimal connections for y% of the queries.

Assume we have 200 queries and found 800 connections. If variant (H) has a quality loss in connections $Q_{conn}(H) = 10\%$ and a $Q_{query}(H) = 25\%$ queries with worse quality, it lost 80 optimal connections. These were distributed over 50 of the 200 queries.

9.4.2.3 Measurement of Speedups

Baseline Variant
A baseline implementation without speed-up techniques requires between 15 and 20 million extractions from the priority queue and nearly 5 minutes of runtime per query. Our 10 reference runs for all 5,000 queries would take half a year to complete. We do not deem the improvement compared to this version a fair measure of the speedup.

	a_{time}^i	a_{ic}^i	a_{cost}^i	a_{sec}^i	$rel_i(AB)$ Pareto	$rel_i(AB)$ relaxed
i						
1	1	0	0	0	0	$rel_{time}(AB)$
2	0	1	0	0	0	0
3	0	0	1	0	0	0
4	0	0	0	1	0	0

Table 9.7: The coefficients a_c^i and relaxation terms $rel_i(A, B)$ in Formula 9.1 with $k = 4$ and $r = 4$ for rule sets Pareto dominance (P) and relaxed Pareto dominance (R).

Reference Version

We want to measure the effect of each setting/heuristic in the whole setup. Hence, and due to the unfair measure mentioned above, we will not take the baseline variant without the speedup techniques and add either all techniques individually or one after another. Instead we start with a fully optimized version without heuristics and only change the parameters currently under investigation. So when testing lower bounds, for example, we will disable the lower bounds for each of the four criteria separately and look in detail at the effect of using different ways to obtain lower bounds on the number of interchanges (from different graphs and with different options to the algorithm determining lower bounds).

Our reference version uses the optimal setting among our parameters for lower bounds, goal-direction and priority queue type and no heuristics at all, thus delivering optimal quality at the best possible speed. Throughout this chapter, the base version will be marked with a star (★) in all tables in which it appears.

9.5 Advanced Pareto Dominance

9.5.1 Pareto to Relaxed Pareto to Advanced Pareto

In this section, we will specify the applied versions of *Pareto dominance*, *relaxed Pareto dominance*, and *advanced Pareto dominance* as introduced in Chapter 2.3.3. We look at the following criteria c_{iA} of a connection A:

- travel time ($c_1 = time$),

- number of interchanges ($c_2 = ic$),

- price ($c_3 = price$), and

- reliability of interchanges ("security"[i], cf. Section 6.3) ($c_4 = sec$).

---

[i]We did not want to confuse the reader using *rel* for reliability and the relaxation functions, thus the choice of *sec* for security.

9.5 Advanced Pareto Dominance

For ease of reference we restate our advanced Pareto formulation to compare two connections A and B with k criteria and r equations, $1 \leq i \leq r$ (recall that $\preccurlyeq$ stands for not greater in all and smaller in at least one of the inequalities):

$$(i) \quad \sum_{j=1}^{k} \alpha_{c_j}^i c_{jA} + rel_i(A,B) \preccurlyeq \sum_{j=1}^{k} \alpha_{c_j}^i c_{jB} \quad (9.1)$$

Pareto Dominance (P) To formulate Pareto dominance in Formulation 9.1, we use the parameters in Table 9.7 with $k = 4$ and $r = 4$. We have $\alpha_{c_j}^i = 1$ for $i = j$ and $\alpha_{c_j}^i = 0$, otherwise.

Relaxed Pareto Dominance (R) To relax the criterion travel time to have less influence between connections the larger their time difference at departure or arrival is, we use the following function (cf. Section 2.3.1):

$$rel_{time}(A,B) = \frac{time_A}{2 \cdot time_B} \cdot \min\{|d_A - d_B|, |a_A - a_B|, \omega(A,B)\} \quad (9.2)$$

where a_A, d_A, a_B, and d_B are the arrival and departure times of connections A and B and

$$\omega(A,B) = \begin{cases} 0 & \text{if } A \text{ overtakes } B \\ 100,000 & \text{otherwise} \end{cases}$$

to void the relaxation if A overtakes B.

To obtain relaxed Pareto dominance in Formulation 9.1, we use the parameters in Table 9.7 with $k = 4$ and $r = 4$. We have $\alpha_{c_j}^i = 1$ for $i = j$ and $\alpha_{c_j}^i = 0$, otherwise.

Note that with the relaxation term $rel_{time}(A,B) = 0$ the same parameters describe classical Pareto dominance.

Advanced Pareto Dominance (A_W) The wages W for advanced Pareto dominance according to our standard profile are the following (see also Table 9.13):

ic one interchange is worth 30 minutes ($\delta_{ic} = 30$)

cost 4 Euros per hour ($\delta_{cost} = 15$)

sec one additional minute per 1% reliability ($\delta_{sec} = -1$)

Note that, as the last criterion is to be maximized, its cost is negative. Our rule set (A_W) for advanced Pareto dominance is similar to the rule set (I) in Section 2.3.3. Except here the number of interchanges also has a wage δ_{ic} associated with it (in the second row), identical to the criteria price and reliability of interchanges. Set (A_W) uses the parameters in Table 9.8.

i	a^i_{time}	a^i_{ic}	a^i_{cost}	a^i_{sec}	$rel_i(AB)$
1	1	0	0	0	$rel_{time}(AB)$
2	δ_{ic}	1	0	0	0
3	δ_{cost}	0	1	0	0
4	δ_{sec}	0	0	1	0

Table 9.8: The coefficients a^i_c and relaxation terms $rel_i(A,B)$ in Formula 9.1 with $k = 4$ and $r = 4$ for rule set advanced Pareto dominance ($A_\mathcal{W}$).

Final Version of Advanced Pareto Dominance (A) We want to find connections almost achieving the hourly wages in multiple criteria, here criteria cost, number of interchanges, and reliability of interchanges, therfore we add a fifth (in)equality (analogously to the discussion in Section 2.3.3). Thus, we have $k = 4$ and $r = 5$.

Additionally, the compensation for the difference in departure and arrival time might depend on all criteria instead of just one criterion. To that end we will use the following relaxation function for a suitable $\gamma > 0$:

$$rel_5(A,B) = \gamma \cdot \frac{\sum_{j=1}^{k} a^i_{c_j} A_{c_j}}{\sum_{j=1}^{k} a^i_{c_j} B_{c_j}} \cdot \min\{|d_A - d_B|, |a_A - a_B|, \omega(A,B)\} \qquad (9.3)$$

This function is placed in the fifth equation and replaces the relaxation $rel_{time}(A,B)$ previously in the first equation.

Our rule set (A) for advanced Pareto dominance (similar to rule set (III) in Section 2.3.3) uses the parameters in Table 9.9.

We will use rule set (A) as our base version and fall back on rule set ($A_\mathcal{W}$) only for a special consideration. Namely, when comparing different sets of wages as previewed in Section 2.4, as we want the relaxation in the first criterion only for that purpose.

9.5.2 Tests with Dominance

In this section, we will test the influence of the different definitions of dominance. We will look at the combination of criteria, and of some of the rows in rule set (A). Additionally,

i	a^i_{time}	a^i_{ic}	a^i_{cost}	a^i_{sec}	$rel_i(AB)$
1	1	0	0	0	0
2	0	1	0	0	0
3	δ_{cost}	0	1	0	0
4	δ_{sec}	0	0	1	0
5	1	$\overline{\delta}_{ic}$	$\overline{\delta}_{cost}$	$\overline{\delta}_{sec}$	$rel_5(AB)$

Table 9.9: The coefficients a^i_c and relaxation terms $rel_i(A,B)$ in Formula 9.1 with $k = 4$ and $r = 5$ for rule set (A).

9.5 Advanced Pareto Dominance

we will examine different wage sets applying rule set ($A_\mathcal{W}$) for our standard customer, a businessman or a handicapped person traveling in a wheelchair.

9.5.2.1 Pareto Vs. Relaxed Pareto Vs. Advanced Pareto

We compared the profiles Pareto (P), relaxed Pareto (R), and advanced Pareto (A) (see Table 9.10). Relaxing the criterion travel time from (P) to (R) increases the runtime by 15% and the number of all significant operations by nearly 9% and results in 50% more connections. As expected, advanced Pareto is much faster, it requires only one sixth or seventh of the runtime, respectively. Besides, it determines less connections. The other profiles calculate 4 (relaxed Pareto) or nearly 3 (Pareto) times as many optima in the end, but filtered according to advanced Pareto dominance, advanced is (of course) the best. The quality for (R) is only worse in 13.5% of the queries, whereas (P) is worse in 72.12%.

Since (P) disregards alternatives created by the relaxations, its poor quality was to be excepted. The fifth equation protects connections that achieve desired wages if we combine more than one criterion and thus creates new optima. This and the differences between the relaxations in (R) and (A) explain the discrepancies between those two versions.

9.5.2.2 Influence of the Criteria

In this section we want to measure the share of computational complexity of each of the criteria. To this end we either activated or deactivated the criteria price, reliability of interchanges and number of interchanges (see Table 9.11). Of course, it is not reasonable to deactivate criterion travel time. We observe that the number of advanced Pareto optima decreases as we deactivate criteria.

Number of interchanges ic
Toggling the criterion ic only (odd rows and their subsequent rows), the number of optima is less affected, than toggling any other of the criteria. The biggest difference is together with

Profile	Optima avg	Runtime avg in ms	ratio in %	PQ extracts avg	ratio in %	Labels created avg	ratio in %
Pareto	22.48	2,466.08	100.00	192,178	100.00	305,426	100.00
relaxed	33.57	2,857.06	115.85	209,140	108.83	331,947	108.68
*advanced	8.45	412.14	16.71	57,926	30.14	90,921	29.77

Table 9.10: The influence of using profiles Pareto (P), relaxed Pareto (R), or advanced Pareto (A) for dominance testing. Runtime, number of significant operations and the average number of solutions.

#	Criteria				Optima	Runtime		PQ extracts		Labels created	
	time	price	rel	ic	avg	avg in ms	ratio in %	avg in k	ratio in %	avg in k	ratio in %
1★	✓	✓	✓	✓	8.45	412.1	100.0	57.93	100.0	90.92	100.0
2	✓	✓	✓		8.20	507.3	123.1	72.33	124.9	106.14	116.7
3	✓	✓		✓	6.49	219.8	53.3	34.87	60.2	54.74	60.2
4	✓	✓			5.07	143.9	34.9	28.47	49.2	42.35	46.6
5	✓		✓	✓	4.67	121.6	29.5	20.61	35.6	33.15	36.5
6	✓		✓		4.39	138.4	33.6	25.73	44.4	39.66	43.6
7	✓			✓	3.82	71.4	17.3	11.01	19.0	17.72	19.5
8	✓				3.11	71.6	17.4	11.04	19.1	18.17	20.0

Table 9.11: The influence of toggling the criteria ticket cost (price), reliability (rel), and number of interchanges (ic). Runtime, number of significant operations, and the average number of solutions.

time and price (from #3 to #4), where we get 1.42 optima less without interchanges, in all other combinations the difference is only 0.71, 0.28, or 0.25 optima.

Interestingly, *time* and *price* is the only combination, where enabling *ic* increases the runtime (by about 55%), for all other combinations the additional criterion *ic* speeds up the search. This is due to the fact that travel time and reliability of interchanges are correlated with the number of interchanges, whereas the price is not.

Additionally, *ic* is severely limited to a range of usually no more than 2 to 5 different values for the optimal results to a given query. There are no queries for which one optimal connection is a direct one and another one has 7 interchanges.

Reliability of interchanges *rel* and ticket cost *price*

The combinations *time*+*price* (#4) and *time*+*rel* (#6) have nearly identical runtime, so *price* and *rel* appear to be equally complicated. However, disabling only *rel* (#3) in the standard version speeds up the search by 46%, whereas disabling *price* (#5) nets us over 70% due to the correlation with *ic* that only *rel* exhibits.

There are not as many additional optima for *rel* (e.g. 0.85 from #7 to #5 or 1.96 from #3 to #1) as for *price* (e.g. 2.67 from #7 to #3 or 3.78 from #5 to #1). However, some of the latter originate again from the missing correlation with criterion *ic*, as seen above (e.g. 1.42 additional optima from #4 to #3).

9.5.2.3 Other Criteria

We introduced the search for special offers and the criterion sleeping time in night trains in Chapter 6. Here, we want to answer the question: How does the performance in the respective sections relate to that observed in this section? In Section 9.1 and Section 9.2, we

9.5 Advanced Pareto Dominance

used relaxed Pareto dominance with three or four criteria, therefore the runtimes have to be compared to our relaxed Pareto experiment (cf. Table 9.10 in the previous section).

Comparison to the Search for Special Offers In Section 6.2 we discussed the search for special tariffs, discounts or fix prices. The tests were run using three real criteria (time, number of interchanges, and price) and artificial ones (extendibility to a connection eligible for a certain special offer). The results were presented in Section 9.1. The approx. 170k priority queue extractions and a runtime of 1.7 seconds are about 80% of the priority queue operations and 60% of the runtime of the relaxed Pareto reference version with our four criteria.

Comparison to the Search for Night Trains The search for night trains introduces a different fourth criterion in Section 6.4. The required runtime as observed in Section 9.2 was comparable, albeit slightly faster, as the criterion sleeping time is easier to handle than the criterion reliability of interchanges. There are much less connections "protected" during dominance due to their sleeping time, than there are differences in the reliability score high enough to warrant considering more alternatives.

9.5.2.4 Influence of the "Rows"

In rule set (A) we have five rows ($r = 5$). Instead of measuring the impact of the criteria as in the previous section, we now want to have a closer look at the influence of the "rows" in advanced Pareto dominance. We give runtime and the numbers of significant operations without row 5 (w/o 5), without rows 3+4 (w/o 3+4) and for rows 1 or 5 only in Table 9.12. Note that we have to change to the relaxation term rel_{time} instead of zero in the first row, if row 5 with the relaxation term rel_5 is disabled.

We observe that the variants w/o 5 and w/o 3+4 have a worse quality for about half of the queries, but w/o 3+4 misses double the amount of optimal connections. Not surprisingly

Rows	Runtime avg	Runtime ratio in %	PQ extracts avg	PQ extracts ratio in %	Labels created avg	Labels created ratio in %	Quality loss conn in %	Quality loss query in %
all★	413.53	100.0	57,926	100.0	90,921	100.0	-	-
w/o 5	350.64	84.8	52,169	90.1	82,029	90.2	15.6	49.4
w/o 3+4	232.28	56.2	37,375	64.5	58,662	64.5	28.2	54.6
only 5	143.98	34.8	26,689	46.1	40,843	44.9	64.5	79.2
only 1	71.6	17.4	11,037	19.1	18,168	20.0	69.7	83.6

Table 9.12: The influence of the rows in advanced Pareto dominance (A). Runtime, number of significant operations, the average number of solutions and quality loss in connections (conn) and queries (query).

wage	unit	Basic profile $\mathcal{W}$	Business customer $\mathcal{B}$	Handicapped person $\mathcal{H}$
δ_{ic}	min / ic	30	10	120
δ_{sec}	min / %	-1	-0.5	-2
δ_{cost}	min / €	15	2.4	15
$\overline{\delta}_{cost}$	€ / h	4	25	4

Table 9.13: Differing wages for our profiles standard ($\mathcal{W}$), business customer ($\mathcal{B}$) and handicapped person ($\mathcal{H}$) in advanced Pareto dominance ($A_\mathcal{W}$).

after that observation, w/o 3+4 is also much faster.

In variants *only 1* and *only 5* about two thirds of optimal connections are missing and for for fifths of the queries we have worse quality. Both variants share similar scores but found different connections. Optimizing the weighted sum in *only 5* is about twice as demanding as optimizing only the first row with travel time and the other relaxation term.

9.5.2.5 Advanced Pareto Dominance with Different Wages

Next, we will examine different wage profiles for rule set ($A_\mathcal{W}$). Besides our standard profile ($\mathcal{W}$) we will look at profiles suited for a business customer ($\mathcal{B}$) or a handicapped person ($\mathcal{H}$).

Profile Businessman We assume that the proposed wages $\mathcal{W}$ are suitable to find attractive connections for most passengers. However, if we know more about a customer in advance, say a businessman with a much higher priority on the travel time than on anything else, we may raise the importance of time in our wages, for example changing to the business customer profile $\mathcal{B}$ in Table 9.13. Now we will spend at most 10 minutes to save one interchange instead of 30 minutes.

Using the advanced Pareto dominance profile ($A_\mathcal{W}$) with either of the two profiles and filtering the resulting connections according to profile $\mathcal{B}$, the quality of the result set is identical. Of course, the result sets are not identical in the first place, but there is no advanced Pareto optimal connection in one set that is not also present in the other with respect to profile $\mathcal{B}$.

Profile		Runtime avg in ms	Runtime ratio in %	PQ extracts avg	PQ extracts ratio in %	Labels created avg	Labels created ratio in %
business	$\mathcal{B}$	156.97	100.00	25,111	100.00	39,977	100.00
standard	$\mathcal{W}$	387.06	246.59	53,688	213.80	84,528	211.44

Table 9.14: Searching for connections for customer businessman using different wage profiles and rule set ($A_\mathcal{W}$). Runtime and number of significant operations.

Profile		Runtime		PQ extracts		Labels created		Quality loss	
		avg	ratio in %	avg	ratio in %	avg	ratio in %	conn in %	query in %
handicap	$\mathcal{H}$	473.62	100.00	61,346	100.00	97,141	100.00	-	-
standard	$\mathcal{W}$	387.06	81.72	53,688	87.52	84,528	87.02	14.34	38.74

Table 9.15: Searching for connections for a handicapped customer using different wage profiles and rule set ($A_\mathcal{W}$). Runtime, number of significant operations, and quality loss in connections (conn) and queries (query).

On the other hand, Whereas the runtime decreases significantly for the business customer profile, as the search does not have to provide that many cheaper or other alternatives (cf. Table 9.14). With the standard wage profile more than double the runtime is required. A search with wage profile $\mathcal{B}$ is not more complicated than a two criteria search, e.g. *time+rel* or *time+price* as seen in Section 9.5.2.2. With 4.95 optima on average we are in a similar range as well.

Our approach does not have to be informed about the customer, it will always find the best results for the customers. Additionally, as demonstrated, it may profit from advance knowledge about the preferences of certain customers and disregard alternatives that are not interesting for these anyway.

Profile Handicapped Although we are quite confident in our least common parameter set, there might still be customers that are not optimally served with it. Think of elderly people, a handicapped person in a wheelchair or a class of children on a school trip. These customers might want to put greater emphasis on the number of interchanges and request a higher reliability of interchanges in order to avoid the hassle of a missed connection. A suitable set of parameters $\mathcal{H}$ is given in Table 9.13. Contrary to the business customer whose wages (or more precisely their absolute values) were all smaller than in the standard profile, we have increased the importance of two of the criteria. So we can no longer expect to find all attractive alternatives for this group of costumers using our standard wages.

In Table 9.15 we see a comparison between the searches with wages $\mathcal{W}$ or $\mathcal{H}$. The runtime increases by about 20% for the more complicated wages. Instead of 7.7 optimal results, there are 9.13 optimal results on average. Searching with standard wages we miss one seventh of the optimal connections and produce worse results for nearly 40% of the queries.

This quality drawback can be overcome by adding a special search mode to the user interface. Standard wages are used for all standard queries, should a person in a wheelchair query for a connection, the special search mode uses wage profile $\mathcal{H}$. Note that a search for a connection accommodating a person in a wheelchair might even restrict the search to trains which are accessible in a wheelchair providing ramps or lifts at the stations.

Strategy	Runtime avg in ms	Runtime ratio in %	PQ extracts until 1st in k	PQ extracts avg in k	PQ extracts ratio in %	Created avg in k	Created ratio in %	Dominated node in k	Dominated term in k
none	14,532	100.0	221.4	1,160	100	1,603	100	419	-
goal	11,643	80.1	9.8	1,002	86	1,484	93	474	-
domTerm	6,720	46.2	221.4	753	65	764	48	306	82.7
domTerm LB	2,620	18.0	246.2	290	25	431	27	117	24.1
both★	412	2.8	7.3	58	5	91	6	22	11.1

Table 9.16: The influence of the strategies goal-direction (*goal*) and domination by terminal (*domTerm*). Runtime, number of significant operations, extractions from the priority queue before the first connection was found and number of labels dominated at the node level (node) and by terminal labels (term).

9.6 Goal-Direction and Domination by Terminal

We have seen in Chapter 8 that a multi-criteria Dijkstra may profit from two fundamental speedup techniques, namely goal-direction (*goal*) and *domination by labels at the terminal*. The latter was tested either without (*domTerm*) or with lower bounds (*domTerm LB*).

In this section, we use *realistic assumptions* on journeys through Germany to be able to obtain reasonable runtime and numbers of significant operations without those essential techniques. These assumptions are:

- No journey is longer than 36 hours.[ii]

- And no journey has more than 10 interchanges.

Additionally, once a first connection C_1 with travel time $time_1$ is found during search, we set the maximum allowed travel time to the minimum of $2 \cdot time_1 + 100$ minutes and 36 hours. Every partial connection exceeding these bounds (or guaranteed to exceed these bounds, since its current value plus lower bound exceeds them) is dropped and no longer regarded. Without those assumptions we reach query times of several minutes, as already mentioned for our baseline variant in Section 9.4.2.3. Note that these assumptions are not necessary during regular searches, we only use them to demonstrate the effects in this section.

Toggling Goal-Direction and Domination by Terminal Enabling none or only one of the techniques has a tremendous effect, as depicted in Table 9.16. We limited the processing time to 60s, which was not necessary for our standard algorithm using both strategies. But without *domination by labels at the terminal* the search was stopped 196 (*none*) and 68 (*goal*) times, respectively. Except in the stopped runs, where no or less results were produced, the quality was identical.

[ii]The bound of 36 hours is also used for Dial's data structure.

Of the created labels 24% (*both*), 26% (*domTerm*), 27% (*domTerm LB*), and 32% (*none*) were dominated on the node level. After about 220,000 extractions from the priority queue on average the first solution was found without *goal*. With it, less than 10,000 extractions were required. Although producing the first result faster, strategy *goal* only marginally improved the runtime. This improvement is based on more dominations on the node level due to the better creation sequence of labels with goal-direction. 7% (*domTerm*) or 6% (*domTerm LB*) of the created labels were dominated by labels at the terminal, combined with *goal* even 12% were dominated, as the first results for domination were found much earlier.

While *domTerm* alone improved the search speed by a factor of two, using lower bounds for this technique (*domTerm LB*) results in another factor of 2.5. Together with *goal-direction*, runtime decreases further to below one sixth.

These two fundamental techniques are an essential step to making multi-criteria search possible in online-scenarios, as they speed up the search by a factor of 35, from way over ten seconds to less than a second.

9.7 Lower Bounds

In this section, we will investigate the effectiveness of lower bounds. We will look in detail at the different station graphs and interchange graphs to determine lower bounds on travel time, number of interchanges, ticket cost and reliability of interchanges. These lower bounds are used for *goal-direction* (cf. Section 8.3) and *domination by terminal* (cf. Section 8.4), as well as for pruning the search space (cf. Section 8.5.5). We have already seen, in the previous section, that the first two techniques are essential for multi-criteria search. *Goal-direction* is impossible without lower bounds and *domination by terminal* with lower bounds is much more efficient than without them.

9.7.1 Station Graphs

Lower bounds on the travel time can be determined from the different kinds of station graphs as introduced in Section 8.5.1. The algorithm to obtain these bounds can either be single direction or bidirectional (B) without or with (T) triangle inequalities (cf. Section 8.5.5). A pruning step (P) using biconnected components (cf. Section 8.5.5 also) may be used additionally. Results for the test-runs can be found in Table 9.17.

Using the different station graphs, we have nearly identical runtimes. The bigger graphs need longer for the preprocessing but result in better lower bounds, thus reducing the number of significant operations. Since stations are represented by more than one node in all but the *standard* station graph, obtaining pruning information and lower bounds during the search from the extended station graphs is also more costly than on the standard graph, not only the calculation time for the lower bounds. The bidirectional algorithm in itself only yields an average decrease of 3 or 4 operations and quite naturally slightly more than doubles the processing time on the station graph. Thus, runtime even increases. Combined with triangle inequalities the overall saving improves to about 3%. The biconnected components pruning contained in the runtime of the station graphs takes about 8.2ms on the standard graph. There, it enhances the saving to about 10%.

Pruning takes 10.7ms on the *fourhours* graph. We get the lowest number of significant operations for using a bidirectional Dijkstra algorithm with triangle inequalities and biconnected components pruning on that station graph. However, this is not enough to compensate for the 52.6ms increase in preprocessing time over the same calculation on the *standard* graph.

Ticket Cost For the minimal investment of 3.6ms additional preprocessing time on the station graph for ticket cost we determine lower bounds on ticket costs as well (see Section 8.5.1). These bounds save nearly three quarters of the runtime, over 1.2 seconds (see Table 9.18). This reward is so high because ticket cost depends on the travel distance and used train classes and is not related to travel time.

However, we do not intend to apply pruning based on the ticket cost alone. Consequently, we did not test any extended version of obtaining lower bounds on the ticket cost (e.g. bidirectional search on the ticket cost graph).

9.7.2 Interchange Graph

We used the different versions of our interchange graph (presented in Section 8.5.2) to obtain lower bounds on the number of interchanges. The preprocessing on the interchange graph with unified routes is nearly 50% faster than on the standard graph derived from train routes (interestingly the graph has only 30% less nodes and 40% less edges). As on both graphs

SG type	options	Prepro- cessing in ms	Runtime avg in ms	Runtime ratio in %	PQ extracts avg	PQ extracts ratio in %	Labels created avg	Labels created ratio in %
standard	-	3.6	710.61	100.00	92,860	100.00	149,225	100.00
sixhours	-	18.6	708.63	99.72	90,423	97.38	145,442	97.46
rushhours	-	18.7	707.82	99.61	90,172	97.11	145,085	97.23
fourhours	-	27.1	725.27	102.06	89,212	96.07	143,736	96.32
standard	B	7.8	715.53	100.69	92,857	100.00	149,221	100.00
standard	BT	7.8	690.73	97.20	90,909	97.90	144,416	96.78
standard	BTP	16.0	638.32	89.83	84,742	91.26	134,479	90.12
fourhours	BTP	68.6	707.74	99.60	83,000	89.38	134,005	89.80

Options: B = bidirectional Dijkstra / T = triangle inequalities / P = biconnected comp. pruning

Table 9.17: The influence of lower bounds from the station graph. Runtime, number of significant operations, and preprocessing time on the station graph (SG).

9.7 Lower Bounds

Disabled lower bound	Runtime avg in ms	Runtime ratio in %	PQ extracts avg	PQ extracts ratio in %	Labels created avg	Labels created ratio in %
none★	412.14	100.00	57,926	100.00	90,921	100.00
ic reliability	416.69	101.10	59,185	102.17	92,989	102.27
ticket cost	1,627.05	394.78	199,291	344.04	307,418	338.12

Table 9.18: The influence of lower bounds on the reliability of interchanges obtained from the interchange graph and on ticket cost obtained form the cost graph. Runtime and number of significant operations.

the same bounds are calculated, their runtime difference is exactly the difference in the preprocessing. Combined with the better lower bounds from the *fourhours* station graph the additional 50ms of preprocessing for the lower bounds on travel time result in too small an improvement on the number of significant operations to be worthwhile, very similar to the results in the preceeding section for the expanded station graph.

Figure 9.4 illustrates the reduction in search space when using lower bounds obtained from the interchange graph. We see that the search visits fewer stations and branches less. This feature is most prominent near the conurbations Berlin and Cologne.

Speeding Up Searches on the Interchange Graph Using Pruning Information Even the unified interchange graph is about 8 times as big as our station graph, with 8.8k nodes and 22.5k edges in the station graph compared to 75k nodes and 169k edges in the interchange graph using unified routes, cf. Table 8.3 in Section 8.5.2. Consequently, preprocessing is about 7 times slower (3.6ms and 29.6ms). To improve the runtimes on this graph, we may exploit the results obtained from the preceeding lower bound computation on the station graph. All stations that are pruned in the station graph will not be visited during the search.

SG type	ICG options		Preprocessing in ms	Runtime avg in ms	Runtime ratio in %	PQ extracts avg in k	PQ extracts ratio in %	Labels created avg in k	Labels created ratio in %
std	none			638.3	100.0	84.7	100.00	134.5	100.00
std	std		57.4	462.3	72.4	57.9	68.37	90.9	67.63
std	uni		29.6	432.4	67.7	57.9	68.37	90.9	67.63
4hrs	uni		29.6	493.6	77.3	56.5	66.70	89.3	66.37
std★	uni	U	9.6	412.1	64.6	57.9	68.36	90.9	67.61
std	uni	BT	63.5	467.9	73.3	56.8	66.97	89.3	66.41
std	uni	UBT	22.8	423.1	66.3	56.7	66.97	89.3	66.41

Options: B = bidirectional Dijkstra / T = triangle inequalities / U = using pruning information

Table 9.19: The influence of lower bounds from the interchange graph. Runtime, number of significant operations, and preprocessing time on the interchange station graph (ICG).

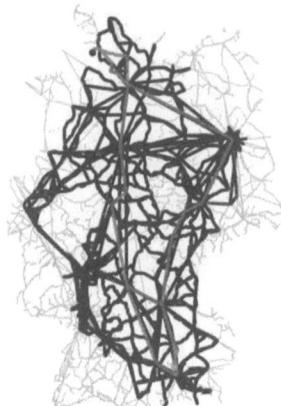 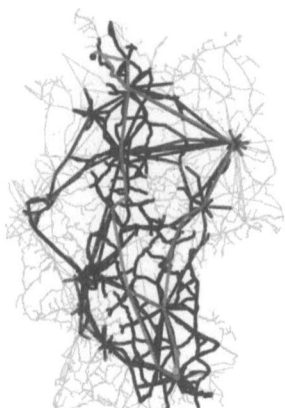

Figure 9.4: Search space without (left) and with lower bounds from the interchange graph (right) for a search from Hebertshausen (south) to Büsum (north).

Therefore, we restrict the computation on the interchange graph to the stations that were not pruned. This technique improves the runtime from 29.6ms to 9.6ms. For the bidirected version runtime could be improved from 63.5ms to 22.8ms. In both cases we are about two thirds faster. The bidirectional interchange graph Dijkstra only saves less than 2% operations, not enough to compensate for the increased preprocessing time.

The best variant spends only 9.6ms preprocessing time on determining lower bounds from the interchange graph and improves the runtime by one third.

Bounds on the Reliability of Interchanges The lower bound on the number of interchanges can be used to obtain an upper bound on the reliability of interchanges. The upper bound of μ^{ic} for the highest reliability factor μ of one interchange and a lower bound on the number of interchanges to the target ic seemed not really tight (cf. the end of Section 8.5.2). Unfortunately our suspicion was justified, we save only 2% of significant operations and 1% runtime (see Table 9.18). We use the bound nonetheless, as we need the number of interchanges as a lower bound anyway and get this tiny improvement for free.

9.7.3 Summary Lower Bounds

Lower bounds on travel time are essential for the algorithm as they enable goal-direction The best performance is the result of using a bidirectional station graph Dijkstra with triangle inequalities and biconnected component pruning on a standard station graph for lower bounds on travel time (in about 16ms) The easy to calculate lower bounds on ticket cost (below 4ms) have a high impact (reducing search time by three quarters). Using the information obtained from the station graph for travel time, lower bounds on the number of interchanges to the target can be calculated in less than 10ms on the interchange graph obtained from unified routes. We get the lower bounds on the interchange reliability for free from the lower bounds on the number of interchanges to the terminal.

The influence of the lower bounds on travel time and interchanges in comparison to the most basic version using lower bounds on the travel time from the *standard* station graph without bidirectional Dijkstra and pruning in the preprocessing can be found in the Appendix in Table B.1.

In summary, all our lower bounds can be calculated in about 30ms. The bounds for travel time and number of interchanges to the terminal are used in goal-direction (as we will see in Section 9.8.2) and lower bounds for all our criteria improve the technique to dominate labels by labels at the terminal. These decrease the average search speed from about 15 seconds (run without both of these techniques in Table 9.16) to less than 0.5 seconds.

9.8 Priority Queue

In this section we will investigate the items introduced in Section 8.8, namely different priority queue types and variants of the "smaller"- relation. Recall the smaller relation from Section 8.8.1:

$$\texttt{smaller}(A, B) : time_A + \theta \cdot lb_{time}(S_A) + \gamma \cdot ic_A < time_B + \theta \cdot lb_{time}(S_B) + \gamma \cdot ic_B.$$

Additionally, we will look at techniques reducing the number of labels in the priority queues.

9.8.1 Priority Queue Type and "Smaller"-Relation

We have already seen the effects of foregoing goal-direction (as for $\theta = 0$) cf. Table 9.16. Consequently, we will test the four priority queue types with $\theta = 1$ and $\gamma = 20$ with and without using the FIFO principle to break ties. The results can be seen in Table 9.20.

All queues with the FIFO property have the same number of significant operations since the order in which labels are processed is identical. The 4–heap requires a quarter more runtime whereas the binary and pairing heaps take over a third longer.

Without FIFO property for breaking ties, for heap data structures the details of the restructuring methods determines the evaluation order of the labels regarded as identical for the smaller relation. Although this ordering saves nearly 5% of the extract operations and over 2% of the number of created labels, it does not suffice to make the heaps competitive. The fastest heap (4–heap) still is 10% slower than Dial's data structure. Interestingly, perturbing labels with the same $\texttt{value}(\cdot)$ in Dial's data structure did not improve the number of significant operations.

PQ type		FIFO Tie-breaking	Runtime		PQ extracts		Labels created	
			avg in ms	ratio in %	avg	ratio in %	avg	ratio in %
dial ★		✓	412.14	100.00				
heap	binary	✓	560.59	136.02	57,926	100.00	90,921	100.00
	4–heap	✓	526.15	127.66				
	pairing	✓	575.06	139.53				
heap	binary		487.75	118.35	55,555	95.91	88,841	97.71
	4–heap		457.17	110.93	55,469	95.76	88,723	97.58
	pairing		527.20	127.92	55,583	95.95	89,042	97.93
	4–heap	lexi	538.28	130.61	66,876	115.45	100,177	110.18

Table 9.20: The influence of different priority queue types. The heaps were tested with and without FIFO tie-breaking. Additionally the 4–heap with lexicographic smaller relation for comparisons. Runtime and number of significant operations.

Lexicographic Lexicographic ordering seems to be a worse choice than the variants using travel time plus weighted number of interchanges as the sorting criterion. Comparing lexicographic ordering for the 4–heap with the runtime for the same heap with or without FIFO property, we observe a significant increase in the number of significant operations, over 10% in created labels and 15% to 20% in priority queue operations. The runtime is about 18% worse than without FIFO.

Due to this poorer performance we did not consider lexicographic ordering for Dial's data structure. Note that the adaption of lexicographic ordering to a value function would require the value to be something like

$$\texttt{value}(A) = (((time_A \cdot 11 + ic_A) \cdot 101) + sec_A) \cdot 201 + cost_A$$

for the reasonable upper bounds of at most 10 interchanges, 100% reliability and no more than 200€ ticket cost. So for travel times of no more than two days, a number of $2880 \cdot 11 \cdot 101 \cdot 201 \approx 640$ million buckets would be required.

Without goal-direction the performance of lexicographic ordering and weighted sum is nearly identical with a slightly lower number of significant operations and 2,588ms on average for lexicographic compared to 2,620ms for our standard smaller relation.

9.8.2 Weight for Interchanges in Goal-Direction

For the best priority queue (Dial's data structure) we tested different values for the weight of the number of interchanges ($\gamma \in \{0, 5, 10, 20, 30, 50, 300\}$). We either used the number of interchanges accumulated so far or this number plus a lower bound on the number of interchanges to the terminal. The resulting runtime and the number of significant operations are given in Table 9.21. First of all we can see that using goal-direction for the number of

Interchanges wage	goal-direction	Runtime avg in ms	ratio in %	PQ extracts avg	ratio in %	Labels created avg	ratio in %
0		479.14	100.00	69,303	100.00	102,147	100.00
5		425.78	88.86	60,921	87.90	94,977	92.98
	✓	422.66	88.21	59,576	85.96	93,113	91.16
10		419.15	87.48	60,723	87.62	94,893	92.90
	✓	416.95	87.02	58,582	84.53	91,854	89.92
20		419.25	87.50	61,116	88.19	95,539	93.53
	✓★	412.14	86.01	57,926	83.58	90,921	89.01
30		429.92	89.73	62,040	89.52	96,897	94.86
	✓	421.12	87.89	58,202	83.98	91,211	89.29
50		439.13	91.65	64,408	92.94	100,300	98.19
	✓	428.55	89.44	59,007	85.14	92,039	90.10
300		511.67	106.79	80,907	116.74	123,275	120.68
	✓	459.46	95.89	63,112	91.07	96,763	94.73

Table 9.21: The influence of different weights for the number of interchanges in the smaller relation with and without using goal-direction for interchanges as well.

interchanges as well always improves the search speed. The wage of choice seems to be $\gamma = 20$. It achieves the lowest number of labels created and extracted and likewise the fastest search times. We save about 14% of the processing time with this choice of γ.

If we choose the real large value $\gamma = 300$ we are essentially using the number of interchanges as our most important criterion in goal-direction and travel time as a secondary criterion. However, this alone does not seem to be a good move.

9.8.3 Reordering the Priority Queue

The strategy to reorder the priority queue once the first optimal connection is found was presented in Section 8.8.3. We start using goal-direction according to the criterion travel time using the weight $\gamma = 20$ as determined in the previous section. As soon as the first (and fastest) connection is found, we change the ordering in the priority queue. For the remainder of the search we use $\gamma = 300$, making the number of interchanges the dominant criterion and travel time the secondary one. In Table 9.22 we see the resulting runtimes and the number of significant operations in comparison to the variants using either $\gamma = 20$ or $\gamma = 300$ throughout the whole search.

Naturally, the standard version and *reorder* find the first and fastest solution at the same time. When the first solution is found, about 19,000 labels are stored in the priority queue. These have to be reordered according to the new sorting criterion. The second result in *reorder* is obtained earlier than in the standard version. Remember that these results are not identical, *reorder* determines the results with the least number of interchanges as result

Weight for interchanges γ	Runtime avg in ms	ratio in %	PQ extracts 1st	2nd	avg	ratio in %	Labels created avg	ratio in %
20★	412.14	100.00	7,284	9,772	57,926	100.00	90,921	100.00
20 ↦ 300	448.78	108.89	7,284	8,738	61,283	105.80	94,733	104.19
300	459.46	111.48	3,081	5,070	63,112	108.95	96,763	106.43

Table 9.22: Strategy reordering the priority queue compared to the versions with the initial and final weight for interchanges. Runtime and number of significant operations in total and until the first and second optimal connection were found.

number two. In comparison the version using goal-direction according to the number of interchanges from the beginning, finds its first (and second) connection much earlier. In spite of that the total runtime is higher. Even with the additional cost for reordering, variant *reorder* achieves a runtime between the two. Unfortunately, goal-direction according to the number of interchanges, either completely or after reordering does not pay off, as the number of significant operations, as well as runtime, is worse than that of the standard version.

9.8.4 Decreasing the Number of Labels in the PQ

In this section we will study the techniques to skip departure nodes (*skip*) presented in Section 8.6.2, bypass departure nodes (*bypass*) from Section 8.6.3 and avoid inserting minimum labels (*avoid*) introduced in Section 8.8.4. Runtime and the number of significant operations can be found in Table 9.23.

Techniques *skip* and *bypass* Both do not enter departure nodes into the priority queue, therefore they have nearly identical numbers of extract operations. However, the labels are still created in *skip*. Even around 4% more are created as the sequence of labels is different from the extraction sequence in the standard version. Once *skip* decides to take a train, its departure event is processed immediately after the entering edge. Since the departure has

Strategy	Labels not inserted avg	in %	Runtime avg in ms	ratio in %	PQ extracts avg	ratio in %	created avg	ratio in %
none★	-	0.00	412.14	100.00	57,926	100.00	90,921	100.00
skip	21,052	36.34	434.37	105.39	40,304	69.58	94,633	104.08
bypass	-	0.00	370.71	89.95	40,624	70.13	74,057	81.45
avoid	8,952	15.45	410.14	99.52	49,054	84.68	91,106	100.20

Table 9.23: The influence of techniques: skip departure nodes, bypass departure nodes and avoid inserting minimum labels. Runtime, number of significant operations, and the number of labels that were not inserted into the priority queue.

one interchange more, in the standard version another label might be processed in between.

Bypass only saves 10% of the runtime although saving roughly 30% of the extractions and 18.5% of the label creations. This is due to the fact, that the combined edge types are harder to evaluate than e.g. a stay-in-train edge. It is simply always available and no checks have to be performed and only the travel time and nothing else of the new label has to be updated. Consequently, the average work per label creation or edge inspection increases.

Technique *avoid* Avoiding about 15% of the operations on the priority queue does not result in reduced computation time. This is due to the additional comparisons and the fact that using a FIFO queue for the labels that are equal or better than the current minimum in the queue is not much different from (and thus not faster than) determining and using the right FIFO queue in an array of FIFO queues in Dial's data structure.

9.9 Reliability of Interchanges

The required effort to search for more reliable connections has been investigated together with toggling the criteria number of interchanges and ticket cost in Section 9.5.2.2. In this section we will look at the influence of different numbers of equivalence classes for the criterion (as introduced in Section 6.3.3) and of setting the maximal effective reliability for a single interchange to values between 90% and 99%.

9.9.1 Number of Equivalence Classes

We discretized the float for reliability of interchanges to differing numbers of equivalence classes (10, 25, 50, 100, 500, and 1000), see Table 9.24 for results. The quality was compared to the version with 1,000 equivalence classes. For reference we also inserted a version without reliability as an advanced Pareto criterion (cf. Section 9.5.2.2).

Equivalence classes	Runtime		PQ extracts		Labels created		Quality loss	
	avg in ms	ratio in %	avg	ratio in %	avg	ratio in %	conn in %	query in %
1,000	433.10	100.00	59,272	100.00	93,071	100.00	-	-
500	432.84	99.94	59,173	99.83	92,914	99.83	0.04	0.26
100★	412.14	95.16	57,926	97.73	90,937	97.71	0.33	1.86
50	408.37	94.29	57,003	96.17	89,565	96.23	1.78	9.16
25	400.32	92.43	55,439	93.53	87,300	93.80	4.09	18.18
10	353.25	81.56	50,632	85.42	80,035	85.99	8.13	28.46
-	219.83	50.76	34,873	58.84	54,744	58.82	28.93	60.04

Table 9.24: The number of equivalence classes for the criterion reliability of interchanges. Runtime, number of significant operations, the average number of solutions and quality loss in connections (conn) and queries (query).

Maximal reliability $\hat{\mu}$ in %	Runtime avg in ms	Runtime ratio in %	PQ extracts avg	PQ extracts ratio in %	Labels created avg	Labels created ratio in %
90	334.90	81.26	48,756	84.17	76,415	84.05
91	343.65	83.38	50,054	86.41	78,542	86.38
92	359.40	87.20	51,183	88.36	80,340	88.36
93	370.63	89.93	52,894	91.31	83,014	91.30
94	383.34	93.01	54,192	93.55	85,036	93.53
95	395.21	95.89	55,648	96.07	87,369	96.09
96★	412.14	100.00	57,926	100.00	90,921	100.00
97	449.61	109.09	60,763	104.90	95,577	105.12
98	483.28	117.26	64,014	110.51	100,840	110.91
99	556.01	134.91	69,501	119.98	110,100	121.09

Table 9.25: Varying the maximal effective reliability $\hat{\mu}$ for an interchange. Runtime and number of significant operations compared to the standard version with $\hat{\mu} = 96\%$.

Enabling quality (with 10 classes) gives as the biggest improvement in quality as well as the highest runtime increase. More classes lead to a higher number of significant operations and longer runtime. Quality also increases monotonically. Note that the decrease in the number of significant operations is all but exactly the same for priority queue extractions and label creations.

We loose optimal connections in additional 10% of the queries when changing from 100 to 50 to 25 to 10 classes. However, setting the number of classes to 500 or even 1,000 is costly but does hardly pay off in quality. On the one hand, the runtime improvement from 100 to 50 classes is small and quality drops significantly. Increasing above 100 classes, on the other hand, is not worthwhile at all, quality improves only slightly, yet runtime increases by over 20ms. Thus, we decided eventually to go with the natural choice of 100 equivalence classes for the criterion,

9.9.2 Maximal Effective Reliability

Recall the definition of the *maximal effective reliability* $\hat{\mu}$ and the truncated reliability function $sec'(\cdot)$ in Section 6.3.3.2. We tested the values $\hat{\mu} \in [90\%, 99\%]$ and compared to $\hat{\mu} = 96\%$ as the reference version (see Table 9.25). As the quality measurement depends on the definition of reliability of interchanges, it does not make sense to compare the quality of test runs based on differing definitions, therefore we restrict this comparison to runtime and the number of significant operations.

For the step size of 1% of $\hat{\mu}$ we observe the following increases in the number of significant operations and runtime. The increase in the number of significant operations for $\hat{\mu} \in [90\%, 95\%]$ is between 2% and 3% runtime increases between 2% and 4%. From $\hat{\mu} = 95\%$ to $\hat{\mu} = 96\%$ the number of significant operations and runtime increase by 4%, between

$\hat{\mu} = 96\%$ and $\hat{\mu} = 98\%$ the number of significant operations increases by ca. 5% and runtime by 9%. The final step towards $\hat{\mu} = 99\%$ costs nearly 10% significant operations and 17% more runtime.

The higher increase in both significant operations and runtime for the later steps is due to the increasing differences between $\theta(\hat{\mu}+1\%) - \theta(\hat{\mu})$ for bigger $\hat{\mu}$. As already mentioned when introducing $\hat{\mu}$, this increase is 1 to 2 minutes from 90% to to 96% and as much as 3,6, or even 15 minutes in the following steps. In the test, whether label a is dominated by label b, we always use the maximal effective reliability for the last interchange of a. Selecting higher $\hat{\mu}$ more connections are "protected" from dominance due to a still possible improvement in their reliability rating. As the aforementioned differences in $\theta(\hat{\mu})$ grow, so do the number of protected alternatives and, thus, the increases in runtime and the number of significant operations.

9.10 Heuristics

In this section we will evaluate the following heuristics: *bitonic search*, *mass transportation*, *routes blocking*, *important stations*, the insertion of *shortcuts* into the graph, and various combinations. Each of these techniques may fail to find all optimal connections, therefore we will present the quality loss in all remaining tables.

9.10.1 Bitonic Search

The results for the heuristic *bitonic search* (introduced in Section 8.10) are shown in Table 9.26. Of more than 40,000 connections found in the standard version, only 2% are not bitonic, e.g. use the products ICE, IC, RE, IC or ICE, IC, ICE in that order. Exactly the same number of optimal connections are lost. Interestingly they are distrubuted over nearly 400 queries, therefore the quality loss in queries is 7.8%. The *bitonic* heuristic actually finds alternatives for the forbidden non-bitonic connections, but these are worse than the bitonic connections. The search for these alternatives even results in a tiny bit more operations (around 0.2%) and, together with the (albeit quick) bookkeeping and testing for the bitonic property, this heuristic is 0.5% slower.

The positive result is that most optimal connections are indeed bitonic and missing the non-bitonic ones might be acceptable. So instead of a speed-up we gained a structural insight that may prove useful for the future. Should bidirectional search for multi-criteria-optimization become a feasible option, bitonic search might improve the approach.

9.10.2 Mass Transportation

The heuristic prohibiting leaving means of mass transportation at a station under certain conditions (cf. Section 8.9.1) produces the results in Table 9.26. The variants based on the number of interchanges in mass transportation to this station (*ic*) is by far the fastest as it rejects the most exits of all variants. Unfortunately its quality is really bad. If the decision is based on the travel time (*time*) we still save nearly one third of the runtime but we still loose quality for more than a third of the queries.

Using advanced Pareto dominance (*advP*) is by far the best variant of this heuristic, although still lacking optimal connections for one seventh of the queries. The additional test for advanced Pareto dominance, for which label lists at the stations have to be maintained, is quite costly. Despite saving about 30% of label creations and 20% of the operations on the priority queue, the runtime improvement stays below 10%.

Experienced quality loss. For example, in a connection ICE, mass transportation, IC the alternatives using different subways in the half hour available for traveling from the arrival station of the ICE to the departure station of the IC, usually do not create interesting alternatives. Provided the alternatives of using mass transportation do not differ in travel time (for *time*) or the number of interchanges (for *ic*) between two stations, the first possibility to arrive at a station using mass transportation will always dominate all later arrivals with mass transportation from the same previous non mass transportation edge/label except in *advP*. But only as long as interchange reliability is not an issue, this is correct. However, if we consider interchange reliability, taking a later subway may result in less buffer time at the departure station of the second train therefore a balanced distribution of buffer times maximizes the interchange reliability in the example from above. The reliability of interchanges is only covered by variant *advP*, hence that variant attains the best quality.

9.10.3 Routes Blocking

Table 9.27 shows the data for the heuristic disallowing the use of trains that belong to routes already used. The variants maintain lists of allowed routes for the individual stations (*station*), for each of the train edges arriving at a station (*edge*), or for distinct arrival labels at a station (*label*) as introduced in Section 8.9.2.

| Heuristic | | Runtime | | PQ extracts | | Labels created | | Quality loss | |
type	variant	avg in ms	ratio in %	avg	ratio in %	avg	ratio in %	conn in %	query in %
none★	-	412.1	100.0	57,926	100.0	90,921	100.0	-	-
bitonic	-	414.1	100.5	58,050	100.2	91,059	100.2	2.1	7.8
mass	ic	190.8	46.3	26,436	45.6	36,261	39.9	40.1	63.8
mass	time	278.4	67.5	38,610	66.7	54,434	59.9	14.0	35.0
mass	advP	378.6	91.9	45,479	78.5	65,122	71.6	3.5	14.2

Table 9.26: Heuristics bitonic search (*bitonic*) and mass transportation (*mass*) in its variants. Runtime, number of significant operations, and quality loss in connections (conn) and queries (query).

9.10 Heuristics

Heuristic variant	Runtime avg in ms	Runtime ratio in %	PQ extracts avg	PQ extracts ratio in %	Labels created avg	Labels created ratio in %	Quality loss conn in %	Quality loss query in %
off★	412.14	100.00	57,926	100.00	90,921	100.00	-	-
station	123.20	29.89	19,391	33.48	25,370	27.90	51.38	70.92
edge	302.10	73.30	42,866	74.00	63,524	69.87	17.39	34.42
label	398.09	96.59	48,865	84.36	75,390	82.92	0.76	3.52

Table 9.27: Different variants of the routes blocking heuristic. Runtime, number of significant operations, and quality loss in connections (conn) and queries (query).

Variant *station* misses optimal connections for twice as many queries as *edge*. The *station* variant looses half of the optimal connections, *edge* only one sixth. The only variant with acceptable quality is *label* with less than 1% lost optimal connections and only 3.5% negatively affected queries. The variants *station* and *edge* save ca. 70% or 30% of runtime and the number of significant operations, respectively. Although *label* decreases the number of significant operations by over 15%, its speed-up is less than 4%.

Intended only as a reference model, the poor quality of *station* is not surprising at all. It is totally unaware of the way used to a station and allows each leaving route to be used only once. Both the interval instead of a single starting point and the multi-criteria approach do not harmonize with the simple idea behind this heuristic in its basic version.

Variant *edge* disregards the exact characteristics of reaching a station and only distinguishes the different last trains to it. We overcome all these problems with version *label*. Now each partial connection reaching a station may continue its travel and is not impeded by the fact that another partial connection has already reached the station (as in *station*) or that another partial connection ending with the same train (as in *edge*) has reached the station.

Eliminating alternatives using a later train serving the same route only minimally reduces the quality. Taking the later train increases the reliability of interchanges score at that station. However, only if the later train still permits a reasonable connection, an optimum is lost. Remember the number of minutes θ after which the maximal possible reliability rating is achieved for an interchange. We could improve the heuristic by allowing all trains of a route upto and including the first train departing at least θ minutes after the arrival at that station. Thus, taking an even later train belonging to that route would not increase interchange reliability. Unfortunately, the bookkeeping already requires enough additional calculation time to nearly void the positive effect on the runtime that we do not expect a remaining runtime improvement after modifying the heuristic and yet increasing the effort involved.

Combining Mass Transportation and Routes Blocking

We combined the *mass transportation* (versions *time* (MT) and *advanced Pareto* (MP), introduced in Section 8.9.1) and *routes* (versions *edge* (RE) and *label* (RL), introduced in Section 8.9.2). The results are presented in Table 9.28.

Heuristic		Runtime		PQ extracts		Labels created		Quality loss	
mass	routes	avg in ms	ratio in %	avg	ratio in %	avg	ratio in %	conn in %	query in %
off★	off	412.14	100.00	57,926	100.00	90,921	100.00	-	-
time	edge	227.29	55.15	30,498	52.65	41,429	45.57	24.61	46.92
time	label	290.31	70.44	33,013	56.99	45,737	50.30	14.33	35.74
advP	edge	292.60	71.00	35,261	60.87	48,209	53.02	18.63	37.70
advP	label	365.17	88.60	39,410	68.04	55,546	61.09	4.07	15.88

Table 9.28: Combination of different variants of the mass transportation and routes blocking heuristics. Runtime, number of significant operations, and quality loss in connections (conn) and queries (query).

Not surprisingly, the worst quality is obtained when combining (MT) and (RE), the weaker versions. The quality is decided by these weaker version, as we observe for the combinations (MT, RL) and (MA, RE) nearly identical quality as for (MT) or (RE) alone. Both combinations result in similar numbers of significant operations, runtime, and quality. They are faster than (RE) alone, but slower than (MT). See Table 9.26 for results of the *mass transportation* heuristic alone and Table 9.27 for the *routes* heuristic.

Using the best versions (MA) and (RE) in tandem, we get nearly the same quality as for (MA), (worse for an additional 1.6% of the queries). So we conclude that some of the optimal connections that (MA) looses are also lost by (RL). For example after using one means of mass transportation from station S to station S', entering a later one of the same line at S prime is prohibited by the *routes* heuristic whereas leaving that one at S' is prohibited by the *mass transportation* heuristic. With (MA) and (RE), we are only minimally faster than (MA) alone (less than 15ms). Although the runtime is 33ms faster than for (RL) alone, this improvement is not worth loosing quality for over 5 times as many queries.

9.10.4 Important Stations

We tested both variants of the *important stations* heuristic (cf. Section 8.7). For the *routes* version we require a station to be served by at least 5,10, or 15 routes (Rx) to be considered important. The *neighbors* version was evaluated for 3,4, or 5 neighbors as the threshold for qualifying as important (Nx). In Table 9.29 we present the results.

For both heuristics the number of significant operations and runtime drop when increasing the thresholds, thus decreasing the number of important stations. When we enable *skip*, i.e. not inserting the labels at unimportant stations into the priority queue, this decreases the number of extractions from the priority queue.

However, as this technique only slightly affects the number of created labels it is not able to improve runtimes by more than 10ms. If only few operations on the PQ are saved, this version is actually slower.

ISH	Skip	Runtime		PQ extracts		Labels created		Quality loss	
		avg in ms	ratio in %	avg	ratio in %	avg	ratio in %	conn in %	query in %
★-	-	412.1	100.0	57,926	100.0	90,921	100.0	-	-
R5		405.7	98.4	55,247	95.4	84,945	93.4	0.51	1.64
R5	✓	411.6	99.9	52,204	90.1	84,845	93.3	0.62	1.94
R10		383.9	93.1	48,188	83.2	75,272	82.8	2.73	6.82
R10	✓	378.8	91.9	40,699	70.3	74,993	82.5	2.93	7.62
R15		332.4	80.6	41,767	72.1	63,682	70.0	5.72	13.26
R15	✓	323.0	78.4	31,653	54.6	63,360	69.7	5.79	13.50
N3		317.8	77.1	44,911	77.5	64,237	70.7	0.76	2.12
N3	✓	317.9	77.1	35,560	61.4	64,371	70.8	0.68	2.02
N4		267.5	64.9	38,971	67.3	53,475	58.8	2.16	5.80
N4	✓	263.3	63.9	26,259	45.3	53,429	58.8	2.33	6.32
N5		242.5	58.8	34,209	59.1	46,934	51.6	4.80	12.04
N5	✓	235.2	57.1	20,243	34.9	46,651	51.3	5.11	12.74

Table 9.29: The influence of the important stations heuristic (ISH) using the neighbors (N) or routes (R) variant with or without skipping nodes at unimportant stations (skip). Runtime, number of significant operations, and quality loss in connections (conn) and queries (query).

When selecting important stations, version *routes* achieves much worse results: To obtain an improvement of 20% for (R15) in runtime, we have to accept a quality loss for 13% of the queries. If we are willing to sacrifice that much quality we can easily decrease the runtime by over 40% with (N5). Alternatively, to speedup the search as much as with (R15) we may use (N3) and get worse result sets for only 2% of the queries.

When introducing the heuristic we saw in Table 8.5 that for (N5) we have about half as many important stations as for (R15), explaining the much faster processing for (N5). However, the clever selection is also important, as for (N3) we categorized nearly 30% of the stations as important and for (R15) only 21.3%, still we achieve similar numbers of significant operations and runtimes.

The quality loss for the *routes* version and for requiring more than 3 neighbors is due to the heuristic nature. However, without regarding the reliability of interchanges, changing only at stations where two routes meet for the first time or separate, is optimality preserving. The few lost connections for (N3) occur due to the criterion reliability of interchanges. If changing between two trains t_1 and t_2 is possible at a number of stations, allowing interchanges only at the important ones may violate optimality. Because at unimportant stations there are typically fewer tracks, therefore the required time for changing trains is smaller. Assume the differences between the arrival of t_1 and the departure of t_2 is always the same, then these shorter interchange times increase the buffer times at unimportant stations and consequently higher reliability ratings can be achieved.

We experimented with constraining the use of the important station heuristic only to the middle part of the journey to improve quality. Next to the source or terminal station we wanted to explore all alternatives and allow changing at any station, to reach important stations from the source or the target from important stations in its vicinity as "good" as possible. Only at a certain distance from source and terminal, the heuristic should be used. We implemented different versions based on a radius around source and terminal or on a hierarchy of classes, but none was as successful as the one we will present in combination with shortcuts next, so we omit details here.

9.10.5 Shortcuts

Next we analyze the technique of *shortcuts* in the graph introduced in Section 8.7.2. The shortcuts can either connect each departures to the final stop of the train (F), the next (*scnext* N) or all subsequent (*scall* A) important stations. For the selection of important stations we used the *important station* heuristic investigated in the previous section in the *routes* or *neighbors* variant. A station needs to be served by at least 5 or 10 routes (Rx) or have at no less than 3 or four neighbors (Nx). Due to the bad quality of higher thresholds in the preceeding investigation, we limited ourselves to this values. The results can be found in Table 9.30. Some of the findings are easier observed in Table B.2 in the appendix, where we summarize the relation between important station heuristic and shortcuts with various parameters.

Shortcuts to the last stop. Adding the shortcuts to the last stops of trains generates many long edges and the created partial connections cover large distances quickly. However, without using the blocking technique for shortcuts (X), these are only explored as additional edges and increase the number of significant operations and runtime. If the blocking technique is used (B), the runtime is reduced drastically, but quality suffers unacceptably. This technique only suits as a reference model.

Blocking technique to improve the quality. Measuring the quality of the shortcuts to the next important station, we observed a better quality than for the important station heuristic alone. The best possible way to improved the quality of the *important station* heuristic (better than distance or hierarchy based approaches) comes naturally with the technique *shortcuts*. The optimal reason to allow changing even at unimportant stations seems to be that a shortcut bypassing the terminal or a station from which the terminal is reachable via a foot path exists at that station. If however, the *important station* heuristic is activated together with shortcuts, changing close to the terminal is still only possible at important stations. Additionally, potentially existing footpaths to the terminal station are never used at unimportant stations, since leaving the train is only allowed at important stations. Consequently, the quality is nearly identical to that of the *important station* heuristic, albeit the search runs faster (cf. Appendix B.2).

9.10 Heuristics

ISH	SC	P	Runtime		PQ extracts		Labels created		Quality loss	
			avg in ms	ratio in %	avg	ratio in %	avg	ratio in %	conn in %	query in %
★-	-		412.1	100.0	57,926	100.0	90,921	100.0	-	-
-	F	B	84.8	20.6	7,923	13.7	10,965	12.1	67.71	77.92
-	F	X	583.0	141.5	59,861	103.3	107,684	118.4	2.29	9.56
N3	N		275.6	66.9	33,411	57.7	53,250	58.6	0.11	0.38
N4	N		210.9	51.2	25,054	43.3	40,136	44.1	1.74	4.56
R5	N		424.4	103.0	55,296	95.5	86,873	95.5	0.04	0.20
R10	N		391.6	95.0	48,483	83.7	76,540	84.2	0.73	2.22
N3	A		596.2	144.7	37,851	65.3	86,024	94.6	1.37	4.90
N4	A		394.9	95.8	27,609	47.7	58,625	64.5	3.48	9.88
R5	A		1401.6	340.1	67,763	117.0	194,022	213.4	1.14	4.10
R10	A		1105.2	268.2	58,784	101.5	157,732	173.5	2.07	6.72

Parameters P: B/X = with/without blocking according to shortcuts

Table 9.30: The influence of the shortcuts heuristic using the neighbors (N) or routes (R) variant of the important station heuristic (ISH) to determine the shortcuts (SC) to the final station (F), or the next (N), or all (A) important stations. Runtime, number of significant operations, and quality loss in connections (conn) and queries (query).

Shortcuts to the next important station. With the improvement over the *important station* heuristic from above, *scnext* scores excellent quality results, especially with (R5) and (N3). The number of significant operations for shortcuts according to *neighbors* are around half that of the reference version. Unfortunately if the shortcuts are based on *routes*, the runtime is actually higher than for the plain *important station* heuristic (cf. Appendix B.2).

The quality is better than for the plain *important station* heuristic for about 1.5% to 2.5% of all the queries. Comparing versions (N3) and (N4), we might not want to accept the 10 times as high loss in quality for saving another 15% runtime. Version (N4) achieves the lowest number of significant operations and runtime, another 15% drop compared to (N3).

Shortcuts to all subsequent important stations. For version *scall* we added between 3.1 (N5) and 8.7 (R5) shortcuts per node (observed in Section 8.7 in Table 8.5). As expected, the huge number of additional edges tremendously increases the runtime, mainly due to the large number of additionally created labels. Only for version R5 we have more priority queue extractions than without shortcuts. If the shortcuts are based on routes, the number of created labels double.

For version (N3) we actually created nearly the same number of labels and save one third of priority queue operations. The complicated additional testing still results in nearly 50% higher runtime. Remember that e.g. stay-in-train edges are only feasible if the reached departure node has any leaving shortcut edge bypassing a terminal station. Without this test the number of significant operations and runtime increase even more (figures omitted).

For all definitions of important stations, *scall* is much slower and delivers worse quality than *scnext*. The only variant that is at all faster (only 4%) than the reference setup without shortcuts is (N4), simultaneously delivering the worst quality. In summary, *scall* is not a practicable technique at all.

Best version. The undisputed winner of all variants with and without shortcuts and the *important station* heuristic is (N3) with shortcuts to the next important station. Its number of significant operations are over 40% lower than for the reference version and the runtime improvement is about one third. This version has nearly no quality deficit; it missed an optimal connection in less than 20 of our 5000 queries.

9.10.6 Combination of the Four Heuristics: Important Station, Shortcuts, Mass Transportation, and Routes

In this section we combined the *important station* heuristic with and without shortcuts with the *mass transportation* and *routes* heuristics. According to the outcome, when combining the heuristics *mass transportation* and *routes* in Section 9.10.3, we tested the best versions of the last two heuristics only, namely *advanced Pareto* for *mass transportation* and *labels* for the *routes* heuristic. To determine the important stations we set the threshold to 3 or 4 for the neighbors version of the *important station* heuristic. Shortcuts were inserted to the next important station only.

The *mass transportation* heuristic (M) is dominant in case of quality, all combinations with it loose optimal connections for additional 14% of the queries, the same number as for this heuristic alone. Activating the *routes* heuristic (R) we experience a quality loss for an additional 4% of the queries for either definition of important station with or without shortcuts. This is identical to the loss for *routes* alone. If the *mass transportation* heuristic is already activated, we loose optimal connections for an additional 1.5% of the queries (identical to the combination of (R+M)). Heuristic (M) yielded a higher improvement in runtime than (M) without combinations, this can be observed in combination with the *important station* heuristic with or without shortcuts, too. The combination of all heuristics is always the fastest version. For the neighbors version N4 with shortcuts we receive the fastest version, but it also achieves the worst quality.

From these results we can see that both (R) and (M) achieve their speedup due to pruning other partial connections than the *important station heuristic* Therefore the runtime improvement is still recognizable in combinations. Sadly, the quality loss also adds up, as different connections are missing from the results.

Unfortunately, neither of the combinations creates better variants. All combinations with N3 are slower than N4 (with shortcuts) alone without improving quality. The fastest versions of all looses 6% of optimal connections distributed over nearly 20% of the queries. This is too much. So we should stay with shortcuts N3 and its near optimal quality. If we needed to

9.11 Detailed Figures for the Reference Version

Heuristic ISH	SC	R	M	Runtime avg in ms	Runtime ratio in %	PQ extracts avg in k	PQ extracts ratio in %	Labels cr. avg in k	Labels cr. ratio in %	Quality loss conn in %	Quality loss query in %
★_	-	-	-	412.1	100.0	57.9	100.0	90.9	100.0	0.0	0.0
N3				317.8	77.1	44.9	77.5	64.2	70.7	0.8	2.1
N3			√	279.4	67.8	36.8	63.5	49.2	54.1	4.4	15.9
N3		√		294.9	71.5	38.3	66.1	54.2	59.7	1.7	6.0
N3		√	√	256.1	62.1	31.3	54.1	41.6	45.8	4.9	17.4
N3	√			275.6	66.9	33.4	57.7	53.3	58.6	0.1	0.4
N3	√		√	241.4	58.6	26.4	45.6	39.0	42.9	3.7	14.4
N3	√	√		261.6	63.5	28.9	49.8	45.3	49.8	0.9	4.0
N3	√	√	√	229.2	55.6	23.2	40.1	33.8	37.1	4.2	16.1
N4				267.5	64.9	39.0	67.3	53.5	58.8	2.2	5.8
N4			√	233.4	56.6	32.6	56.3	42.4	46.6	6.0	19.0
N4		√		248.7	60.3	33.1	57.2	45.2	49.8	3.4	10.3
N4		√	√	217.6	52.8	27.4	47.3	35.6	39.1	6.4	20.3
N4	√			210.9	51.2	25.1	43.3	40.1	44.1	1.7	4.6
N4	√		√	184.3	44.7	19.9	34.4	29.9	32.9	5.5	17.9
N4	√	√		208.9	50.7	22.0	37.9	34.7	38.1	3.0	9.2
N4	√	√	√	177.1	43.0	17.8	30.6	26.2	28.8	6.0	19.4

Table 9.31: Combination of the most prominent important station heuristic (ISH) variants based on the number of neighbors (N3 and N4) with or without shortcuts (SC) and the routes (R) heuristic (version *labels*) and the mass transportation (M) heuristic (version *advancedPareto*). Runtime, number of significant operations, and quality loss in connections (conn) and queries (query).

decrease search speed for whatever reason, we would have to select shortcuts with N4 with the best tradeoff in speedup for quality.

9.11 Detailed Figures for the Reference Version

9.11.1 Configuration

Our reference version, as mentioned in Section 9.4.2.3 and used throughout this chapter, has the following configuration. Each value was determined to be the best setting and discussed in the respective section.

It employed parameter set (A) for advanced Pareto dominance with our four criteria travel time, number of interchanges, ticket cost, and reliability of interchanges. We had 100 equivalence classes and set the maximal effective reliability to $\hat{\mu} = 96\%$ for the last criterion.

Lower bounds were computed for all criteria. On the standard station graph a bidirectional Dijkstra with triangle inequalities and biconnected component pruning delivered lower bounds for travel time. These results were exploited to speed up the calculation on the unified interchange graph in order to obtain bounds on the number of interchanges and the reliability of transfers. Lower bounds on ticket cost were delivered by a single-directed Dijkstra on the appropriate station graph. All the bounds were used for domination by terminal.

The priority queue was Dial's data structure. Goal-direction was active with the criterion travel time plus $\gamma = 20$ times the number of interchanges (goal-directed on both criteria with criterion plus lower bound on that criterion).

9.11.2 Detailed Number Of Significant Operations

During the search process on average 90,921 labels are created. About 20% at arrival nodes and 40% each at departure and change nodes.

Of these labels 32,924 are dominated either at the node level (66%) or by terminal labels (34%). Interestingly over half of these (53%) are at the change level and only 6% at arrival nodes. As labels at arrivals are only created if the corresponding departure was not dominated, the number of labels at arrival nodes is very small. 57,967 labels are inserted in to the priority queue and later removed. This is also the average of the maximum number of labels in use during a search. About one fourth are at arrival nodes, the rest are evenly distributed between departure and change nodes. We create 196 start labels and get 27 terminal labels per query. In the final filtering step nearly 19 of the candidates are removed to obtain the set of optimal results. Before the last edge partial connections may still be incomparable and the real prices are only computed at the terminal. Thus, the number of optima is considerably smaller than the number of terminal labels.

Runtimes In Figure 9.5 we see the runtimes for the standard version (standard) and the best heuristic, using *shortcuts* to the next *important station* determined with the *neighbors* threshold three (SC N3). On the x-axis we give the runtime in milliseconds. On the y-axis the percentage of queries that require at least this much runtime can be found. For the average of 412ms for (standard) we can see that only 29.1% of all queries are slower. Only 20.4% are slower using (SC N3). 95% of all queries are answered within about 1.5 seconds (standard) (1560ms) or 1 second (1045ms) for (SC N3).

Space Requirements The graph sizes were already given in Table 8.1. We have 2.1 million nodes and 2.9 million edges. On average there are 58k labels in use at the same time during a search. Note that all labels that have been removed from the priority queue are still needed, as they may be part of one or more connections and be required to reconstruct these connections. For some of the longer queries we needed as much as 500k labels, but managed to stay below 1GB of memory consumption.

9.11 Detailed Figures for the Reference Version

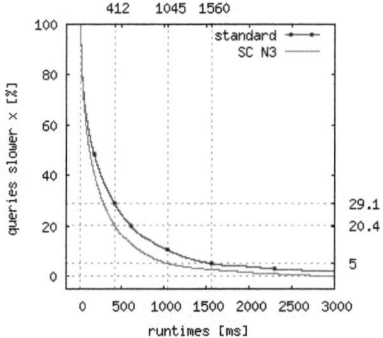
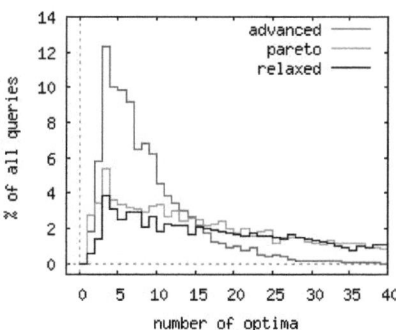

Figure 9.5: Runtime distribution (left): the y-axis gives the percentage of queries that require at least the runtime found on the x-axis. Frequency of the number of Pareto, relaxed Pareto and advanced Pareto optima (right).

9.11.3 Number of Optima

Pareto Vs. Relaxed Vs. Advanced The distribution of the number of optima using either Pareto dominance (P), relaxed Pareto dominance (R), or advanced Pareto dominance (A) is shown in Figure 9.5 (right). The average number of optima is 22.48 (P), 33.57 (R), and 8.45 (A), respectively (as already stated in Table 9.10). For all versions of dominance we see peaks for 3 optima, but much less pronounced for (P) and (R).

The large number of Pareto Optima in (P) is especially notable for longer and more complicated journeys. As the number of interchanges increases, the distribution of buffer times creates more alternatives. Additionally, first or last parts of a journey may utilize local trains like RB or S-Bahn, resulting in different travel times, and a larger set of stations where interchanges can take place. Furthermore, various options to take either ICE or IC/EC trains in the middle part result in differing prices and travel times.

The relaxation in (R) makes more connections incomparable, and consequently the number of optima increases by about half. Really large numbers of alternatives appear with higher frequency in this version (outside of the graphic).

Undesired optima are removed by (A). Recall from the motivation in Chapter 2 some connections that are only 10 Cents cheaper but take an hour longer. With the trade-offs for ticket cost and reliability of interchanges in advanced Pareto dominance, we determine 3 to 6 optima for many queries (41.4%). For two thirds of the queries we obtained 2 to 9 optima.

9.12 Significant Operations

In Section 9.4.2, we introduced the number of created labels and extractions from the priority queue as *significant operations* and indicators for the runtime of the algorithm.

Runtimes and number of significant operations behaved similarly for many test-cases. An increase or decrease in one could be found in the other, as well. Different ratios for the increase in runtime were mirrored in the number of significant operations. (e.g. a decrease to 34% or 17% in runtime and a decrease to ca. 44% or 20% in the number of significant operations in Table 9.11).

From the differences in the characteristics when changing priority queue types, we could observe that the heaps have more overhead per operation on the queue than Dial's data structure (cf. Section 9.8.1). The techniques *avoid inserting minimum labels* and *skip departure nodes* decreasing the number of operations on the priority queue did not improve runtimes (cf. Section 9.8.4). Only for technique *bypass departure nodes* that also reduced the number of created labels we observed a speed-up effect. We can conclude, that the operations on Dial's data structure do not dominate the runtime.

A discrepancy in the proportion of runtimes and number of extract operations from the priority queue could also be detected for the *shortcuts* heuristic. For variant (N4) runtimes were much higher for *scall* than for *scnext* even for a nearly identical number of priority queue operations (cf. Table 9.30). The version using shortcuts to all subsequent stations (*scall*) created much more labels, which explained the higher runtimes.

The more involved heuristics have some overhead in evaluating edges and labels. Some of them require extensive bookkeeping and the maintenence of additional data structures. Due to these facts the average effort per operation increases. Consequently, for many of these techniques the differences in the numbers of created/extracted labels differs significantly from the effect on the runtime. This was especially noticeable for the more complex meta data structures for the heuristics *routes blocking* and *mass transportation* (cf. Section 9.10.2 and Section 9.10.3). The observed differences can be interpreted as an indicator to measure the overhead involved. This was also done for the evaluation of different priority queue types (see above).

9.13 Analysis of Heavy-Weight Searches

All queries that still take long to compute exhibit one of the following properties:

- They are queries with destination on an island off shore,

- or they start and end in regions with dense mass transportation networks.

9.13 Analysis of Heavy-Weight Searches 191

Reaching Islands The ferry connection is problematic with searches toward islands. If ferries to that island operate on a regular basis (in intervals between 15 minutes and 3 hours), there is no problem. When the ferries have really low frequencies, searches tend to visit larger parts of Germany than necessary. Say the earliest partial connection reaches the ferry port just a few minutes after the ferry left, but the next will leave in five hours. During these five hours, alternatives explore long detours through Germany, although no other way to the terminal than this ferry exists. Until the next ferry is finally reached, partial connections that have amassed up to five hours additional travel time through Germany have been created. Starting at those islands on the other hand is easy. While waiting some hours for the next ferry, not many partial connections are created because of the limited public transportation networks on these small islands.

To overcome this problems we will investigate using bidirectional search. In contrast to standard searches for which an arrival interval is either too hard to obtain or too large for bidirectional search, we get the suitable points in time (not even intervals anymore) from the ferry schedule. If we encounter a search for which the only possible route uses a ferry, we enter a *ferry search mode*. Note that obtaining this information is easily realizable within our biconnected pruning approach (cf. Section 8.5.5) as both ferry ports are articulation points in this case. Within our ferry search mode, we search from the arrival events of the ferry to our destination and backwards from the departure events to our source station. By using bounds irrelevant arrivals may be discarded early, e.g. if the lower bound on the travel time to the ferry port is too high to reach the departure from within the departure interval at the source station.

Mass Transportation Problem For all queries we have on average less than 200 start labels. Queries starting in regions with dense mass transportation networks need more than 1,000 start labels. For example in Berlin, we have source-/target equivalences that allow us to start at all the major hub stations within the city and many departures of trains and of even more means of mass transportation in the departure intervals. Differing routes through these mass transportation networks are considered and many labels with relatively little travel time are created. Within the first few steps of algorithm execution there is no possibility to dominate these labels. Next to terminal stations in centers of mass transportation alternatives are explored that leave high speed trains one or two stations earlier than the fastest connection. They use means of mass transportation for the rest of the journey, achieving better prices. Thus, they cannot be dominated as well.

These insights motivated our *mass transportation* (cf. Section 8.9.1) and *routes* heuristics (cf. Section 8.9.2). However, as the computational results in Section 9.10.6 revealed, *shortcuts* to the next important station based on the number of *neighbors* (see Sections 8.7 and Sections 8.7.2) performed better. Stations that are served only by one or more lines of mass transportation (e.g. S-Bahn stops) are automatically bypassed in shortcuts. No additional

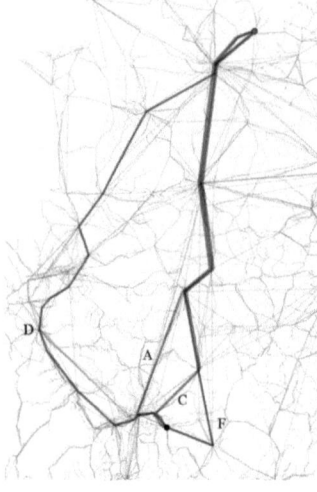

Name	Depar-ture	Criteria				Path
		time in h	ic	sec in %	cost in €	
fast	10:07	5:28	2	57	114	F
fast'	11:07	5:28	2	57	114	F
cheap	11:38	5:30	3	33	101	C
cheap'	11:07	5:31	3	41	101	C
alt	10:07	5:52	2	84	113	A
direct	10:43	7:04	0	100	107	D

Figure 9.6: Fast, convenient, and cheap connections for a query from Lübeck (north) to Aschaffenburg (south). The traveled routes (left) and characteristics of the connections (right).

alternatives are created by changing between means of mass transportation. Superior to the *routes* heuristic, even changing to different routes at unimportant stations is impossible.

9.14 Example Connections

To illustrate that advanced Pareto optimal alternatives actually take different routes through Germany we look at an example query from Lübeck (north) to Aschaffenburg (south) with a departure interval between 10:00 and 12:00. The paths and characteristics of the calculated connections can be found in Figure 9.6. Note that all except path (D) start identically and branch after over half of the distance, although different types of trains are used. A somewhat direct path (C) results in the least expensive connections (cheap) with 3 interchanges. The fastest connections (F) take a detour over Würzburg. They save 2 minutes, are more reliable and 13€ more expensive. Besides, there is a direct IC connection via Köln (D) that is rather slow. An additional alternative takes path (A) and increases the reliability over the fastest connection by almost 30%. Only the direct connection is without ICE but has the longest detour. The cheaper connections use RE or RB for a part of the journey and thus save money.

9.15 Conclusion

In this chapter we have evaluated the search for special offers and night trains and later presented an in-depth analysis of our algorithm.

Special Offers The focus of our approach to search for special offers was to demonstrate how a large variety of different tariff classes can be incorporated into a multi-objective shortest path framework for travel information. We successively integrated a combined search for regular tariffs and contingent-based tariffs into MOTIS. In our computational experiments we observed that a multi-objective search with a mixture of tariff rules can be done almost as fast as just with one regular tariff. Sometimes the contingent-restricted versions run even faster, because the special offers apply to fast connections. In that case, less effort has to be put into searching cheap connections.

We also observed that our simple model to represent regular fares within Germany is not as accurate as desired. Hence, future work should concentrate on improved approximations of regular fares. A tighter approximation would allow stricter dominance rules. We do expect considerable savings of computational time from stricter dominance rules.

Night Trains Our computational study shows that a specialized night train search delivers many more attractive connections than an ordinary search. We have observed a trade-off between quality of the solution sets and computation time. Our implementation of a multi-criteria search with one additional criterion fails to find a good night train connection in a few cases, but it is the most efficient one. The pre-selection approach with a fast feeder computation never failed and delivers almost optimal quality. Both variants are fast enough to be applied in on-line information systems. With additional tuning the runtime can probably be reduced further, while maintaining high quality.

We see two promising perspectives for applying our algorithms in practice. The first is the scenario for which this section was written: the user explicitly asks for a night train connection. Then we would recommend using the pre-selection approach with fast feeder computation (Algorithm C), which delivers excellent quality. The second scenario is an ordinary query with a start interval in the evening. Here, it would be an option to run MOTIS with an additional criterion (Algorithm D) but without spending too much additional computation time. If this search finds attractive night train connections, these can be offered as alternatives to those computed for the query interval.

Overall We have thoroughly analyzed the speed-up techniques and heuristics introduced in Chapter 8. The impact of several of these techniques on the search space is visualized for an exemplary search in Section B.3 on page 233 in the appendix.

We have seen that the techniques *goal-direction* and *domination by labels at the terminal* are essential for online capabilities. We are able to efficiently determine lower bounds for *goal-direction* and *domination by terminal* for all of our criteria and prune the search space accordingly, in less than 30ms. Selecting the right priority queue type and tuning the weights and criteria used in *goal-direction* further improved processing times. Contrary to single-criterion search the time spent on the priority queue is not among the dominant factors.

The reference version using optimal settings without heuristics achieves an average runtime of 412ms and answers 95% of the queries within 1.5 seconds.

Respecting the additional criterion reliability of interchanges produced additional results. The computational cost for adding the criterion is lower than for ticket cost. This is mainly to the correlation with the number of interchanges which the latter does not exhibit.

Of all heuristics the one with best quality for performance tradeoff is shortcuts with the *important station heuristic* based on the *neighbors* threshold. We may use threshold N4 to speed up searches to about a fifth of a second (210ms) on average at only little quality loss. The best choice is threshold N3 with nearly indiscernible quality loss and one third runtime improvement over our reference version.

Our baseline version without any speed-up techniques required several minutes per query. With our best setup and *shortcuts* N3 we reach an average runtime of 275ms and answered 95% of the queries in at most 1 second.

Chapter 10

A Time-Dependent Timetable Information System

Our fully realistic multi-criteria prototype MOTIS is based on a time-expanded graph because it appears to be easier to model all side constraints arising in practice in this framework. However, the major drawback of time-expanded graphs, in comparison to time-dependent models, is the higher space consumption, in particular if highly periodical regional mass transit has to be included. In addition, the time-dependent graph model seems easier to adapt in case of dynamic graph changes due to train delays. These reasons motivate our investigation of the time-dependent graph model in this chapter. It is based on the publication [DMS08].

Related Work and Our Contribution

To the best of our knowledge, no complete, realistic system has been built for exact multi-criteria search of all Pareto optimal solutions in the time-dependent graph model. In [PSWZ08], Pyrga et al. consider constant transfer times and traffic days, but other aspects of real timetables, like footpaths and special transfer rules, are not considered. In this chapter, we describe a first prototype for multi-criteria search of all Pareto optima within a fully featured, real timetable. Its search results are guaranteed to be optimal. We provide an extensive computational study showing the impact of several speed-up techniques. Even though the number of possible speed-up techniques is severely restricted, in order to guarantee the optimality of all search results, the performance of our prototype is already comparable to time-expanded systems, but consumes much less space.

Most previous research (in particular [PSWZ08]) has concentrated on the earliest arrival problem from a given point in time. But here we focus on a many-source shortest path version, because in a pre-trip search for train connections, a user usually wants to specify a *time interval* in which the journey should start. This implies that we have to perform a simultaneous search from multiple starting times. In a time-expanded graph model, this can be handled very easily: One simply adds a "super-source" and edges of length zero to all start events, thereby reducing the search to a single-source search. In time-dependent graphs, however, solving the many-source shortest path problem is more subtle if travel time is used as an optimization criterion. Consider two sub-paths from the source to some intermediate node. Then, path p_1 with start time s_1 and travel time t_1 dominates another path p_2 with start time s_2 and travel time t_2, with respect to travel time, only if $t_1 < t_2$ and $s_1 \geq s_2$. Otherwise, both paths are incomparable. This leads to weaker dominance during search than for the earliest arrival problem, and consequently to more non-dominated solutions which can be offered to customers. It is therefore remarkable that we still achieve a reasonable performance.

Our approach can easily be extended to further criteria. In order to exemplify this, the "reliability of transfers" is investigated as an additional criterion. The reliability of transfers is a property of a connection that captures the probability of catching all trains within the connection (cf. Chapter 6.3). Since possible train delays cannot be ignored, such a criterion is of great practical importance.

Overview The remainder of this chapter is organized as follows. In Section 10.1, we introduce the time-dependent graph model and describe the adaptations needed in order to make it suited for fully realistic timetables. A modification of Dijkstra's algorithm that makes it capable of minimizing multiple criteria is introduced in Section 10.2. Several speed-up techniques that do not violate the optimality of the search results are proposed. The results of the experimental analysis of our time-dependent search system are presented in Section 10.3. We analyze the impact of the proposed speed-up techniques on performance. The prototype is then compared to our search on a time-expanded graph using MOTIS. The final aspect of our discussion covers the relationship between performance and the number of search criteria. Finally, Section 10.4 summarizes our results and gives an outlook on future work.

10.1 Realistic Time-Dependent Graph Model

In this section we will describe a time-dependent graph model as introduced in [PSWZ08, BJ04, PSWZ04a]. Although a basic version for constant interchange times has already been presented in Chapter 4, here we will start off with a very basic time-dependent model and extend it in the following to a fully realistic model.

We assume the timetable to consist of a set $\mathcal{T}$ of trains, a set $\mathcal{S}$ of stations, and a set $\mathcal{E}$ of elementary connections. An *elementary connection* $e \in \mathcal{E}$ describes a connection between two adjacent train stations without intermediate stops. Such a connection contains a departure station $\text{from}(e) \in \mathcal{S}$, an arrival station $\text{to}(e) \in \mathcal{S}$, a departure time $\text{d}(e)$, and an arrival time $a(e)$. In addition to that, each elementary connection has several properties like train class, traffic days and train number. Each train $tr \in \mathcal{T}$ is an ordered list of elements of $\mathcal{E}$. A *train connection* is composed of an ordered list of elementary connections which must be consistent with the sequence of departure and arrival stations.

10.1.1 Basic Time-Dependent Model

For each station $S \in \mathcal{S}$ in the timetable there is a node $v(S) \in V$ in the basic time-dependent graph $G = (V, E)$. We call these nodes *station nodes*. There is an edge $e_{AB} = (v(A), v(B)) \in E$ if the set $\mathcal{E}_{AB} := \{e \in \mathcal{E} | \text{from}(e) = A \land \text{to}(e) = B\}$ is non-empty. The characteristics of all elementary connections in $\mathcal{E}_{AB}$ are attributed to this single edge e_{AB}. Each edge has multiple length functions, one for each optimization criterion. These length functions are time-dependent: Depending on the time t at which the edge is to be used, different connections in $\mathcal{E}_{AB}$ may be favorable. In general, this is implemented with an iterator which computes edge lengths "on-the-fly" and returns all necessary variants with different characteristics.

If we only consider travel time and make the assumption that a connection $e_1 \in \mathcal{E}_{AB}$ may *not* overtake another connection $e_2 \in \mathcal{E}_{AB}$ in the sense that $d(e_1) \geq d(e_2)$ and $a(e_1) < a(e_2)$, then the connection with the earliest departure after time t is the one chosen from $\mathcal{E}_{AB}$. Its travel time length is precisely $a(\text{rel}(\mathcal{E}_{AB}, t)) - t$, where $\text{rel}(\mathcal{E}_{AB}, t) := \arg\min_{e \in \mathcal{E}_{AB}, d(e) \geq t} d(e)$ is the relevant connection in $\mathcal{E}_{AB}$ at time t.

10.1.2 Transfers

In the basic model, transfers between different trains are not modeled differently than two consecutive elementary connections with the same train. In order to allow for our search to count the number of transfers and in order to assign a duration to transfers, the model has to be extended as follows. We assume here for simplicity that a constant transfer time is provided for each station.

In order to still be able to take advantage of the fact that multiple elementary connections are modeled by a single edge, it is necessary to group train connections into *routes*. The set of routes forms a partition of $\mathcal{T}$ such that two connections are in the same route if and only if they share equal stations and properties. The departure and arrival times of two connections in the same route may differ as well as their traffic days. Using this partition, each station is represented by several *route nodes* in addition to its station node. The station node is used only to connect the route nodes and has no edges to nodes from other stations. The expanded model is depicted in Figure 10.1.

One route node is required for each route that arrives or departs at the station. For all connections in the same route, the corresponding route node plays the role of the station node in the basic model. The assumption that connections may not overtake each other can now be restricted to connections within a route. If we have overtaking elementary connections

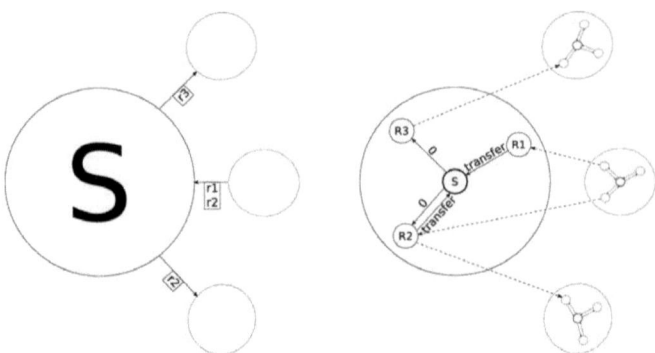

Figure 10.1: Extension of a simple time-dependent graph (left) to support transfers. The timetable has three routes r1, r2, r3 so that the extended station (right) has three route nodes.

within a route, the route can simply be split up in order to separate the two elementary connections (and so we can get rid off this assumption). If the route has a connection that arrives at the station, an edge connecting the route node to the station node is introduced; if the route has a connection that departs from the station, an edge connecting the station node to the route node is introduced. One of these two edges needs to carry the transfer costs at the station and is called *transfer-edge*, the other has a transfer cost of 0. In the following we choose the edges from route nodes to station nodes as transfer-edges. This is called *exiting transfers* as opposed to *entering transfers*. We will see, that our choice is preferable due to performance advantages of the multi-criteria search.

10.1.3 Fully Realistic Model

We propose the following extensions to make the model fully realistic.

10.1.3.1 Foot-Paths

In a real environment it is possible to walk from one station to another if the two stations lie in geographic proximity. Realistic models therefore contain foot-paths to model this. Foot-paths are tuples (A, B, c) that represent a possibility to walk between stations A and B within c minutes. We assume, that c already contains all transfer costs at both A and B, so that no additional cost for switching trains arise. Foot-paths are special in that their length is constant in time. Figure 10.2 (a) shows the modifications that are needed in order to model a foot-path (A, B, c). It is not sufficient to simply add an edge from the station node of A to the station node of B with length c. This is because no additional transfer costs have to be paid when using a foot-path. Reducing c by the transfer cost at A, does not correctly model

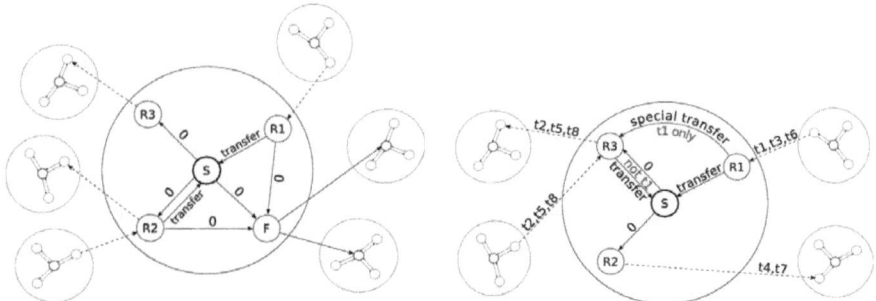

Figure 10.2: (a) Illustration of a station with two foot-edges in the time-dependent model. (b) Modifications to the graph for a station with a special transfer from train t_1 to train t_2.

the costs when the journey starts at A. To circumvent these problems, an additional *foot-node* is added to the stations subgraph.

10.1.3.2 Special Transfer Rules

Another feature of realistic timetables are special transfer rules, that change the transfer time between two specific trains. The general transfer time of a station may be increased or decreased that way, depending on the real-world situation at the station. Two trains that use the same platform may for instance have a reduced transfer time. For each transfer rule several changes to the graph have to be made. Consider a special transfer time to get from train t_1 to train t_2 at station A. Let X denote the route node of A for t_1 and Y the route node of A for t_2. The station node for A is denoted by S. We assume that all special transfers are reasonable, i.e. it is not possible to reach a train departing before t_2 at Y if we arrived with t_1. However, there are cases in which it is explicitly made impossible to reach t_2 by setting the time of the special transfer higher than the usual transfer time. Figure 10.2 (b) shows the changes that have to be applied to the model when a special transfer rule is introduced. A new edge leads from X to Y carrying the special transfer cost. This edge may only be used after using t_1. The existing edges from S to Y and from Y to S have to be restricted so that they may *not* be used if t_1 is the last used train. This way Y cannot be reached from X without using the special transfer and the special transfer may not be used as shortcut to get to another route.

10.2 Multi-Criteria Dijkstra and Speed-Up Techniques

10.2.1 Algorithm

We use a multi-criteria version of Dijkstra's algorithm on our time-dependent graph. It is very similar to the one presented in Chapter 5 on Page 58). The differences in the implementation mainly concern the details discussed in that chapter, the pseudocode version remains unchanged.

10.2.2 Speed-Up Techniques

Some of the speed-up techniques from our time-expanded version (cf. Chapter 8) are applicable in a time-dependent version as well. We will now briefly mention some of these and introduce two new and rather technical optimizations that have some impact on the search within the time-dependent graph.

Lower Bounds The techniques *domination by labels at the terminal* (cf. Sections 8.4 and 8.5.3) and *goal-direction* (cf. Sections 8.3 and 8.5.4), producing the labels for domination earlier in the search process, harmonize well with time-dependent search. These techniques utilize lower bounds for the distance of some node to the target node. These bounds can be available for some or all criteria. A general way of obtaining bounds is to simplify the graph enough to make it possible to search quickly. In a simplified auxiliary graph, a single-criterion backward search is performed in order to obtain lower bounds for all nodes and one criterion. In order to be able to perform a backward search, any time-dependency must be eliminated.

We have implemented two different versions of simplified graphs with different properties. The more efficient one uses the graph of the basic time-dependent model in which only travel time can be optimized and transfers are costless. Time-dependency is removed by replacing variable edge costs with their minimal cost over time. This graph is suited for obtaining lower bounds for travel time only. Another simplification procedure keeps the complete graph and only substitutes time-dependent edges with constant ones as in the first approach. The resulting graph is more complicated but yields tighter bounds and can also be used for transfers.

Avoid Hopping and Label Forwarding Two phenomena that often arise when searching the time-dependent graph can be eliminated in order to improve performance. The first one is that labels propagate back to the node which they originated from. In this case the labels are immediately dominated. The search can easily be adapted to forbid *"hopping"*, i.e. the back-propagation of labels. The other phenomenon is due to the fact that all edges between station and route nodes in our graph have a cost of zero for all criteria. Because of this, newly created labels often have the same values for the single criteria as the label they originated from. Therefore, they are lexicographically minimal in the priority queue from the moment on they are inserted. We can thus avoid inserting them and simply hold them back until the current label has been processed completely. Before extracting further labels from the queue, the labels that are held back can be processed. This is similar to the technique *avoid inserting minimum labels* from Section 8.8.4 and happens rather often as a result of the aforementioned fact.

10.3 Computational Study

In the following, we analyze the performance of our multi-criteria search algorithm. We apply the aforementioned speed-up techniques and compare our prototype to a time-expanded approach. For the main part of our experiments we selected two relatively unrelated criteria, namely travel time and the number of transfers. Later we also show the influence on performance when adding an additional criterion to the search.

10.3.1 Train Network and Test Cases

The train network used in this study is derived from the train schedule of all trains within Germany of 2007 (56,994 trains, 8916 stations). The time-dependent graph has about 240,000 nodes and 670,000 edges while the corresponding time-expanded graph uses about 3,479,000 nodes and 5,633,000 edges. Three different sets of test cases were used. Each test case contains a source and a target station for the search, a date and a start time interval on that date. The first set of test cases is a synthetic one. It contains 1,000 randomly created tests that allow for arbitrary start time intervals (referred to as *random cases*). In this test set intervals of several hours are possible, it is intended as a stress test. The second set also contains 1,000 randomly created tests which however have more realistic start time intervals of exactly one hour (*realistic cases*). The third set contains about 14,000 tests that were obtained from a snapshot of real connection queries provided by Deutsche Bahn AG (*real cases*).

10.3.2 Computational Environment

All computations were executed on an AMD Athlon(tm) 64 X2 dual core processor 4600+ with 2.4 GHz and 4 GB main memory running under Suse Linux 10.2. Our C++ code has been compiled with g++ 4.1.2 and compile option -O3.

10.3.3 Experiments

We first analyze the impact of single speed-up techniques. As a main indicator for performance we use several operation counts on representative operations, most importantly on the number of created labels, as well as on the number of labels which pass the domination tests and are inserted into the priority queue. We also provide CPU times, however, since our system is just a prototype to demonstrate feasibility of the approach, no serious effort was spent on fine-tuning the code in order to improve runtime directly.

| Algorithmic | Labels | | Runtime |
variant	created	inserted	average
base-line variant	1,236,744	636,393	4.730s
optimized version	207,976	47,967	1.050s

Table 10.1: Comparison of the base-line variant with an optimized version (realistic cases).

10.3.3.1 Impact of Exact Speed-Up Techniques

We start with a *base-line variant* which is the generalized Dijkstra algorithm on the fully realistic graph model without using any optimization techniques and choosing exiting transfers (cf. Section 10.1.2). Our first investigation compares this base-line variant with an optimized version which includes domination by early results as well as goal direction. The lower bounds are obtained from the basic time-independent graph (cf. Section 10.2.2). In addition to that, avoidance of hopping and label forwarding are used. Table 10.1 shows the combined impact of these techniques on performance. We observe an improvement of a factor of about six with respect to the number of created labels and a factor of 13 with respect to the number of insertions into the priority queue. A more careful analysis reveals the individual impact of the low level optimizations of avoiding the hopping of labels and their forwarding along costless edges (cf. Section 10.2.2). This can be seen in Table 10.2.

We can also observe that the choice between entering and exiting transfers (cf. Section 10.1.2) makes a notable difference in performance. Together a factor of nearly two is achieved in the number of created labels and a factor of over three is achieved in the number of inserted labels. Note that the runtimes of the different sets of queries cannot be compared. The real cases use start time intervals of three hours while the realistic cases use

| Cases | Strategy | Labels | | Runtime |
		created	inserted	average
1,000 random	enter	1,232,592	545,416	7.049s
	exit	1,072,187	552,012	5.990s
	avoid	682,925	552,014	5.453s
	+forw	682,897	146,766	4.690s
1,000 realistic	enter	385,982	160,200	1.606s
	exit	315,565	160,516	1.311s
	avoid	207,984	160,514	1.183s
	+forw	207,976	47,967	1.050s
14,076 real	enter	386,764	176,540	2.360s
	exit	343,248	177,193	2.098s
	avoid	212,503	177,192	1.932s
	+forw	212,516	45,114	1.570s

Table 10.2: Performance improvement when entering or exiting carries the transfer cost (*enter* and *exit*) and for the techniques avoid hopping (*avoid*) or avoid hoping and forwarding labels (*+forw*).

10.3 Computational Study

Heuristic for Lower Bounds		Labels		Runtime
time	transfers	created	inserted	average
none	none	420,803	92,305	1.839s
simple	none	207,976	47,967	1.050s
complex	none	205,260	45,886	1.003s
simple	complex	207,813	47,939	1.106s
complex	complex	205,101	45,866	1.159s

Table 10.3: Performance when using several combinations of the simple and the complex graph in order to obtain lower bounds (realistic cases).

one hour. This leads to an average number of about six non-dominated solutions for the real cases, but only an average of about two for the realistic cases. Therefore, different runtimes are to be expected. Although the average number of created labels is similar for both sets of instances, the actual distribution of the number of created labels has a significantly larger variance for the real cases.

As explained in Section 10.2.2, there are several ways of obtaining lower bounds. The last results used the basic time-dependent graph. However, by using the more complex approach, lower bounds can be obtained for other criteria as well, like the number of transfers. Unfortunately, the lower bounds on the number of transfers do not improve the search sufficiently to overcome the effort of determining the bounds in the first place, as can be seen in Table 10.3.

An improvement can still be achieved with tighter bounds on the travel time. Compared to not using any heuristic, we obtain an improvement of factor about two. The most efficient variant of these bounds — the complex graph with travel time bounds only — will from here on be used as our *standard variant* for further comparisons.

10.3.3.2 Further Speed-Up by Realistic Assumptions

One of the strengths of our approach is the guaranteed optimality of the search results. We are not willing to sacrifice this advantage by using speed-up techniques that violate optimality. The only exception are optimizations that use realistic assumptions in order to limit the search

Algorithmic variant	Labels		Runtime
	created	inserted	average
standard	205,260	45,886	1.003
max. travel time = 24h	180,910	30,893	0.845s
max. travel time = 15h	141,602	16,175	0.631s
max. travel time = 10h	83,162	6,999	0.406s
$\gamma = 5$	182,535	32,030	0.865s
$\gamma = 3$	144,678	17,015	0.653s
$\gamma = 2$	84,125	6,890	0.415s

Table 10.4: Limiting the maximum travel time to a constant (24h, 15h, 10h) or a multiple of the travel time of the fastest connection ($\gamma \in \{2,3,5\}$) (realistic cases).

Algorithmic variant	Labels created	Labels inserted	Runtime average
standard	205,260	45,886	1.003
max. waiting time = 5h	167,914	19,751	0.777
max. waiting time = 3h	151,680	15,441	0.637

Table 10.5: Limiting the maximum waiting time (realistic cases).

to certain reasonable ranges for the criteria. The results of applying some of these techniques are shown in the following.

There are two ways of restricting the allowed travel time. Firstly it can be restricted by a fixed upper limit like 24 hours. This helps a lot for long connections but does not help at all for short ones. A more adaptive restriction is to limit the allowed travel time to γ times the time of the fastest connection, where γ is a variable parameter of our algorithm. This improves the search a lot for short queries. Our results are summarized in Table 10.4. To limit the number of transfers did not show a notable effect on performance in our tests. A maximum of five allowed transfers did not yield a better performance, even though it makes some Pareto optimal connections impossible. Hence we dropped the limit on the number of transfers completely. A reasonable limitation can be put on the maximum waiting time at a station since long waiting periods are very unattractive for most passengers. This especially improves the search for connections running over night. The improvement can be seen in Table 10.5. Finally, the single limits can be applied together in different ways. We applied *conservative limits* of 24 hours for maximum travel time, five hours for maximum waiting time and $\gamma = 5$ and *tight limits* of ten hours for maximum travel time, three hours for maximum waiting time and $\gamma = 2$. The improvements can be found in Table 10.6.

In summary, together with the exact speed-up techniques, a speed-up factor of about 20 over the base-line version has been achieved with respect to the number of created labels and a factor of 138 with respect to the number of insertions.

10.3.3.3 Comparison with a Time-Expanded Approach

In general, we expect a better performance of the time-dependent approach than of the time-expanded one. It is unclear however, whether this can be achieved in a multi-criteria setting. In order to answer this question, we compare the performance of our time-dependent approach with the time-expanded search incorporated in MOTIS. As the time-dependent sys-

Algorithmic variant	Labels created	Labels inserted	Runtime average
standard	205,260	45,886	1.003s
conservative limits	156,515	17,827	0.685s
tight limits	63,261	4,605	0.335s

Table 10.6: Performance improvement when combining limits (realistic cases).

10.3 Computational Study

Algorithm	Version	Limits	Labels inserted
time-expanded	optimized	conserv.	92,538
time-expanded	optimized	tight	64,782
time-dependent	optimal	none	44,133
time-dependent	real. assump.	tight	11,913

Table 10.7: The number of labels inserted into the priority queue on average for both the time-dependent and the time-expanded search (real cases).

tem was developed as a proof of concept only, it makes not much sense to compare runtimes. We restrict our analysis to the comparison of the number of labels inserted into the priority queue. Note that the version of MOTIS we compare to employed the concept of relaxed Pareto optimality and not yet the advanced Pareto approach (cf. Chapter 2 for theory and Section 9.5.2.1 for the computational results). This version comes closest to the concept of dominance used in our time-dependent system.

As can be seen in Table 10.7, the time-dependent approach creates much fewer labels. When using realistic assumptions, the time-dependent system adds 5.4 times less labels into the priority queue. However, it should be noted, that the time-dependent approach requires additional effort to compute actual edge lengths on-the-fly. Thus, we expect (and empirically observe) similar runtimes for both approaches. As expected, the memory consumption of the time-expanded graph is a lot higher than that of the time-dependent one. In our tests, MOTIS needed nearly 1GB while the time-dependent graph used only 281MB.

10.3.3.4 Adding an Additional Criterion: Reliability of Transfers

The preceeding experiments were performed using travel time and the number of transfers as only search criteria. An interesting question is how the performance worsens when further criteria are introduced. This was explored by adding the "reliability of transfers" as a further criterion (cf. Section 6.3).

The reliability of a single transfer is a function of the *buffer time* which is the available time exceeding the minimum transfer time at the station. This means that a passenger will catch the connecting train unless the incoming train is delayed by more than the buffer time. There

Criteria	Labels created	Labels inserted	Runtime avg	Optima avg
time	99,284	19,401	0.454s	1.28
time, transfers	205,260	45,886	1.003s	2.34
time, transfers, reliability[50]	990,664	160,254	5.726s	6.76
time, transfers, reliability[20]	853,742	149,366	4.727s	5.67
time, transfers, reliability[10]	772,822	142,615	4.138s	4.66

Table 10.8: Relationship between the number of criteria and performance on 1000 realistic test cases. Different numbers of discretization steps are used for reliability of interchanges.

are many plausible ways to map a buffer time t into a reliability measure. In this chapter, we use

$$\text{reliability} : t \mapsto \mu - e^{(\log(\mu-\eta)-\frac{1}{\alpha}x)}$$

with parameters $\eta = 0.6$, $\alpha = 8$, $\mu = 0.99$ so that the maximal reliability of a single transfer is 99% and a buffer time of 0 minutes leads to 60% reliability. The reliability of connections with several transfers is defined as the product of the reliabilities of each single transfer.

This yields a continuous reliability measure which we further transformed into a discrete one by subdividing the interval of [0,1] into 50, 20, and 10 equivalence classes of equal width. Table 10.8 summarizes the performance of the search when using different numbers of criteria. The addition of the number of transfers as second criterion leads to a slow-down of factor two, the addition of reliability of transfers as third criterion leads to a slow-down of another factor four if we use 10 equivalence classes.

As we can see (similar to the results in Section 9.9), increasing the number of equivalence classes increases computational time, as more connections have to be followed instead of being dominated by another connection formerly in the same equivalence class.

10.4 Conclusions and Future Work

In this chapter, we have presented our prototype for a time-dependent, multi-criteria search system that works in a fully realistic scenario. We have shown how to introduce the most important features of real timetables and how to improve performance significantly. We have provided the results of our experimental analysis that show that a speed-up factor of 20 with respect to the number of label creations and 138 with respect to the number of label insertions can be achieved under realistic assumptions. A comparison to the time-expanded approach was done, indicating that the new approach clearly is competitive. Finally, we discussed the impact on performance when adding further criteria to the search.

In order to make the time-dependent approach able to replace current online search systems, its performance needs to be improved further. If possible, optimality should be maintained. It remains a challenge to design better speed-up techniques for multi-criteria search. Another goal is to extend our prototype to a dynamic scenario with train delays (as introduced for MOTIS in Chapter 7).

Chapter 11

Developed Software Tools

In this chapter, we will present various user interfaces to demonstrate that MOTIS really is a full-fledged time table information system and not just a prototype showcasing theoretical results.

First, we will present two graphical user interfaces. The first supports searching for connections (MOTIS Search GUI) with nearly the same interface as customers are used to. The second one is our Connection Controller and Alternatives System (CoCoAS) for proactive route guidance, as already mentioned in Chapter 7. Afterwards, we will briefly mention other visualization tools. We will close with a look at the "big picture", containing all the components introduced in this thesis.

11.1 GUI Architecture

11.1.1 MOTIS Backbone

All GUIs are connected to one or more MOTIS servers. These servers may optionally have access to delay information as introduced in Chapter 7. Communication is handled via HTTP-Interfaces transmitting queries and results in XML. Administrative commands and affirmations are handled analogously.

11.1.2 GUIs

The Search and CoCoAS GUIs are accessible as web sites with any current browser on a laptop or smart-phone. We decided to use the framework "Ruby on Rails". The applications run in apache with passenger extension. For CoCoAS an additional MySQL database forms the persistence layer.

11.2 Search GUI

The MOTIS Search GUI provides all the possibilities every electronic timetable information system offers, and more. The user has to enter at least source and destination stations and the desired time τ of departure or arrival. As most users are accustomed to specifying a single point in time, we create an interval $[\tau - 15min, \tau + 105min]$ from this. Additional query options include the following:

- only direct connections,

- some prominent attribute combinations
  (bike transportation possible, with restaurant/bistro, handicapped accessible),

- train class restrictions (none, no high-speed trains, only regional trains), and

- search for additional alternatives, with...

    - higher interchange reliability (toggling criterion reliability of interchanges cf. Section 6.3)

    - increased sleeping comfort (toggling search for night trains cf. Section 6.4).

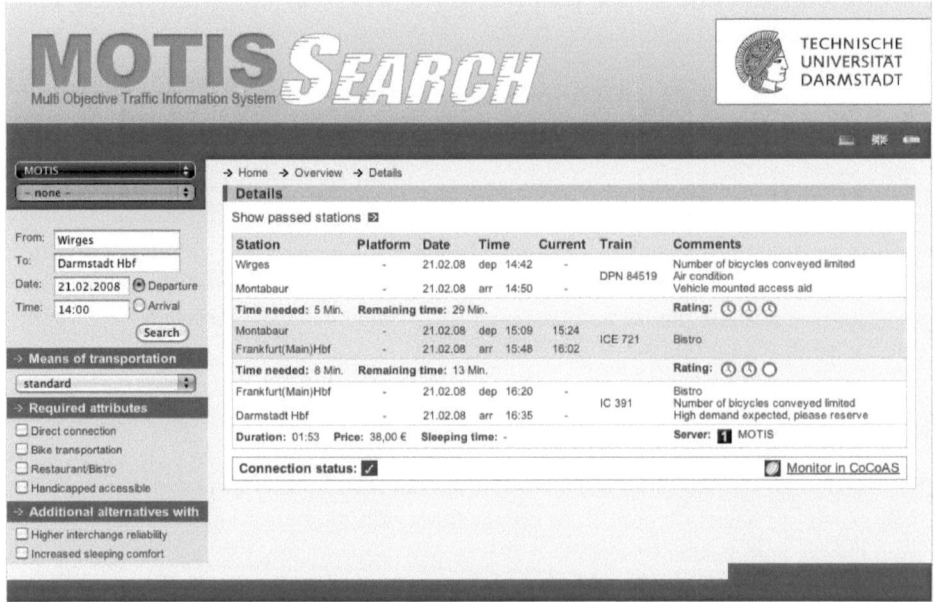

Figure 11.1: Details of a connection from Wirges to Darmstadt main station (Hbf)

11.2 Search GUI

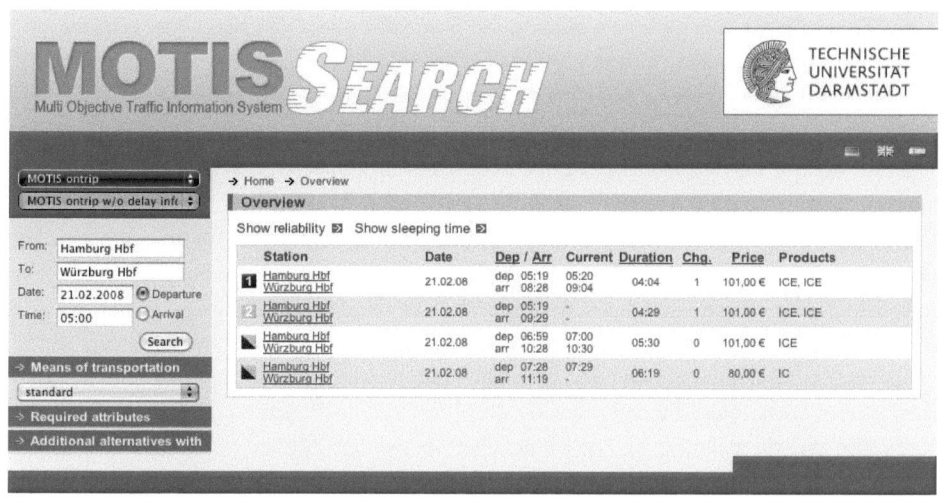

Figure 11.2: An on-trip query from Hamburg main station (Hbf) to Würzburg main station (Hbf). The comparison display (top) shows connections determined by on-trip search with (blue) and without (yellow) delay information. Details for the fastest connection (bottom).

The GUI presents an overview of the search results (cf. Figures 11.2 and 5.3) and details for a selected connection (in Figure 11.1 for a query from my home town Wirges to the city of my university).

Furthermore, we have a multi-server display for the comparison of the results delivered by various servers. These individual types of servers may be different search algorithms (MOTIS or our time-dependent prototype), with or without access to delay information, differently parameterized versions of the same server (e.g. diverse optimization-criteria), servers with access to delay information and varying internal states (say one at 9:00 the other already at 9:05), or interpret queries as on-trip or pre-trip. The comparison display is helpful to developers for single case analysis of differences as well as for motivating the need for the multi-criteria approach and our new criteria, e.g. reliability of interchanges.

In the single- and multi-server view the current and scheduled times are available for servers with access to delay information (e.g. delayed ICE 721 in Figure 11.1). Additionally, the connection status is verified in such a server and displayed in the bottom line.

For the connection in Figure 11.1 we see the departure and arrival times according to the schedule and, for the delayed ICE 721, the updated event times. Without the delay, an earlier connecting train would have been reached at Frankfurt main station.

In Figure 11.2 we see the comparison display for an on-trip search. Assume a passenger is at station Hamburg at 5:00 in the morning (maybe he missed a connecting train). He queries MOTIS for a connection to Würzburg. The two selected servers are MOTIS with (blue #1) and without delay information (yellow #2). Connections are marked according to the server that found them. The first and second were found by server #1 and #2, respectively. The last two were found by both servers. Note that server #1 added delay information to the results one, three, and four. The connection that reaches Würzburg first was determined by server #1. It arrives 25 minutes earlier than the connection from server #2. The last two connections have less interchanges, the last is cheaper. Therefore, these alternatives are shown. Note that the travel time is counted starting at 5:00. The first and best connection has an initial waiting time of 20 minutes before it departs at 5:20 (bottom figure). The interchange in Kassel-Wilhelmshöhe is only possible due to the delay of the connecting ICE 531. A server without delay information would not have been able to find this connection.

When introducing reliability of interchanges in Section 6.3, we saw a multi-server display in Figure 6.1, comparing two servers with and without reliability of interchanges as an optimization criterion. The scores for reliability of a single interchange or the whole connection are symbolized by intuitively understandable graphics, here clocks for interchanges (cf. Figures 6.2 and 11.1) and stars in Figure 6.1, (the more the better).

11.3 Connection Controller and Alternatives System

We implemented a proactive route guidance system, that constantly checks the status of travel plans, offering information about status changes and supporting the search for alternatives, called Connection Controller and Alternatives System (CoCoAS). This system offers a new service to the public and demonstrates the benefits provided by a system with delay information as introduced in Chapter 7.

The system basically works as follows: A user can register a planned trip obtained from any timetable information system for controlling. Starting some time before the actual departure of the connection, the connection is continuously checked for status changes. Recall from Chapter 7 the potential states of a connection:

- Journeys can either be still valid (i.e., they can be executed as planned),

- they can be affected such that the arrival at the destination is delayed, or

- they may no longer be possible.

Whenever a status change occurs (or some predetermined change within a certain status, e.g. a significant increase or decrease of the delay time in the second case), or only when the status changes to "broken" and an action is required, the system informs the customer about it via SMS or e-mail.

Now the customer may log on to our web site (per notebook or smart-phone) and inspect his connection, the current delay, and how endangered the interchanges are. If the interchange takes place one hour in the future and we have 1 minute less than the required interchange time, we may still have hope. On the other hand, a forecast arrival after the departure of the connecting train should most certainly trigger the search for an alternative.

In case alternatives are requested, the system determines the current position of the customer, either in a train or waiting at a station. More precisely the current position should actually mean the position at the time the passenger is ready to travel. Customers may specify the time needed before being able to change trains. More preparation time might be required when traveling with luggage or children, than when only carrying a newspaper. In case a train change is planned at the station anyway or the passenger is already standing at a platform, this time is zero.

With this position the corresponding type of on-trip query is executed. The on-trip queries guarantee to only deliver valid alternatives. Instead of querying a system at a station after already missing the connecting train, this type of system allows the alternatives to be determined while there are still many more possibilities. The following types of alternatives may be presented:

- *Different change.* Change at a station originally planned for changing trains but to another train.

- *Earlier change.* Change trains before arriving at a station originally planned for changing trains.

- *Later change.* Stay longer in the train and change at a station after one originally planned for changing trains.

- *Different start.* Sometimes problems with a connection are known before the passenger has boarded the first train. In such cases, alternatives that require taking a different first train, maybe even some minutes earlier to reach the destination in time, can be produced by our system. Our system requires the earliest time a user could arrive at the station and the time needed from notification to reaching the station to provide such alternatives as well.

Note that the planned interchange mentioned above does not need to be the broken interchange, it may be any interchange not after the broken one. The calculated alternative is then merged with the original connection up to the starting point of the alternative, resulting in an alternative from source to destination. Even in the case of *different change* the system can produce better connections than any system without delay information. The other cases are not supported by any commercial system right now.

After selection of the best alternative, this becomes the connection currently supervised and the customer receives status message for this connection from now on.

Incidentally, our system may not only reduce the delay at the final station, it may also allow passengers to arrive earlier, in case an interchange arises due to a delayed connecting train. If a train is delayed by 10 minutes, changing to this train may become feasible. So instead of taking the next train of that route scheduled to leave 50 minutes later (a periodicity of one hour assumed), changing to the delayed train greatly reduces waiting time at that station. Thus, the passenger arrives 50 minutes earlier.

Example To outline the whole process let us give a real example. Assume a customer wanted to travel from Kaiserslautern to Mönchengladbach and selected a connection with two interchanges, an interchange in Koblenz and one in Düsseldorf.

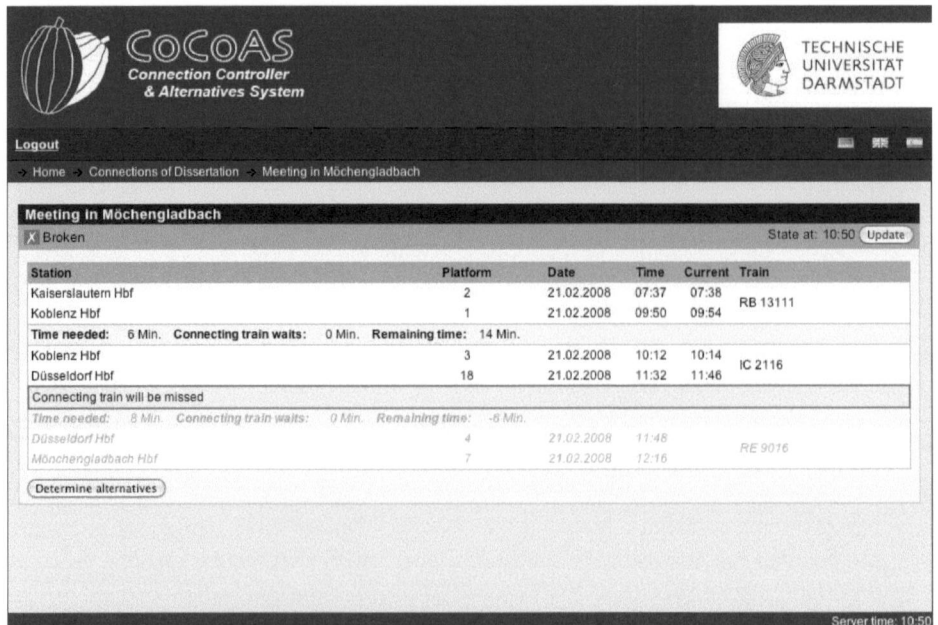

Figure 11.3: CoCoAS example: Connection status at 10:50 - broken. 6 minutes are missing to complete the interchange in Düsseldorf.

11.3 Connection Controller and Alternatives System

Original connection								
Station	Date	Time	Current	Dur	Changes	Products	Status	State at
Kaiserslautern Hbf Mönchengladbach Hbf	21.02.2008	07:37 12:16	07:38	04:38	2	RB, IC, RE	X	10:50

Alternatives								
Station	Date	Time	Current	Dur	Changes	Products	Status	State at
Kaiserslautern Hbf Mönchengladbach Hbf	21.02.2008	07:37 12:20	07:38 12:25	04:47	2	RB, IC, RE	!	10:50
Kaiserslautern Hbf Mönchengladbach Hbf	21.02.2008	07:37 12:46	07:38	05:08	2	RB, IC, S	✓	10:50

Figure 11.4: CoCoAS example: Overview of the alternatives for the broken connection

- The first change went well but at 10:45, he receives a message that his train change in Düsseldorf may fail.

- He logs on to our CoCoAS site and sees that 6 minutes are missing (at 10:50) to successfully complete the interchange (see Figure 11.3).

- He requests alternative connections (see Figure 11.4).
  The first connection has him change in Köln at 11:15 (delayed) before the problematic interchange in Düsseldorf, resulting in an arrival less than 10 minutes delayed. With the other connection he would change in Düsseldorf to a later train, arriving 30 minutes later than planned.

- He prefers the alternative changing earlier in Köln (see Figure 11.5).

- The customer prepares to change in Köln at 11:15 and rechecks the status at 11:11. In the meantime, the IC was further delayed, now ten minutes are missing to catch the connecting train in Düsseldorf. The customer sees no chance to make up the delay until his connecting train leaves in Düsseldorf. He selects the first alternative and changes in Köln.

Alternative						
Station	Platform	Date	Time	Current	Train	
Kaiserslautern Hbf	2	21.02.2008	07:37	07:38	RB 13111	
Koblenz Hbf	1	21.02.2008	09:50	09:54		
Time needed: 6 Min. Connecting train waits: 0 Min. Remaining time: 14 Min.						
Koblenz Hbf	3	21.02.2008	10:12	10:14	IC 2116	
Köln Hbf	-	21.02.2008	11:05	11:15		
Change earlier.						
Time needed: 9 Min. Connecting train waits: 0 Min. Remaining time: 7 Min.						
Köln Hbf	-	21.02.2008	11:25	11:31	RE 11312	
Mönchengladbach Hbf	-	21.02.2008	12:20	12:25		

(Select alternative)

Figure 11.5: CoCoAS example: Details of the first alternative at 10:50.

- CoCoAS supervises the remainder of the journey without triggering any action. The final train increased its delay by one minute. In the end the customer arrives delayed at 12:26 with the help of our system instead of 12:16 as originally planned. Changing differently in Düsseldorf he would have arrived 20 minutes later, at 12:46.

Without our system, determining to change to the delayed RE 4711 in Köln would have been difficult, especially since the arrival at Köln was at 11:25 in the end. Had the customer queried any online timetable information system for a train leaving after 11:25, he would not have seen RE 4711 at all, since according to schedule it would have already left. Alternatives determined without delay information from Köln arrived no earlier than 13:20, resulting in a worse alternative than changing trains in Düsseldorf. Should the change at Köln have become impossible, the customer would have been informed about that, since the new connection was under supervision once it was selected.

11.4 Others

MOTIS Visualization We have already seen some figures from our MOTIS visualization tool, which is basically a version of MOTIS with QT drawing abilities. It is capable of visualizing the search process in real-time, coloring inspected edges and visited or pruned nodes. We also use it for drawing maps of visited or pruned stations according to all implemented heuristics and to visualize the search results (e.g. different routes taken by the connections). The visualization aided in the development (and improvement) of search and speedup techniques. It was used to create the Figures 6.3, 8.2 (left), 8.5, 9.3, ??, 9.4, and 9.6 (left).

RailViz: Visualization of delay information Our student Christian Weber has built a simulation and visualization tool for delayed trains "RailViz" in his on-going Bachelor thesis. In Figure 11.6 we see a screen-shot of the system. The current simulation time is 7:01. On the left hand side all ICE trains in Germany are drawn. The smaller map around Hannover main station (Hbf) on the right shows all kinds of trains. Trains are either arrows pointing in their travel direction or squares if they are standing in stations. The trains arriving or departing within the last and next 5 minutes are shown in the station window for Hannover on the right. The delays are color coded from dark green for on time to light green, yellow, orange, and red for significantly delayed. The simulation advances time in adjustable steps. Steps may either be executed one by one or continuously via a timer. Note that the screen-shot in Figure 11.6 has simply been converted to gray-scale printing.

The tool is fed by delay information processed in our real-time information server (as introduced in Chapter 7). This visualization with moving trains and changing color codes produces intuitively understandable impressions of the current situation and the developments throughout Germany and at specific stations.

11.5 System Architecture: The Big Picture

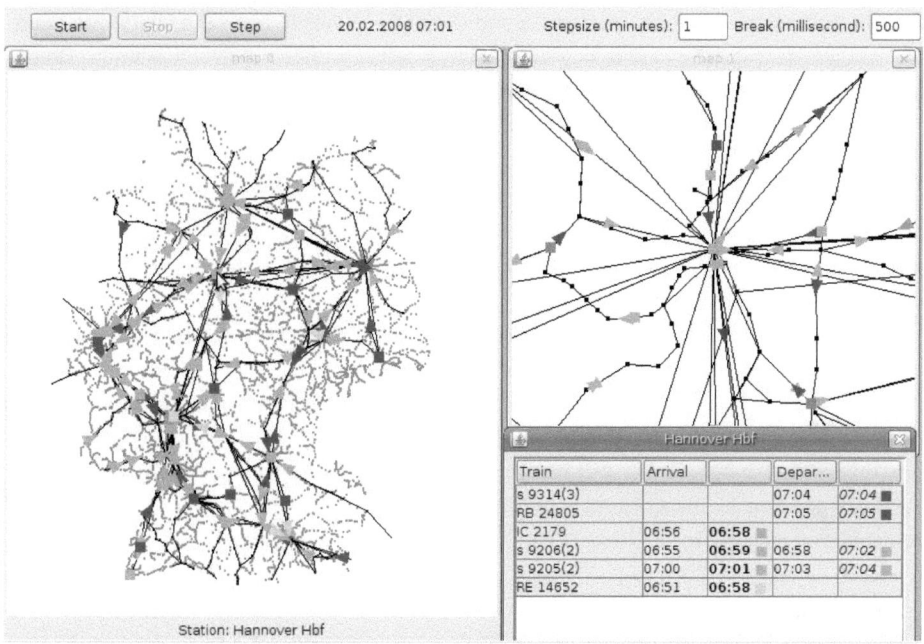

Figure 11.6: A screen-shot of RailViz: Visualization of delay information. The tool shows high-speed trains in Germany (left map) and all trains around Hannover (right map and text area). Delays are color coded (green: on time, red: significantly delayed - here in gray-scale)

11.5 System Architecture: The Big Picture

In Figure 11.7, we see all the components of the MOTIS system. The topmost layer consists of the applications which interact with the user. All requests from the interaction layer are routed by the *load balancer* to the appropriate server in the computational layer. This layer is composed of the search servers and the *real-time information server*.

A customer contacts the system through one of our GUIs. Depending on the requested service, he either consults the timetable information system via the MOTIS Search GUI (from Section 11.2) or CoCoAS (see below). The GUIs can be accessed from any web-enabled device, e.g. PC, laptop, smart-phone, and other mobile devices.

The GUIs communicate with our load balancer in XML via HTTP. Behind the load balancer are the timetable information servers: several MOTIS instances (see Chapter 5), our time-dependent prototype (introduced in Chapter 10), and, maybe, a third party system. We actually connected third party servers which, of course, do neither offer all features of our system, nor do they support all search forms. Within our servers the schedule is represented either as a time-expanded or time-dependent graph (cf. Chapter 4).

The load balancer selects appropriate and available servers to answer a query. For example, a status decision test cannot be processed by a server without delay information. On the other hand, a timetable request for next week should not be answered by such a server.

The multi-server architecture for delay information (as introduced in Chapter 7) is visible in the lower part. The real-time information server continuously receives status messages about trains. These are processed in the *dependency graph* and prepared for transmission. On request, the server updates one of our search servers. The update cycles can be scheduled to guarantee the availability of service. Recall that a search server spends only 0.1% of the time on updating and maintenance.

The CoCoAS system (introduced in Section 11.3) regularly checks the status of registered connections. Connections may be registered via the MOTIS Search GUI. They may attain a delay or, in the worst case, break. The latter happens in case of canceled connecting trains or if the delay of a train is too high to change to the connecting train. Once our system determines that a connection will break, it informs the customer via e-mail or SMS. The customer logs on to the CoCoAS interface and obtains optimal recommendations for the remainder of his journey.

11.5 System Architecture: The Big Picture

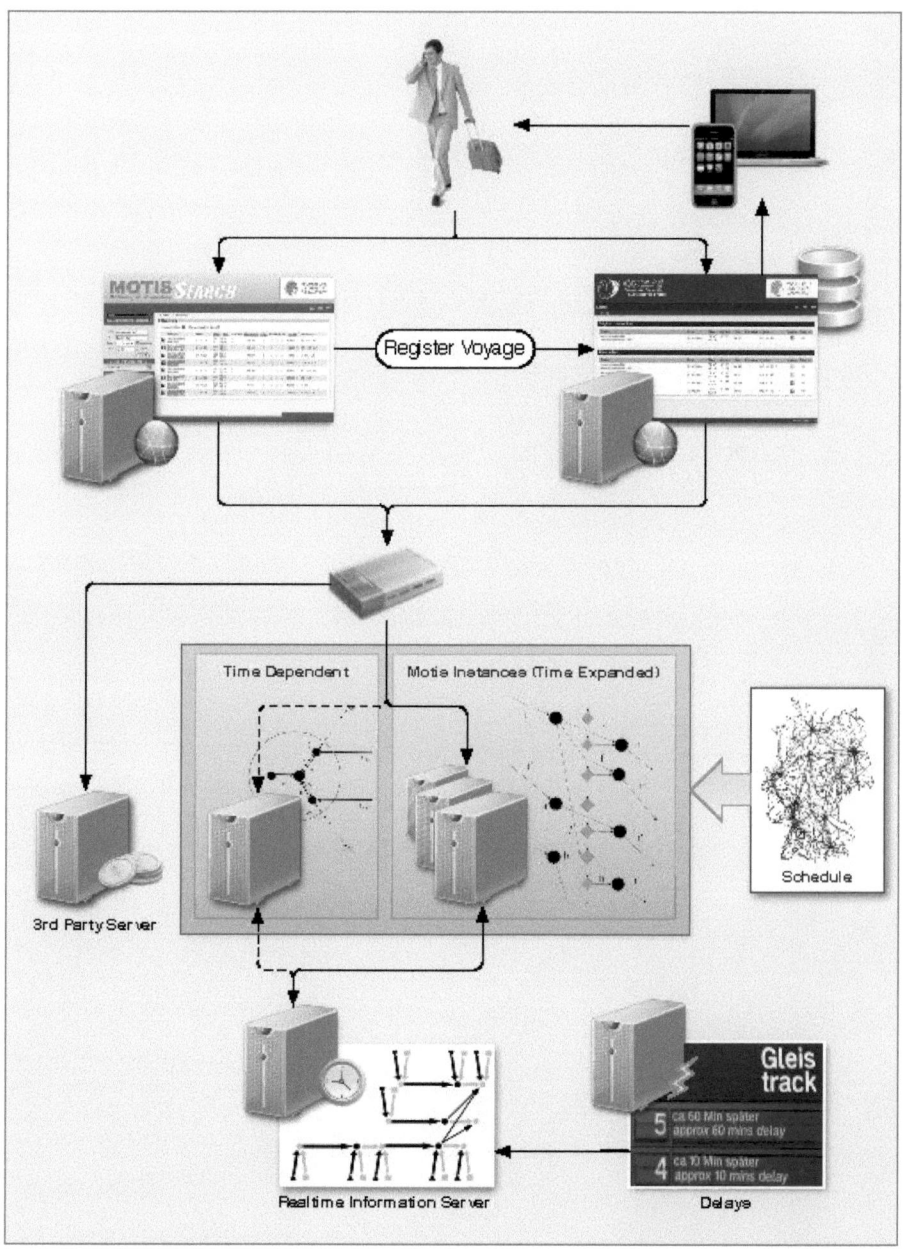

Figure 11.7: The system architecture of MOTIS.

Chapter 12

Conclusion and Outlook

Conclusion

In this thesis, we have presented MOTIS (Multi Objective Traffic Information System), our fully realistic, multi-criteria timetable information system, and the concepts and innovations it is based on.

Multi-Criteria To improve the capability and efficiency of multi-criteria searches we have developed an enhanced approach to multi-criteria optimization: *advanced Pareto optimality*. It delivers more interesting alternatives that classical approaches fail to determine. At the same time, it not only removes unattractive solutions from the result sets but increases search speed by not exploring paths towards those undesired alternatives. Our universal formulation of advanced Pareto optimality allows the modeling of other multi-criteria approaches like weighted sum, classical Pareto dominance, and our earlier concept of relaxed Pareto dominance. Thus, it is a universal model for multi-criteria optimization.

Additional Criteria We investigated the search for cheaper connections respecting different regular tariff systems and even special offers. We have seen that searching for special offers and regular fares simultaneously is not much more expensive (in terms of runtime) than the search for regular fares alone. For high availability of contingents, the existence of special offers for many connections even reduces runtimes. Little extra search effort has to be spent on cheaper alternatives, once the faster connections have a fixed or reduced price.

The newly introduced concept of *reliability of transfers* is a complex measurement and required non-trivial engineering to be used as an additional criterion. However, especially when dealing with delays, its importance even surpasses ticket costs, as the ticket is already paid. We observed that the criterion reliability of transfers is even easier to optimize than ticket costs, mainly due to its correlation with the least complicated criterion: number of interchanges.

We presented two approaches to the search for night trains and see two possibilities to apply them. If a customer explicitly asks for night train connections, the specially tailored enumerative night train search (with faster feeder computation) delivers excellent quality. In case the departure interval for a regular query lies in the evening, our second approach with its additional criterion may automatically be activated without spending too much extra computation time. Should attractive night train connections be found, they can be offered as alternatives to the results produced for the regular query.

Graph and Algorithm The time-expanded graph model has been extended to become a fully realistic model of the true schedule. We have evolved a generalization of Dijkstra's algorithm to efficiently determine all optimal solutions with respect to advanced Pareto optimality. We presented an extensive study of speed-up techniques that are feasible in our complex scenario and harmonize well with dynamic changes to the graph as results of delays. Our methodology and speed-up techniques enable us to answer queries in a quarter of a second on average, a tremendous speed-up compared to several minutes for a naive implementation. 95% of all queries can be processed in less than one second. In comparison to other approaches, our algorithm delivers superior accuracy at competitive runtimes.

Incorporating Delays We developed a model to efficiently compute and update the delays in our system. With the introduced *dependency graph* we can calculate secondary delays and propagate delays due to connecting trains waiting for their feeders. Restructuring the graph requires lots of local changes. By means of a careful case distinctions we were able to achieve an average update time of $17\mu s$ per required node shift. The efficient computations on the dependency graph and update achieve simulation times of less than 2 minutes for a whole day with over 6.3 million update messages.

The issues arising with traffic days have been addressed. We proposed changing the graph model to only incur an increase in memory usage for the event nodes while keeping the size of the change level small.

We have built a multi-server architecture with dedicated search servers and one (or more) update servers that inform the others upon request about delay information. Each individual search server spends only the tiniest amount of time on updating the graph and changing the schedule between days. Every single one is available for searching 99.9% of the day. Load balancing guarantees availability of the service at all times.

Time-Dependent Prototype Our investigation of the time-dependent model has yielded a prototype implementation with competitive runtime for the concept of relaxed Pareto optimality. This prototype is also fully realistic. We are currently working on reducing the size of the graph and improving the functionality in conjunction with delays of that system.

MOTIS System Apart from the core algorithm and graph model, we have introduced frontends and visualization tools. The MOTIS Search GUI and visualization tools aid in the development and presentation of results and improvements. Our Connection Controller and Alternatives System (CoCoAS) provides the new service of proactive route guidance. It constantly updates the status of registered connections and informs the passenger of foreseen problems (e.g. missed connecting trains). It provides more and better alternatives than any other system can currently do.

Outlook

Further attention should be devoted to the following topics.

Further Speed-Up Potential

Recall that many trains do not operate every day. A lot of space may be saved if every slave in a cluster within our multi-server architecture is only responsible for a certain set of traffic days. For example, if we consider only three subsequent weekdays instead of the complete period of one year, the number of arcs is reduced to roughly one third of its original size. A train company may easily collect statistical data about how many days/weeks in advance a traffic connection is typically inquired, and therefore balance the load of the cluster.

The analysis of heavy-weight searches (Section 9.13) exposed two kinds of demanding queries. The issues with ferries to islands can easily be overcome by backward searches from the reachable ferry departures, as explained therein.

For the search starting or ending near "centers of mass transportation" we see another solution technique, based on a similar principle. It might be beneficial not to search from all possible starting points within the given departure intervals. Instead, we could determine the reasonable departures of long-distance trains and search towards those events. Consider a train route that is operated every hour. Many different paths through the mass transportation network towards the departure station do not constitute attractive alternatives. Instead, we could summarize the means of mass transportation on something like "transportation edges" that are like footpaths, but model mass transportation. Similar to the treatment of departures after footpaths, we could create departures at the train stations eliminating the need for such a large number of start labels. See below for an approach to model busses and subways, that could also be applied, for example, to the inner-city stops of an S-Bahn.

The success of the *shortcuts* technique based on the definition of *important stations* encourages studying longer and more complex shortcuts, even those that also model changing trains. The unidirectional combination of arc-flags and contraction appears to be promising. Berger et al. experimented on the time-dependent graph model [BDGM09] and realized reasonable preprocessing times. Unfortunately, arc-flags are true for nearly half of the bits, so a tremendous speed-up is not to be expected. Their construction method resulted in bypassing nearly 60% of the stations, while our important station heuristic allowed over 70% of the stations to be bypassed. Note that different definitions of bypassing a station are used here.[i] We plan on doing similar experiments for our time-expanded graph.

Prices

We want to extend our understanding of fare models, e.g. to honeycomb structures for urban mass transportation. A systematic analysis of the possibilities to reproduce tariff models and efficiently search for cheap connections with different models seems worthwhile. An overall improvement of the estimates for ticket cost could increase the application field and decrease the runtime of our algorithm.

Incorporating Urban Mass Transportation

Urban mass transportation is not yet fully included. We would like to extend our model to include the schedules of busses, subways, and streetcars. These means of transportation operate at high frequencies, e.g. the subways in Berlin have departures every 2 to 5 minutes during rush-hour. Simply modeling each of the subway rides as one individual train in the time-expanded model is clearly not possible.

We envision a hybrid model: A separate *layer of mass transportation* could be modeled similarly to footpaths. These *mass-transportation* edges are always available and their length depends on the current time (much like time-dependent edges). Changes between means of mass transportation could be hidden behind the mass-transportation edges. Thus, only stations where it is possible to change from or to the layer of mass transportation need to be regarded during the search. Stations only relevant for mass-transportation are only represented as possible source or target stations.

Multi-Modal Traffic

Routing from door to door is becoming increasingly popular. The point of view is no longer concentrated on transporting a passenger from station A to station B. Railway traffic wants to be part of some attractive way of getting from origin to destination. Here, origin and destination can be home, office, place of a business meeting, vacation resort, etc. *Multi-modal traffic* is not limited to public transportation. A typical trip basically consists of three parts: First, a feeding section towards some railway station. This may either be traveled on foot, by bike, or in a car or taxi. The middle part is within the public transportation system (bus, train, etc.). Finally, a part towards the destination, similar to the start again on foot,

---

[i]and, additionally, stations on region borders could not be bypassed by Berger et el.

by bike, in a car or taxi. One or two of these parts might be missing. Legal combinations are not restricted to using a car or bike on just one end (near the home of the passenger, for example). Wherever services like rental cars or bikes are available, they provide the opportunity of obtaining and using cars or bikes. Alternatively, a connection with one's own bike on the first and third part is possible with bike transportation on the train(s) in between.

Two approaches to multi-modal routing are: a *preselection approach* and an *integrated* model. Within the preselection approach, hand-over points are selected first. Then, routing is done for foot, bike, or car from source to the corresponding hand-over points near the source and from the hand-over points near the destination to the destination. Next, timetable information is used between the hand-over points. This requires many-to-many routing, which is quite complicated. For example, lower bounds cannot be applied straightforwardly for goal-direction and domination by labels at the terminal. Finally, complete journeys are constructed from the individual parts.

Within a fully integrated model, every type of transportation is regarded simultaneously. The individual part by car may only appear at the start and/or end of a journey. Thus, switching from road to rail and back results in a naturally bitonic hierarchy. To determine the car (or bike) parts from one (either source or destination) to all stations within a reasonable distance would require solving a one-to-many shortest path problem on road networks. However, most speed-up techniques for road-networks heavily exploit the one-to-one structure of the traditional routing problem.

Together with the issues still present on the railway (and urban mass transportation) part we consider multi-modal traffic a really exciting research topic for the future.

Appendix A: Transitivity

A.1 The Time Difference Formula

In this section we will show that the relaxation function for travel time as introduced in Section 2.3.1 is indeed transitive. Let d_X, a_X, and t_X denote the departure time, arrival time, and travel time of a connection X, respectively. We can now restate Inequality 2.1:

$$t_A + \frac{t_A}{2 \cdot t_B} \cdot \min\{|d_A - d_B|, |a_A - a_B|, \omega(A, B)\} < t_B, \tag{A.1}$$

with

$$\omega(A, B) = \begin{cases} 0 & \text{if } A \text{ overtakes } B \\ 100,000 & \text{otherwise} \end{cases}$$

to void the relaxation if A overtakes B.

We will use the notation $\psi_{XY} = \min\{|d_X - d_Y|, |a_X - a_Y|, \omega(X, Y)\}$ for two connections X and Y.

To prove transitivity we assume $A <_r B$ and $B <_r C$, thus we have

$$t_A + \frac{t_A}{2 \cdot t_B} \cdot \psi_{AB} < t_B \text{ and } t_B + \frac{t_B}{2 \cdot t_c} \cdot \psi_{BC} < t_C \tag{A.2}$$

Insight 1. As $\psi_{XY} \geq 0$ and $t_X, t_Y \geq 0$ for all X, Y, from the equations in (A.2) immediately follows

$$t_A < t_B < t_C.$$

Insight 2. Again from the equations in (A.2) we have:

$$t_C > t_A + \frac{t_A}{2 \cdot t_B} \cdot \psi_{AB} + \frac{t_B}{2 \cdot t_C} \cdot \psi_{BC}$$

$$> t_A + \frac{t_A}{2 \cdot t_B} \cdot \psi_{AB} + \frac{t_A}{2 \cdot t_C} \cdot \psi_{BC} \quad \text{as } t_A < t_B$$

$$> t_A + \frac{t_A}{2 \cdot t_B} \cdot \frac{t_B}{t_C} \cdot \psi_{AB} + \frac{t_A}{2 \cdot t_C} \cdot \psi_{BC} \quad \text{as } \frac{t_B}{t_C} < 1$$

$$= t_A + \frac{t_A}{2 \cdot t_C} \cdot \psi_{AB} + \frac{t_A}{2 \cdot t_C} \cdot \psi_{BC}$$

$$= t_A + \frac{t_A}{2 \cdot t_C} \cdot (\psi_{AB} + \psi_{BC})$$

If we manage to show that $\psi_{AB} + \psi_{BC} \geq \psi_{AC}$ holds, we have proven transitivity.

Insight 3. Let $d_X \leq d_Y$ and $t_X < t_Y$. Then, $a_X = d_X + t_X < d_Y + t_Y = a_Y$. Since

$$a_Y - a_X = (d_Y + t_Y) - (d_X + t_X) = \underbrace{d_Y - d_X}_{\geq 0} + \underbrace{t_Y - t_X}_{> 0} > \underbrace{d_Y - d_X}_{\geq 0},$$

and no overtaking takes place ($\omega(X,Y) = 100{,}000$ in ψ_{XY}), we get $\psi_{XY} = d_Y - d_X$ in that case.

Insight 4. Let $d_X \geq d_Y$ and $t_X < t_Y$.

4a) Since for $a_X \geq a_Y$:

$$a_X - a_Y = (d_X + t_X) - (d_Y + t_Y) = \underbrace{d_X - d_Y}_{\geq 0} + \underbrace{t_X - t_Y}_{< 0} < \underbrace{d_X - d_Y}_{\geq 0}.$$

and no overtaking takes place ($\omega(X,Y) = 100{,}000$ in ψ_{XY}), we get $\psi_{XY} = a_X - a_Y$.

4b) For $a_X < a_Y$, connection X overtakes connection Y and we have $\omega(X,Y) = 0$, thus $\psi_{XY} = 0$.

Case Distinction We will now start a case distinction according to the ordering of the departure times, as listed in Table A.1, inserting the possible terms for ψ_{XY} as seen in Insights 3 and 4:

Case 1. $d_A \leq d_B \leq d_C$

$$\psi_{AB} + \psi_{BC} = d_B - d_A + d_C - d_B = d_C - d_A = \psi_{AC}$$

A.1 The Time Difference Formula

Case	Departure times	ψ_{AB}	ψ_{BC}	ψ_{AC}
1	$d_A \leq d_B \leq d_C$	$d_B - d_A$	$d_C - d_B$	$d_C - d_A$
2	$d_A \leq d_C \leq d_B$	$d_B - d_A$	$a_B - a_C$ or 0	$d_C - d_A$
3	$d_B \leq d_A \leq d_C$	$a_A - a_B$ or 0	$d_C - d_B$	$d_C - d_A$
4	$d_B \leq d_C \leq d_A$	$a_A - a_B$ or 0	$d_C - d_B$	$a_A - a_C$ or 0
5	$d_C \leq d_A \leq d_B$	$d_B - d_A$	$a_B - a_C$ or 0	$a_A - a_C$ or 0
6	$d_C \leq d_B \leq d_A$	$a_A - a_B$ or 0	$a_B - a_C$ or 0	$a_A - a_C$ or 0

Table A.1: Case distinction according to the ordering of the departure times of three connection A, B, and C. For two connections X and Y the possible values for ψ_{XY} are given according to Insights 3 and 4.

Case 2. $d_A \leq d_C \leq d_B$ i) $a_B \geq a_C$ and $\psi_{BC} = a_B - a_C$ (Insight 4a), then

$$\psi_{AB} + \psi_{BC} = d_B - d_A + \underbrace{a_B - a_C}_{\geq 0} \geq d_B - d_A \underbrace{\geq}_{d_B \geq d_C} d_C - d_A = \psi_{AC}.$$

ii) $a_B < a_C$, and $\psi_{BC} = 0$ (Insight 4b), then

$$\psi_{AB} + \psi_{BC} = d_B - d_A + 0 \underbrace{\geq}_{d_B \geq d_C} d_C - d_A = \psi_{AC}.$$

Case 3. $d_B \leq d_A \leq d_C$

i) $a_A \geq a_B$ and $\psi_{AB} = a_A - a_B$ (Insight 4a), then

$$\psi_{AB} + \psi_{BC} = \underbrace{a_A - a_B}_{\geq 0} + d_C - d_B \underbrace{\geq}_{-d_B \geq -d_A} d_C - d_A = \psi_{AC}.$$

ii) $a_A < a_B$, and $\psi_{BC} = 0$ (Insight 4b), then

$$\psi_{AB} + \psi_{BC} = d_C - d_B + 0 \underbrace{\geq}_{-d_B \geq -d_A} d_C - d_A = \psi_{AC}.$$

Case 4. $d_B \leq d_C \leq d_A$

As $t_C > t_B$, $a_C \geq a_B$ always holds.

i) $a_B \leq a_C \leq a_A$ and $\psi_{AB} = a_A - a_B$ (Insight 4a) and $\psi_{AC} = a_A - a_C$ (Insight 4a)

$$\psi_{AB} + \psi_{BC} = a_A - a_B + \underbrace{d_C - d_B}_{\geq 0} \geq a_A - a_B \underbrace{\geq}_{-a_B \geq -a_C} a_A - a_C = \psi_{AC}$$

ii) $a_B \leq a_A \leq a_C$ and $\psi_{AB} = a_A - a_B$ (Insight 4a) and $\psi_{AC} = 0$ (Insight 4b)

$$\psi_{AB} + \psi_{BC} = \underbrace{a_A - a_B}_{\geq 0} + \underbrace{d_C - d_B}_{\geq 0} \geq 0 = \psi_{AC}$$

iii) $a_A \leq a_B \leq a_C$ and $\psi_{AB} = 0$ (Insight 4b) and $\psi_{AC} = 0$ (Insight 4b)

$$\psi_{AB} + \psi_{BC} = 0 + \underbrace{d_C - d_B}_{\geq 0} \geq 0 = \psi_{AC}$$

Case 5. $d_C \leq d_A \leq d_B$

As $t_B > t_A$, $a_B \geq a_A$ always holds.

i) $a_C \leq a_A \leq a_B$ and $\psi_{BC} = a_B - a_C$ (Insight 4a) and $\psi_{AC} = a_A - a_C$ (Insight 4a)

$$\psi_{AB} + \psi_{BC} = \underbrace{d_B - d_A}_{\geq 0} + a_B - a_C \geq a_B - a_C \underbrace{\geq}_{a_B \geq a_A} a_A - a_C = \psi_{AC}$$

ii) $a_A \leq a_C \leq a_B$ and $\psi_{BC} = a_B - a_C$ (Insight 4a) and $\psi_{AC} = 0$ (Insight 4b)

$$\psi_{AB} + \psi_{BC} = \underbrace{d_B - d_A}_{\geq 0} + \underbrace{a_B - a_C}_{\geq 0} \geq 0 = \psi_{AC}$$

iii) $a_A \leq a_B \leq a_C$ and $\psi_{BC} = 0$ (Insight 4b) and $\psi_{AC} = 0$ (Insight 4b)

$$\psi_{AB} + \psi_{BC} = \underbrace{d_B - d_A}_{\geq 0} + 0 \geq 0 = \psi_{AC}$$

Case 6. $d_C \leq d_B \leq d_A$

As we have six possible sequences for the arrivals of A, B, and C, we summarized the resulting values for ψ_{XY} in Table A.2.

Case	Arrival times	ψ_{AB}	ψ_{BC}	ψ_{AC}
6 i)	$a_C \leq a_B \leq a_A$	$a_A - a_B$	$a_B - a_C$	$a_A - a_C$
6 ii)	$a_C \leq a_A \leq a_B$	0	$a_B - a_C$	$a_A - a_C$
6 iii)	$a_B \leq a_C \leq a_A$	$a_A - a_B$	0	$a_A - a_C$
6 iv)	$a_B \leq a_A \leq a_C$	$a_A - a_B$	0	0
6 v)	$a_A \leq a_C \leq a_B$	0	$a_B - a_C$	0
6 vi)	$a_A \leq a_B \leq a_C$	0	0	0

Table A.2: Case distinction according to the ordering of the arrival times for case 6 of the preceeding table.

A.1 The Time Difference Formula

6i) $a_C \leq a_B \leq a_A$

$$\psi_{AB} + \psi_{BC} = a_A - a_B + a_B - a_C = a_A - a_C = \psi_{AC}$$

6ii) $a_C \leq a_A \leq a_B$

$$\psi_{AB} + \psi_{BC} = 0 + a_B - a_C \underbrace{\geq}_{a_B \geq a_A} a_A - a_C = \psi_{AC}$$

6iii) $a_B \leq a_C \leq a_A$

$$\psi_{AB} + \psi_{BC} = a_A - a_B + 0 \underbrace{\geq}_{-a_B \geq -a_C} a_A - a_C = \psi_{AC}$$

6iv) $a_B \leq a_A \leq a_C$

$$\psi_{AB} + \psi_{BC} = \underbrace{a_A - a_B}_{\geq 0} + 0 \geq 0 = \psi_{AC}$$

6v) $a_A \leq a_C \leq a_B$

$$\psi_{AB} + \psi_{BC} = 0 + \underbrace{a_B - a_C}_{\geq 0} \geq 0 = \psi_{AC}$$

6vi) $a_A \leq a_B \leq a_C$

$$\psi_{AB} + \psi_{BC} = 0 + 0 = 0 = \psi_{AC}$$

This concludes the case distinction for *Case 6*.
Thus, all cases from Table A.1 have been considered.

Finally, we have shown that

$$A <_r B \text{ and } A <_r C \Rightarrow A <_r C.$$

A.2 The Hourly Wage Tightening

Connection	time	cost
A	180 min	30€
B	120 min	26€
C	100 min	27€

X	Y	diff(X, Y)	diff(X,Y)·δ_{cost}
A	B	60	5€
B	C	0	0€
A	C	0	0€

Table A.3: Three example connections (left) and the resulting tightening terms in Inequality (A.3) for $\delta_{cost} = 5$€ (right).

We will use the connections in Table A.3 (left) to show that transitivity does not hold if we use tightened dominance on ticket cost as introduced in Section 2.3.2 as the only criterion. Let us restate Inequality 2.2 for ease of reference:

$$cost_A - \frac{\max\{time_A - time_B, 0\}}{60} \cdot \delta_{cost} < cost_B. \tag{A.3}$$

Connection A with cost $cost_A$ and travel time $time_A$ dominates connection B with $cost_B$ and $time_B$ only if the inequality holds. The values for

$$\text{diff}(A, B) = \frac{\max\{time_A - time_B, 0\}}{60}$$

and diff$(A, B) \cdot \delta_{cost}$ for $\delta_{cost} = 5$ are given in Table A.3 (right). We have $A <_t B$, since

$$cost_A - \text{diff}(A, B) \cdot \delta_{cost} = 30 - 5 = 25 < 26 = cost_B$$

and $B <_t C$ since

$$cost_B - \text{diff}(B, C) \cdot \delta_{cost} = 26 - 0 < 27 = cost_C.$$

However, due to $cost_A - \text{diff}(A, C) \cdot \delta_{cost} = 30 - 0 \not< 27 = cost_C$ and $A \not<_t C$, hence transitivity does not hold.

Appendix B: Speed-Up Techniques

B.1 Lower Bounds

In Table B.1 the influence of the lower bounds on travel time and interchanges and different ways to obtain them can be found. All numbers are in comparison to the most basic version with lower bounds on the travel time from the *standard* station graph using a unidirectional algorithm without pruning in the preprocessing (from the computational study in Section 9.7).

SG options		ICG options		Runtime avg in ms	Runtime ratio in %	PQ extracts avg	PQ extracts ratio in %	Labels created avg	Labels created ratio in %
standard	-	-	-	710.6	100.00	92,860	100.00	149,225	100.00
sixhours	-	-	-	708.6	99.72	90,423	97.38	145,442	97.46
rushhours	-	-	-	707.8	99.61	90,172	97.11	145,085	97.23
fourhours	-	-	-	725.3	102.06	89,212	96.07	143,736	96.32
standard	B	-	-	723.5	101.82	92,857	100.00	149,221	100.00
standard	BT	-	-	690.7	97.20	90,909	97.90	144,416	96.78
standard	BTP	-	-	638.3	89.83	84,742	91.26	134,479	90.12
fourhours	BTP	-	-	707.7	99.60	83,000	89.38	134,005	89.80
standard	BTP	std	-	462.3	65.06	57,941	62.40	90,942	60.94
standard	BTP	uni	-	432.4	60.85	57,941	62.40	90,942	60.94
fourhours	BTP	uni	-	493.6	69.47	56,521	60.87	89,253	59.81
standard★	BTP	uni	U	412.1	58.00	57,926	62.38	90,921	60.93
standard	BTP	uni	BT	467.9	65.85	56,754	61.12	89,311	59.85
standard	BTP	uni	UBT	423.1	59.54	56,749	61.11	89,301	59.84

Options: B = bidirectional Dijkstra / T = triangle inequalities /
P = biconnected component pruning / U = using pruning information from SG in ICG

Table B.1: The influence of lower bounds from the station graph (SG) and interchange graph (ICG). Runtime, number of significant operations, and preprocessing times on both auxiliary graphs.

ISH	SC	P	Runtime avg	ratio in %	PQ extracts avg	ratio in %	Labels created avg	ratio in %	Quality loss conn in %	query in %
★-	-	-	412.1	100.0	57,926	100.0	90,921	100.0	-	-
N2	-		430.6	104.5	57,937	100.0	90,920	100.0	0.00	0.00
N3	-		317.8	77.1	44,911	77.5	64,237	70.7	0.76	2.12
N3	-	S	317.9	77.1	35,560	61.4	64,371	70.8	0.68	2.02
N3	N	I	269.0	65.3	32,656	56.4	52,186	57.4	0.76	2.12
N3	N		275.6	66.9	33,411	57.7	53,250	58.6	0.11	0.38
N3	A	I	580.3	140.8	36,982	63.8	84,007	92.4	2.13	6.72
N3	A		596.2	144.7	37,851	65.3	86,024	94.6	1.37	4.90
N4	-		267.5	64.9	38,971	67.3	53,475	58.8	2.16	5.80
N4	-	S	263.3	63.9	26,259	45.3	53,429	58.8	2.33	6.32
N4	N	I	201.8	49.0	23,876	41.2	38,278	42.1	2.68	6.94
N4	N		210.9	51.2	25,054	43.3	40,136	44.1	1.74	4.56
N4	A	I	385.4	93.5	26,286	45.4	55,645	61.2	4.70	12.73
N4	A		394.9	95.8	27,609	47.7	58,625	64.5	3.48	9.88
N5	-		242.5	58.8	34,209	59.1	46,934	51.6	4.80	12.04
N5	-	S	235.2	57.1	20,243	34.9	46,651	51.3	5.11	12.74
R5	-		405.7	98.4	55,247	95.4	84,945	93.4	0.51	1.64
R5	-	S	411.6	99.9	52,204	90.1	84,845	93.3	0.62	1.94
R5	N	I	406.8	98.7	53,680	92.7	83,343	91.7	0.56	1.82
R5	N		424.4	103.0	55,296	95.5	86,873	95.5	0.04	0.20
R5	A	I	1337.9	324.6	64,721	111.7	183,274	201.6	1.76	5.96
R5	A		1401.6	340.1	67,763	117.0	194,022	213.4	1.14	4.10
R10	-		383.9	93.1	48,188	83.2	75,272	82.8	2.73	6.82
R10	-	S	378.8	91.9	40,699	70.3	74,993	82.5	2.93	7.62
R10	N	I	375.9	91.2	43,425	75.0	70,171	77.2	3.02	7.44
R10	N		391.6	95.0	48,483	83.7	76,540	84.2	0.73	2.22
R10	A	I	985.4	239.1	50,440	87.1	137,066	150.8	4.79	12.80
R10	A		1105.2	268.2	58,784	101.5	157,732	173.5	2.07	6.72
R15			332.4	80.6	41,767	72.1	63,682	70.0	5.72	13.26
R15		S	323.0	78.4	31,653	54.6	63,360	69.7	5.79	13.50
-	F	B	84.8	20.6	7,923	13.7	10,965	12.1	67.71	77.92
-	F	N	583.0	141.5	59,861	103.3	107,684	118.4	2.29	9.56

Parameters P: St' = skip labels at unimportant stations
 I = use important station heuristic together with shortcuts
 B/N = with/without blocking according to shortcuts

Table B.2: Results for the important stations heuristic (ISH) using the neighbors (N) or routes (R) variant and optionally shortcuts (SC) to the final station (F), or the next (N), or all (A) important stations. Runtime, number of significant operations, and quality loss in connections (conn) and queries (query).

B.2 Important Station and Shortcuts Heuristics

In Table B.2 we summarized all combinations of parameters for the *important station* heuristic and the various definitions of shortcuts. Especially the following points are easier to observe in this table than in the separate Tables 9.29 and 9.30.

- Using shortcuts together with the *important station* heuristic (lines with I), the search runs faster than using only shortcuts and delivers results of the same quality as for the *important station* heuristic.

- When foregoing the *important station* heuristic in combination with shortcuts, the quality increases for 1.5% to 2.5% of the queries for (N3,N4,R5) and even 5% for (R10).

- Version *scnext* with shortcuts based on *routes* is actually slower than the plain *important station* heuristic.

B.3 Search Space

We have seen the impact of toggling the lower bounds from the interchange graph in Figure 9.4 on page 172. In Figure B.1 we visualize the impact of various speed-up techniques on the stations that are visited during an exemplary search. The search was from Löffingen (in the south-west) to Bodenfelde (near the center). Visited stations and train lines are shown in thick lines, those untouched are gray. In the final picture, the paths taken by the determined optimal connections are colored in lightgray. We start with the plain search without any speed-up technique (top left). It already uses the best priority queue and smaller relation. We successively added the following speed-up techniques:

- first goal-direction (cf. Section 8.3) and domination by labels at the terminal (cf. Section 8.4) using simple lower bounds for travel time only (top right),

- then lower bounds for all criteria and the techniques limiting the search horizon (bidirectional Dijkstra and pruning of biconnected components, cf. Section 8.5.5) (bottom left),

- and finally the heuristics important station (cf. Section 8.7) and shortcuts (cf. Section 8.7.2) (bottom right).

The significant reductions in each step are easy to observe. Together with the tremendous decrease of touched nodes at each visited stations, this reduction enables the improvement in runtime from several minutes to about a quarter of a second.

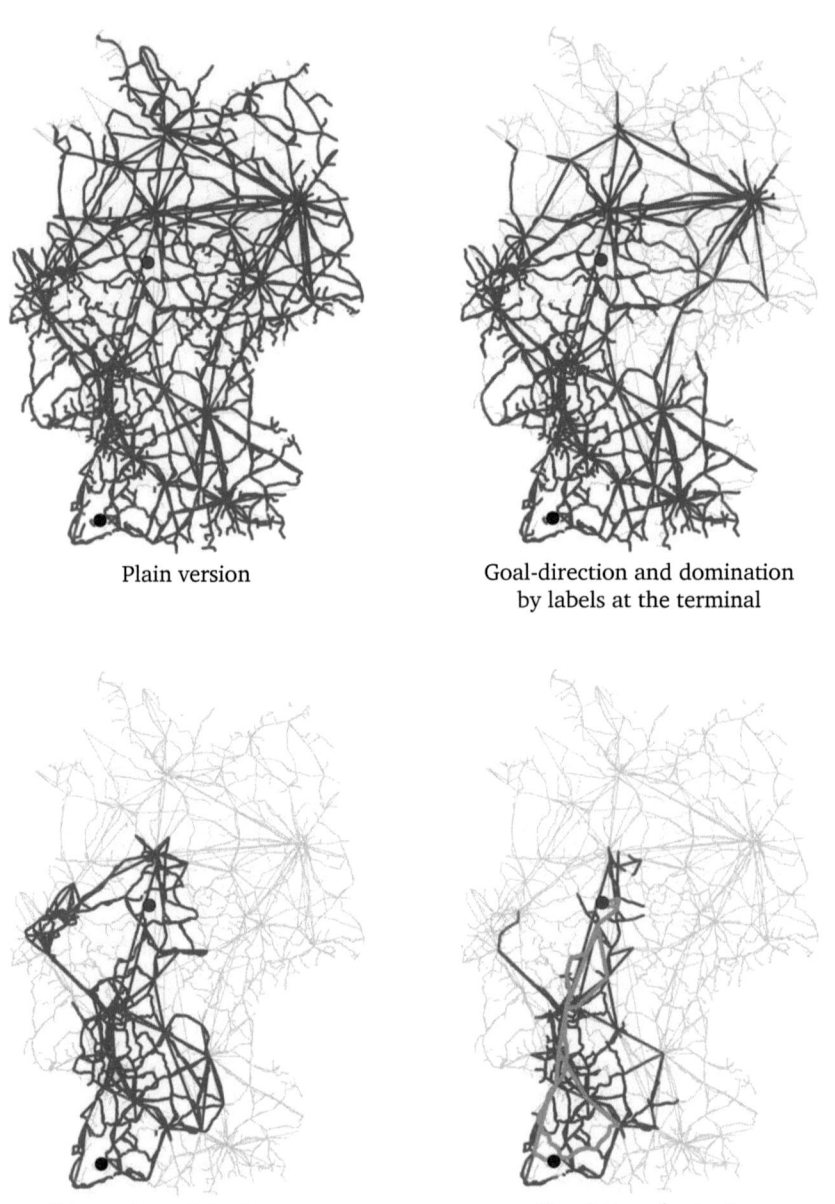

Figure B.1: Reduction of the search space when activating various speed-up techniques.

List of Algorithms

1	Textbook version of Dijkstra's algorithm.	27
2	Dijkstra's algorithm using a priority queue.	29
3	Dijkstra's algorithm using a priority queue without decreaseKey.	34
4	Procedure updateNodeList(...) for Algorithm 5.	38
5	Generalization of Dijkstra's algorithm for the multi-criteria case.	39
6	Floyd-Warshall algorithm.	51
7	Pseudocode for the MOTIS algorithm.	58
8	Pseudocode for the MOTIS algorithm with speed-up techniques.	143

List of Tables

2.1	Examples for Pareto dominance and extensions	14
2.2	Examples for advanced Pareto dominance	21
2.3	Coefficients and relaxation terms for rule set (III)	23
6.1	Parameters and sample values for the reliability function	73
6.2	Maximal attainable reliability in dominance testing	75
7.1	Sizes of the search graph for two days using different models	101
7.2	Properties of the search graph and dependency graph for one day	103
7.3	Number of transfer edges depending on waiting policy and parameters	104
7.4	Simulation a whole day with different policies and parameters	105
7.5	Runtime and operation counts for split server architecture	107
8.1	Number of trains, stations, edges, and nodes for our schedule.	119
8.2	Sizes of different station graphs	125
8.3	Sizes of different interchange station graphs	127
8.4	Number of edges and nodes saved using the "bypass" heuristic	132
8.5	Number of important stations and shortcuts	133
9.1	Size of the time-expanded graph.	148
9.2	Simultaneous search for several tariff types	149
9.3	Results for the fast search for fixed price connections	151
9.4	Key parameters of the schedule and the corresponding graph.	153
9.5	Number of connections found, failures, and runtime for all night train search variants	154
9.6	Pairwise comparison of the first ranked solutions.	156
9.7	Coefficients and relaxation terms for Pareto dominance (P) and relaxed Pareto dominance (R)	160
9.8	Coefficients and relaxation terms for advanced Pareto dominance (A_W)	162
9.9	Coefficients and relaxation terms for advanced Pareto dominance (A)	162
9.10	Influence of Pareto, relaxed Pareto, or advanced Pareto	163

9.11 Influence of criteria: toggling ticket cost, reliability, and number of interchanges 164
9.12 Influence of the rows in advanced Pareto dominance (A). 165
9.13 Differing wages for our profiles standard (W), business customer (B) and handicapped person (H) in advanced Pareto dominance (A_W). 166
9.14 Searching with different wage profiles for business customers 166
9.15 Searching with different wage profiles for handicapped customers 167
9.16 Influence of strategies goal-direction and domination by terminal labels 168
9.17 Influence of lower bounds: station graph 170
9.18 Influence of lower bounds: ticket cost and reliability of interchanges 171
9.19 Influence of lower bounds: interchange graph 171
9.20 Influence of different priority queue types 174
9.21 Influence of different weights for the number of interchanges in the smaller relation 175
9.22 Strategy reordering the priority queue 176
9.23 Influence of techniques: skip departures, bypass departures, and avoid inserting minimum labels 176
9.24 Number of equivalence classes for criterion reliability of interchanges 177
9.25 Varying the maximal effective reliability $\hat{\mu}$ for an interchange 178
9.26 Heuristics bitonic search and mass transportation 180
9.27 Heuristic routes blocking 181
9.28 Combining heuristics mass transportation and routes blocking 182
9.29 Important station heuristic 183
9.30 Shortcuts heuristic 185
9.31 Combining heuristics important station with and without shortcuts, mass transportation and routes blocking 187

10.1 Comparison of the base-line variant with an optimized version 202
10.2 Performance: Different models of transfer costs and the techniques avoid hopping and forwarding of labels 202
10.3 Performance: combinations of the simple and complex graphs to obtain lower bounds 203
10.4 Performance: Limiting the maximum travel time 203
10.5 Performance: Limiting the maximum waiting time 204
10.6 Performance: Combining limits 204
10.7 Priority queue insertions for time-dependent and time-expanded search 205
10.8 Performance: Number of criteria and discretizing the reliability of interchanges 205

A.1 Case distinction according to the ordering of the departure times 227

A.2	Case distinction according to the ordering of the arrival times for case 6 . . .	228
A.3	Transitivity and tightening: hourly wage example	230
B.1	Influence of lower bounds: station graph and interchange graph	231
B.2	Important stations and shortcuts	232

List of Figures

3.1	Example for exponentially many Pareto optimal paths.	36
4.1	Simple time-expanded and time-dependent graph examples	42
4.2	Time-expanded graph with change nodes	44
4.3	Time-dependent graph using train routes	46
5.1	Time-expanded graph in MOTIS	50
5.2	The edge class hierarchy in MOTIS	56
5.3	MOTIS Search GUI: Connections from Darmstadt to Halle	59
6.1	MOTIS Search GUI: Comparison display – reliability of transfers	77
6.2	MOTIS Search GUI: Connections with differing reliability of transfers	78
6.3	Alternative night train connections from Stuttgart to Hamburg.	80
6.4	Selection of pairs of entry and exit points	84
7.1	Sketch of the system architecture.	93
7.2	Illustration of the dependency graph model.	95
7.3	Exemplary changes to the change level	99
7.4	CoCoAS: Alternatives for a broken connection – overview	108
8.1	Visualization for speed-up techniques early termination, goal-direction, and bidirectional search	113
8.2	A graph partitioning for arc flags and a multi-level overlay graph	116
8.3	Example for contraction in the interchange station graph	126
8.4	Pruning results using the station graph	128
8.5	Pruning based on biconnected components	129
8.6	Different ways of chaining nodes on the change level	131
8.7	Bypass departure nodes example.	132
8.8	Shortcuts to the important stations of a train	135
9.1	Distribution of the extract operations for a mixture of fare types	150
9.2	Distribution of the number of Pareto and relaxed Pareto optima	151

9.3 Night train routes in the railway network of Germany 152
9.4 Search space reduction with lower bounds from the interchange graph 172
9.5 Runtime and number of optima for our reference version 189
9.6 Alternative Connections for a Query 192

10.1 Extension of a simple time-dependent graph to support transfers 198
10.2 Modeling foot-edges and special transfer rules 199

11.1 MOTIS Search GUI: Details of a connection 208
11.2 MOTIS Search GUI: Comparison display – on-trip search 209
11.3 CoCoAS: Status check result 212
11.4 CoCoAS: Alternatives overview 213
11.5 CoCoAS: Details of an alternative 213
11.6 RailViz: Visualization of delay information 215
11.7 System architecture: The big picture 217

B.1 Reduction of the search space when activating various speed-up techniques . 234

Bibliography

[AMO93]   R. Ahuja, T. Magnanti, and J. Orlin. *Network Flows*, chapter 4. Prentice-Hall, 1993. (Cited on pages 31 and 34.)

[AMOT90] R. K. Ahuja, K. Mehlhorn, J. Orlin, and R. E. Tarjan. Faster algorithms for the shortest path problem. *Journal of the ACM*, 37(2):213–223, 1990. (Cited on page 35.)

[APW02]   L. Anderegg, P. Penna, and P. Widmayer. Online train disposition: to wait or not to wait? *ATMOS'02, ICALP 2002 Satellite Workshop on Algorithmic Methods and Models for Optimization of Railways, Electronic Notes in Theoretical Computer Science*, 66(6), 2002. (Cited on page 90.)

[BD09]   R. Bauer and D. Delling. SHARC: Fast and robust unidirectional routing. *ACM Journal of Experimental Algorithmics*, 14:2.4–2.29, 2009. (Cited on page 117.)

[BDD09]   E. Berrettini, G. D'Angelo, and D. Delling. Arc-flags in dynamic graphs. In J. Clausen and G. D. Stefano, editors, *ATMOS 2009 - 9th Workshop on Algorithmic Approaches for Transportation Modeling, Optimization, and Systems*, Dagstuhl, Germany, 2009. Schloss Dagstuhl–Leibniz-Zentrum fuer Informatik, Germany. (Cited on page 118.)

[BDGM09] A. Berger, D. Delling, A. Gebhardt, and M. Müller-Hannemann. Accelerating time-dependent multi-criteria timetable information is harder than expected. In J. Clausen and G. D. Stefano, editors, *ATMOS 2009 - 9th Workshop on Algorithmic Approaches for Transportation Modeling, Optimization, and Systems*, Dagstuhl, Germany, 2009. Schloss Dagstuhl–Leibniz-Zentrum fuer Informatik, Germany. (Cited on pages 119, 133, 145, and 221.)

[BDS+08] R. Bauer, D. Delling, P. Sanders, D. Schieferdecker, D. Schultes, and D. Wagner. Combining hierarchical and goal-directed speed-up techniques for DijkstraâĂŹs algorithm. In *Experimental Algorithms*, volume 5038 of *Lecture Notes in Computer Science*, pages 303–318. Springer, 2008. (Cited on page 117.)

[BDSV09] G. V. Batz, D. Delling, P. Sanders, and C. Vetter. Time-dependent contraction hierarchies. In I. Finocchi and J. Hershberger, editors, *ALENEX*, pages 97–105. SIAM, 2009. (Cited on page 118.)

[BFSS07] H. Bast, S. Funke, P. Sanders, and D. Schultes. Fast routing in road networks using transit nodes. *Science*, 316(5824):566, April 2007. (Cited on page 117.)

[BJ04] G. S. Brodal and R. Jacob. Time-dependent networks as models to achieve fast exact time-table queries. In *Proceedings of the 3rd Workshop on Algorithmic Methods and Models for Optimization of Railways (ATMOS 2003)*, volume 92 of *Electronic Notes in Theoretical Computer Science*, pages 3–15. Elsevier, 2004. (Cited on pages 41, 42, 43, and 196.)

[BSS89] J. Brumbaugh-Smith and D. Shier. An empirical investigation of some bicriterion shortest path algorithms. *European Journal of Operational Research*, 43:216–224, 1989. (Cited on pages 37 and 118.)

[CH66] K. L. Cooke and E. Halsey. The shortest route through a network with time-dependent internodal transit times. *Journal of Mathematical Analysis and Applications*, 14:493–498, 1966. (Cited on pages 41 and 118.)

[Del08a] D. Delling. *Engineering and Augmenting Route Planning Algorithms*. PhD thesis, Universität Karlsruhe (TH), Department of Computer Science, 2008. (Cited on page 117.)

[Del08b] D. Delling. Time-dependent SHARC-routing. In D. Halperin and K. Mehlhorn, editors, *ESA*, volume 5193 of *Lecture Notes in Computer Science*, pages 332–343. Springer, 2008. (Cited on pages 118 and 145.)

[Deu09] Deutsche Bahn AG / DB Mobility Logistics AG. Deutsche Bahn DB Mobility Logistics Daten & Fakten 2008, 2009. (Cited on page 1.)

[DGKK79] R. Dial, F. Glover, D. Karney, and D. Klingman. A computational analysis of alternative algorithms and labeling techniques for finding shortest path trees. In *Networks*, volume 9, pages 215–248, 1979. (Cited on page 34.)

[DGWZ08] D. Delling, K. Giannakopoulou, D. Wagner, and C. Zaroliagis. Timetable information updating in case of delays: Modeling issues. Technical report, ARRIVAL, January 2008. (Cited on pages 89, 90, and 118.)

[DH90] J. Divoky and M. Hung. Performance of shortest path algorithms in network flow problems. *Management Science*, 36:661–673, 1990. (Cited on page 34.)

[DI04]   C. Demetrescu and G. F. Italiano. Engineering shortest path algorithms. In C. C. Ribeiro and S. L. Martins, editors, *WEA*, volume 3059 of *Lecture Notes in Computer Science*, pages 191–198. Springer, 2004. (Cited on page 118.)

[DI06]   C. Demetrescu and G. F. Italiano. Experimental analysis of dynamic all pairs shortest path algorithms. *ACM Transactions on Algorithms*, 2(4):578–601, 2006. (Cited on page 118.)

[Dia69]   R. Dial. Algorithm 360: Shortest path forest with topological ordering. In *Communications of ACM*, volume 12, pages 632–633, 1969. (Cited on pages 31, 34, and 137.)

[Dij59]   E. Dijkstra. A note an two problems in connexion with graphs. In *Numerische Mathematik 1*, pages 269–271, 1959. (Cited on pages 26 and 34.)

[Dis07]   Y. Disser. Multi-criteria search for optimal train connections using the time-dependent graph model. Diploma thesis, Technical University of Darmstadt, Department of Computer Science, Nov 2007. (Cited on pages 5 and 60.)

[DMS08]   Y. Disser, M. Müller-Hannemann, and M. Schnee. Multi-criteria shortest paths in time-dependent train networks. In *WEA 2008 7th International Workshop on Experimental Algorithms, Provincetown, MA, USA*, volume 5038 of *Lecture Notes in Computer Science*, pages 347–361. Springer Verlag, 2008. (Cited on pages 5, 60, and 195.)

[DPW08]   D. Delling, T. Pajor, and D. Wagner. Engineering time-expanded graphs for faster timetable information. In M. Fischetti and P. Widmayer, editors, *ATMOS 2008 - 8th Workshop on Algorithmic Approaches for Transportation Modeling, Optimization, and Systems*, Dagstuhl, Germany, 2008. Schloss Dagstuhl - Leibniz-Zentrum fuer Informatik, Germany. (Cited on pages 118, 131, 132, and 139.)

[DSSW09]   D. Delling, P. Sander, D. Schultes, and D. Wagner. Engineering route planning algorithms. In *Algorithmics of Large and Complex Networks*, volume 5515 of *LNCS*, pages 117–139. Springer, 2009. (Cited on page 117.)

[DW07]   D. Delling and D. Wagner. Landmark-based routing in dynamic graphs. In C. Demetrescu, editor, *WEA*, volume 4525 of *Lecture Notes in Computer Science*, pages 52–65. Springer, 2007. (Cited on page 118.)

[DW09a]   D. Delling and D. Wagner. Pareto paths with SHARC. In J. Vahrenhold, editor, *SEA*, volume 5526 of *Lecture Notes in Computer Science*, pages 125–136. Springer, 2009. (Cited on pages 118 and 145.)

[DW09b]   D. Delling and D. Wagner. Time-dependent route planning. In R. K. Ahuja, R. Möhring, and C. Zaroliagis, editors, *Robust and Online Large-Scale Optimization*, volume 5868 of *LNCS*, pages 207 – 230. Springer, 2009. (Cited on page 118.)

[EG00]   M. Ehrgott and X. Gandibleux. An annotated biliography of multiobjective combinatorial optimization. *OR Spektrum*, 22:425–460, 2000. (Cited on page 36.)

[EKZ76]   P. Emde Boas, R. Kaas, and E. Zijlstra. Design and implementation of an efficient priority queue. *Theory of Computing Systems*, 10(1):99–127, 1976. (Cited on page 35.)

[FMS08]   L. Frede, M. Müller-Hannemann, and M. Schnee. Efficient on-trip timetable information in the presence of delays. In M. Fischetti and P. Widmayer, editors, *ATMOS*, volume 08002 of *Dagstuhl Seminar Proceedings*. Internationales Begegnungs- und Forschungszentrum fuer Informatik (IBFI), Schloss Dagstuhl, Germany, 2008. (Cited on pages 5, 60, 87, and 90.)

[FR01]   J. Fakcharoemphol and S. Rao. Planar graphs, negative weight edges, shortest paths, and near linear time. In *Proceedings of the 42nd IEEE Annual Symposium on Foundations of Computer Science (FOCS'01)*, pages 232–241, 2001. (Cited on page 118.)

[Fre08]   L. Frede. A prototype of a dynamic timetabel information system. Diploma thesis, Technical University of Darmstadt, Department of Computer Science, Sep 2008. (Cited on pages 5, 60, and 87.)

[FSST86]   M. L. Fredman, R. Sedgewick, D. D. Sleator, and R. E. Tarjan. The pairing heap: A new form of self-adjusting heap. *Algorithmica*, 1:111–129, 1986. (Cited on page 137.)

[FT84]   M. L. Fredman and R. E. Tarjan. Fibonacci heaps and their uses in improved network optimization algorithms. In *Proceedings of the 25th Annual IEEE Symposium on Foundations of Computer Science*, pages 338–326, 1984. Full paper in Journal of ACM 34 (1987), 596-615. (Cited on page 34.)

[GGJ+04]   M. Gatto, B. Glaus, R. Jacob, L. Peeters, and P. Widmayer. Railway delay management: Exploring its algorithmic complexity. In *Algorithm Theory — SWAT 2004*, volume 3111 of *Lecture Notes in Computer Science*, pages 199–211. Springer, 2004. (Cited on page 90.)

[GH05]   A. V. Goldberg and C. Harrelson. Computing the shortest path: A^* search meets graph theory. In *16th Annual ACM-SIAM Symposium on Discrete Algorithms (SODA '05)*, pages 156–165. 2005. (Cited on pages 113 and 120.)

Bibliography

[GJPS05] M. Gatto, R. Jacob, L. Peeters, and A. Schöbel. The computational complexity of delay management. In *Proceedings of the 31st International Workshop on Graph-Theoretic Concepts in Computer Science (WG 05)*, volume 3787 of *Lecture Notes in Computer Science*, pages 227–238. Springer, 2005. (Cited on page 90.)

[GKW06] A. V. Goldberg, H. Kaplan, and R. F. Werneck. Reach for A*: Efficient point-to-point shortest path algorithms. In *Workshop on Algorithm Engineering & Experiments (ALENEX)*, pages 129–143, 2006. (Cited on page 117.)

[GKW07] A. V. Goldberg, H. Kaplan, and R. F. F. Werneck. Better landmarks within reach. In C. Demetrescu, editor, *WEA*, volume 4525 of *Lecture Notes in Computer Science*, pages 38–51. Springer, 2007. (Cited on page 114.)

[GMS07] T. Gunkel, M. Müller-Hannemann, and M. Schnee. Improved search for night train connections. In C. Liebchen, R. K. Ahuja, and J. A. Mesa, editors, *ATMOS*, volume 07001 of *Dagstuhl Seminar Proceedings*. Internationales Begegnungs- und Forschungszentrum fuer Informatik (IBFI), Schloss Dagstuhl, Germany, 2007. (Cited on pages 5, 60, and 79.)

[GMS09] T. Gunkel, M. Schnee, and M. Müller-Hannemann. How to find good night train connections. *Networks*, 57(1):19–27, 2011. (Cited on pages 5, 60, and 79.)

[Gra04] M. Graue. Timetable information systems: A new approach improving quality and efficiency. Diploma thesis, Technical University of Darmstadt, Department of Mathematics, Nov 2004. (Cited on pages 5, 41, and 59.)

[GS07] A. Ginkel and A. Schöbel. The bicriteria delay management problem. *Transportation Science*, 41(4):pp. 527–538, May 2007. (Cited on page 90.)

[GSSD08] R. Geisberger, P. Sanders, D. Schultes, and D. Delling. Contraction hierarchies: Faster and simpler hierarchical routing in road networks. In C. C. McGeoch, editor, *WEA*, volume 5038 of *Lecture Notes in Computer Science*, pages 319–333. Springer, 2008. (Cited on page 117.)

[Gun07] T. Gunkel. Search algorithms for night train connections under multiple search criteria. Diploma thesis, Technical University of Darmstadt, Department of Computer Science, Feb 2007. (Cited on pages 5, 60, and 80.)

[Gut04] R. Gutman. Reach-based routing: A new approach to shortest path algorithms optimized for road networks. In *Proceedings 6th Workshop on Algorithm Engineering and Experiments (ALENEX)*, pages 100–111. SIAM, 2004. (Cited on page 114.)

[Haf09] HaCon website. http://www.hacon.de/hafas_e/index.shtml, retrieved September, 8th, 2009. (Cited on page 1.)

[Han79] P. Hansen. Bicriteria path problems. In G. Fandel and T. Gal, editors, *Multiple Criteria Decision Making Theory and Applications*, volume 177 of *Lecture Notes in Economics and Mathematical Systems*, pages 109–127. Springer Verlag, Berlin, 1979. (Cited on pages 37 and 118.)

[HD88] M. Hung and J. Divoky. A computational study of efficient shortest path algorithms. *Computers and Operations Research*, 15:567–576, 1988. (Cited on page 34.)

[HNR68] P. E. Hart, N. J. Nilsson, and B. Raphael. A formal basis for the heuristic determination of minimum cost paths in graphs. *IEEE Transactions on Systems Science and Cybernetics*, 4(2):100–107, 1968. (Cited on page 120.)

[Hol08] M. Holzer. *Engineering Planar-Separator and Shortest-Path Algorithms*. PhD thesis, Universität Karlsruhe (TH), Department of Computer Science, 2008. (Cited on page 116.)

[HRT06] H. W. Hamacher, S. Ruzika, and S. A. Tjandra. Algorithms for time-dependent bicriteria shortest path problems. *Discrete Optimization*, 3(3):238–254, 2006. (Cited on page 118.)

[HSW08] M. Holzer, F. Schulz, and D. Wagner. Engineering multilevel overlay graphs for shortest-path queries. *ACM Journal of Experimental Algorithmics*, 13, 2008. (Cited on page 116.)

[HSWW05] M. Holzer, F. Schulz, D. Wagner, and T. Willhalm. Combining speed-up techniques for shortest-path computations. *ACM Journal of Experimental Algorithmics*, 10, 2005. (Cited on page 117.)

[JMS00] O. Jahn, R. Möhring, and A. Schulz. Optimal routing of traffic flows with length restrictions. In K. I. et al., editor, *Operations Research Proceedings 1999*, pages 437–442. Springer, 2000. (Cited on page 35.)

[Joh77] D. Johnson. Efficient algorithms for shortest paths in sparse networks. In *Journal of the ACM*, volume 24, pages 1–13, 1977. (Cited on page 34.)

[Jun06] P. Jung. Speed-up techniques for multi-criteria shortest path search in timetable information systems. Diploma thesis, Technical University of Darmstadt, Department of Computer Science, Apr 2006. (Cited on pages 5, 60, and 119.)

[Key09]	M. H. Keyhani. Verspätungsbehandlung in Bahnfahrplanauskunftssystemen. Bachelor's thesis, Technical University of Darmstadt, Department of Computer Science, Mar 2009. (Cited on pages 5, 60, and 87.)
[KMS07]	E. Köhler, R. H. Möhring, and H. Schilling. Fast point-to-point shortest path computations with arc-flags. In C. Demetrescu, A. V. Goldberg, and D. S. Johnson, editors, *Shortest Paths: Ninth DIMACS Implementation Challenge*. American Mathematical Society, 2007. (Cited on page 115.)
[KV00]	B. Korte and J. Vygen. *Combinatorial Optimization: Theory and algorithms*. Springer, 2000. (Cited on page 26.)
[KW93]	M. M. Kostreva and M. M. Wiecek. Time dependency in multiple objective dynamic programming. *Journal of Mathematical Analysis and Applications*, 173:289–307, 1993. (Cited on pages 41 and 118.)
[Lau04]	U. Lauther. An extremely fast, exact algorithm for finding shortest paths in static networks with geographical background. In *Geoinformation und Mobilität - von der Forschung zur praktischen Anwendung*, volume 22, pages 219–230. IfGI prints, Institut für Geoinformatik, Münster, 2004. (Cited on page 115.)
[Mar84]	E. Q. V. Martins. On a multicriteria shortest path problem. *European Journal of Operations Research*, 16:236–245, 1984. (Cited on pages 37 and 118.)
[Mäu09]	D. Mäurer. Advanced speed-up techniques for multi-criteria shortest path search in timetable information systems. Diploma thesis, Technical University of Darmstadt, Department of Computer Science, Jul 2009. (Cited on pages 5, 60, and 119.)
[Meh07]	K. Mehringskötter. Effiziente Fahrplanauskunft unter Optimierung der Umstiegssicherheit. Bachelor's thesis, Technical University of Darmstadt, Department of Computer Science, Jul 2007. (Cited on pages 5, 60, 71, and 73.)
[MM07]	L. E. Meester and S. Muns. Stochastic delay propagation in railway networks and phase-type distributions. *Transportation Research Part B*, 41:218–230, 2007. (Cited on page 90.)
[MMO91]	J. Mote, I. Murthy, and D. L. Olson. A parametric approach to solving bicriterion shortest path problems. *European Journal of Operational Research*, 53:81–92, 1991. (Cited on page 37.)
[Möh99]	R. H. Möhring. Verteilte Verbindungssuche im öffentlichen Personenverkehr: Graphentheoretische Modelle und Algorithmen. In *Angewandte Mathematik - insbesondere Informatik*, pages 192–220. Vieweg, 1999. (Cited on page 58.)

[MS01]   K. Mehlhorn and G. Schäfer. A heuristic for Dijkstra's algorithm with many targets and its use in weighted matching algorithms. In *Proceedings of 9th Annual European Symposium on Algorithms (ESA'2001)*, volume 2161 of *Lecture Notes in Computer Science*, pages 242–253. Springer, 2001. (Cited on page 123.)

[MS06]   M. Müller-Hannemann and M. Schnee. Paying less for train connections with MOTIS. In L. G. Kroon and R. H. Möhring, editors, *5th Workshop on Algorithmic Methods and Models for Optimization of Railways*. Internationales Begegnungs- und Forschungszentrum für Informatik (IBFI), Schloss Dagstuhl, Germany, 2006. (Cited on pages 5, 59, and 62.)

[MS07]   M. Müller-Hannemann and M. Schnee. Finding all attractive train connections by multi-criteria Pareto search. In F. Geraets, L. G. Kroon, A. Schöbel, D. Wagner, and C. D. Zaroliagis, editors, *4th Workshop on Algorithmic Methods for Optimization of Railways Workshop*, volume 4359 of *Lecture Notes in Computer Science*, pages 246–263. Springer Verlag, 2007.
(Cited on pages 5, 15, 41, 59, 63, and 149.)

[MS09]   M. Müller-Hannemann and M. Schnee. Efficient timetable information in the presence of delays. In R. K. Ahuja, R. Möhring, and C. Zaroliagis, editors, *Robust and Online Large-Scale Optimization*, volume 5868 of *LNCS*, pages 249 – 272. Springer, 2009. (Cited on pages 5, 60, and 87.)

[MSM06] J. Maue, P. Sanders, and D. Matijevic. Goal directed shortest path queries using precomputed cluster distances. In C. Àlvarez and M. J. Serna, editors, *WEA*, volume 4007 of *Lecture Notes in Computer Science*, pages 316–327. Springer, 2006. (Cited on page 113.)

[MSS+05] R. H. Möhring, H. Schilling, B. SchÂĺutz, D. Wagner, and T. Willhalm. Partitioning graphs to speed up DijkstraâĂŹs algorithm. In S. E. Nikoletseas, editor, *Proceedings of the 4th International Workshop on Experimental and Efficient Algorithms (WEA)*, volume 3503 of *Lecture Notes in Computer Science*, pages 189–202. Springer, 2005. (Cited on page 115.)

[MSW02]   M. Müller-Hannemann, M. Schnee, and K. Weihe. Getting train timetables into the main storage. In *Proceedings 3rd Workshop on Algorithmic Methods and Models for Optimization of Railways (ATMOS 2002)*, volume 66 of *Electronic Notes in Theoretical Computer Science*. Elsevier, 2002.
(Cited on pages 5, 47, 56, 59, and 130.)

[MSWZ07] M. Müller-Hannemann, F. Schulz, D. Wagner, and C. Zaroliagis. Timetable information: Models and algorithms. In *Algorithmic Methods for Railway Optimiza-*

tion, volume 4395 of *Lecture Notes in Computer Science*, pages 67–89. Springer Verlag, 2007. (Cited on page 13.)

[MW01] M. Müller-Hannemann and K. Weihe. Pareto shortest paths is often feasible in practice. In *Algorithm Engineering – WAE 2001*, volume 2141 of *LNCS*, pages 185–198. Springer, 2001.
(Cited on pages 36, 37, 41, 82, 85, 118, 123, and 141.)

[MW06] M. Müller-Hannemann and K. Weihe. On the cardinality of the Pareto set in bicriteria shortest path problems. *Annals of Operations Research*, 147:269–286, 2006. (Cited on pages 37, 82, 85, 118, 123, and 141.)

[MZ00] K. Mehlhorn and M. Ziegelmann. Resource constrained shortest paths. In *Proceedings of 8th Annual European Symposium on Algorithms (ESA'2000)*, volume 1879 of *Lecture Notes in Computer Science*, pages 326–337. Springer, 2000. (Cited on pages 35 and 37.)

[MZ01] K. Mehlhorn and M. Ziegelmann. CNOP — a package for constrained network optimization. In *3rd Workshop on Algorithm Engineering and Experiments (ALENEX'01)*, volume 2153 of *Lecture Notes in Computer Science*, pages 17–31. Springer, 2001. (Cited on page 35.)

[Nac95] K. Nachtigal. Time depending shortest-path problems with applications to railway networks. *European Journal of Operational Research*, 83:154–166, 1995. (Cited on page 41.)

[OR90] A. Orda and R. Rom. Shortest-path and minimum-delay algorithms in networks with time-dependent edge-length. *Journal of the ACM*, 37:607–625, 1990. (Cited on page 41.)

[OR91] A. Orda and R. Rom. Minimum weight paths in time-dependent networks. *Networks*, 21:295–319, 1991. (Cited on page 41.)

[PS98] S. Pallottino and M. G. Scutellà. Shortest path algorithms in transportation models: Classical and innovative aspects. In *Equilibrium and Advanced Transportation Modelling*, chapter 11. Kluwer Academic Publishers, 1998. (Cited on page 41.)

[PSWZ04a] E. Pyrga, F. Schulz, D. Wagner, and C. Zaroliagis. Towards realistic modeling of time-table information through the time-dependent approach. In *Proceedings of the 3rd Workshop on Algorithmic Methods and Models for Optimization of Railways (ATMOS 2003)*, volume 92 of *Electronic Notes in Theoretical Computer Science*, pages 85–103. Elsevier, 2004. (Cited on pages 43, 45, 47, and 196.)

[PSWZ04b] E. Pyrga, F. Schulz, D. Wagner, and C. D. Zaroliagis. Experimental comparison of shortest path approaches for timetable information. In L. Arge, G. F. Italiano, and R. Sedgewick, editors, *ALENEX/ANALC*, pages 88–99. SIAM, 2004. (Cited on pages 41 and 47.)

[PSWZ08] E. Pyrga, F. Schulz, D. Wagner, and C. Zaroliagis. Efficient models for timetable information in public transportation systems. *ACM Journal of Experimental Algorithmics*, 12:2.4, 2008.
(Cited on pages 41, 195, and 196.)

[SA00] A. Skriver and K. Andersen. A label correcting approach for solving bicriterion shortest path problems. *Computers and Operations Research*, 27:507–524, 2000. (Cited on page 37.)

[Sch03] A. Schrijver. *Cominatorial Optimization: Polyhedra and Efficiency*, chapter 7. Springer, 2003. (Cited on page 34.)

[Sch04] M. Schnee. High quality search for Pareto-optimal train connections. Diploma thesis, University of Bonn, Department of Computer Science, Feb 2004. (Cited on pages 41 and 59.)

[Sch05] F. Schulz. *Timetable Information and Shortest Paths*. PhD thesis, Universität Karlsruhe (TH), Department of Computer Science, 2005. (Cited on page 41.)

[Sch07] A. Schöbel. Integer programming approaches for solving the delay management problem. In *Algorithmic Methods for Railway Optimization*, volume 4359 of *Lecture Notes in Computer Science*, pages 145–170. Springer, 2007. (Cited on page 90.)

[Sch08] D. Schultes. *Route Planning in Road Networks*. PhD thesis, Universität Karlsruhe (TH), Department of Computer Science, 2008. (Cited on page 117.)

[SS06] P. Sanders and D. Schultes. Engineering highway hierarchies. In *14th European Symposium on Algorithms (ESA)*, volume 4168 of *Lecture Notes in Computer Science*, pages 804–816. Springer, 2006. (Cited on page 117.)

[SS07a] P. Sanders and D. Schultes. Engineering fast route planning algorithms. In C. Demetrescu, editor, *WEA*, volume 4525 of *Lecture Notes in Computer Science*, pages 23–36. Springer, 2007. (Cited on page 111.)

[SS07b] P. Sanders and D. Schultes. Dynamic highway-node routing. In C. Demetrescu, editor, *WEA*, volume 4525 of *Lecture Notes in Computer Science*, pages 66–79. Springer, 2007. (Cited on pages 117 and 118.)

[SWW00] F. Schulz, D. Wagner, and K. Weihe. Dijkstra's algorithm on-line: An empirical case study from public railroad transport. *ACM Journal of Experimental Algorithmics*, 5:12, 2000. (Cited on pages 41, 115, 116, and 124.)

[SWZ02] F. Schulz, D. Wagner, and C. Zaroliagis. Using multi-level graphs for timetable information in railway systems. In *Proceedings 4th Workshop on Algorithm Engineering and Experiments (ALENEX)*, volume 2409 of *LNCS*, pages 43–59. Springer, 2002. (Cited on page 116.)

[The95] D. Theune. *Robuste und effiziente Methoden zur Lösung von Wegproblemen*. Teubner Verlag, Stuttgart, 1995. (Cited on pages 37 and 58.)

[TZ06] G. Tsaggouris and C. D. Zaroliagis. Multiobjective optimization: Improved FPTAS for shortest paths and non-linear objectives with applications. In T. Asano, editor, *ISAAC*, volume 4288 of *Lecture Notes in Computer Science*, pages 389–398. Springer, 2006. (Cited on page 37.)

[War87] A. Warburton. Approximation of pareto optima in multiple-objective shortest path problems. *Operations Research*, 35:70–79, 1987. (Cited on page 37.)

[Wil64] J. Williams. Algorithm 232 heapsort. In *Communications of the ACM*, volume 7, pages 347–348, 1964. (Cited on page 34.)

[Wil05] T. Willhalm. *Engineering Shortest Paths and Layout Algorithms for Large Graphs*. PhD thesis, Universität Karlsruhe (TH), Department of Computer Science, 2005. (Cited on page 115.)

Die VDM Verlagsservicegesellschaft sucht für wissenschaftliche Verlage abgeschlossene und herausragende

Dissertationen, Habilitationen, Diplomarbeiten, Master Theses, Magisterarbeiten usw.

für die kostenlose Publikation als Fachbuch.

Sie verfügen über eine Arbeit, die hohen inhaltlichen und formalen Ansprüchen genügt, und haben Interesse an einer honorarvergüteten Publikation?

Dann senden Sie bitte erste Informationen über sich und Ihre Arbeit per Email an *info@vdm-vsg.de*.

Sie erhalten kurzfristig unser Feedback!

VDM Verlagsservicegesellschaft mbH
Dudweiler Landstr. 99
D - 66123 Saarbrücken

Telefon +49 681 3720 174
Fax +49 681 3720 1749

www.vdm-vsg.de

Die VDM Verlagsservicegesellschaft mbH vertritt

Printed by Books on Demand GmbH, Norderstedt / Germany